MAGICAL REALISM IN WEST AFRICAN FICTION

Magical Realism in West African Fiction provides a far-reaching examination of the cultural politics of this exciting genre, as exemplified in the fiction of three of its West African pioneers, Syl Cheney-Coker of Sierra Leone, Ben Okri of Nigeria and Kojo Laing of Ghana.

Brenda Cooper argues that magical realism arises out of postcolonial, unevenly developed societies, where modern and ancient, and scientific and magical, views of the world co-exist. She examines the plots, themes and narrative techniques of novels that mingle these dimensions of magic, myth and historical reality.

This study contextualizes the art of magical realism within current debates and theories of postcoloniality. Cooper explores the distinct elements of this fictional genre in a West African context, and in relation to

- a range of global expressions of magical realism, from the work of Gabriel Garcia Marquez to that of Salman Rushdie;
- wider contemporary trends in African writing, with particular attention to how the 'realism' of authors such as Chinua Achebe and Wole Soyinka have been connected with nationalist agendas.

Magical Realism in West African Fiction is an invaluable introduction to an increasingly important and popular genre, as well as presenting an engaging and in-depth look at the fictions of three of its most brilliant practitioners. It will be of interest to anyone wanting to expand their knowledge of magical realism, African fiction, and themes of postcoloniality more generally.

Brenda Cooper is Associate Professor in the Centre for African Studies at the University of Cape Town. Her previous book, *To Lay These Secrets Open* (1992), debates the criteria for the evaluation of African fiction. She has produced resources for teaching African literature in schools and colleges, including *Modern African Writing* (1984), *Debates, Dilemmas and Dreams* (1992), and *Nations: Stories of the World for Africa* (1995).

D0420466

Postcolonial Literatures

Edited in collaboration with the Centre for Colonial and Postcolonial Studies, University of Kent at Canterbury, this series presents a wide range of research into postcolonial literatures by specialists in the field. It comprises three strands.

Postcolonial Literatures makes available in paperback important work in the field. Hardback editions of these titles are also available, some published earlier in the *Routledge Research* strand of the series. Titles in paperback include:

Postcolonial Studies: A Materialist Critique by Benita Parry
Magical Realism in West African Fiction: Seeing with a Third Eye by Brenda Cooper
The Postcolonial Jane Austen edited by You-Me Park and Rajeswari Sunder Rajan
Contemporary Caribbean Women's Poetry: Making Style by Denise deCaires Narain

Routledge Research in Postcolonial Literatures is a forum for innovative new research intended for a specialist readership. Published in hardback, titles include:

1. *Magical Realism in West African Fiction: Seeing with a Third Eye* by Brenda Cooper
2. *The Postcolonial Jane Austen* edited by You-Me Park and Rajeswari Sunder Rajan
3. *Contemporary Caribbean Women's Poetry: Making Style* by Denise deCaires Narain
4. *African Literature, Animism and Politics* by Caroline Rooney
5. *Caribbean-English Passages: Intertextuality in a Postcolonial Tradition* by Tobias Döring
6. *Islands in History and Representation* edited by Rod Edmond and Vanessa Smith
7. *Civility, Literature, and Culture in British India: Discipline and identity in the colonial context* by Anindyo Roy
8. *Women Writing the West Indies, 1804–1939: 'A Hot Place, Belonging To Us'* by Evelyn O'Callaghan
9. *Postcolonial Pacific Writing: Representations of the body* by Michelle Keown
10. *Writing Woman, Writing Place: Contemporary Australian and South African fiction* by Sue Kossew

Readings in Postcolonial Literatures will offer collections of important essays from journals or classic texts in the field. Titles include:

1. *Selected Essays of Wilson Harris* edited by Andrew Bundy

MAGICAL REALISM IN WEST AFRICAN FICTION

Seeing with a third eye

Brenda Cooper

Routledge
Taylor & Francis Group

LONDON AND NEW YORK

First published 1998
by Routledge
11 New Fetter Lane, London, EC4P 4EE

Simultaneously published in the USA and Canada
by Routledge
29 West 35th Street, New York, NY 10001

First published in paperback 2004

Routledge is an imprint of the Taylor & Francis Group

© 1998, 2004 Brenda Cooper

Reprinted 2000, 2001

Typeset in Baskerville by Routledge
Printed and bound in Great Britain by Antony Rowe Ltd, Chippenham, Wiltshire

Every effort has been made to ensure that the advice and
information in this book is true and accurate at the time of
going to press. However, neither the publisher nor the authors
can accept any legal responsibility or liability for any errors
or omissions that may be made.

British Library Cataloguing in Publication Data
A catalogue record for this book is available from the British Library

Library of Congress Cataloging in Publication Data
A catalogue record for this book is available on request

ISBN 0–415–18239–5 (hbk)
ISBN 0–415–34061–6 (pbk)

FOR DANIEL
MY ABIKU

CONTENTS

ACKNOWLEDGEMENTS

Martin Hall read, commented upon, believed in and edited the book. For his astute scholarly insights, sweat and love, I give thanks.

Rustum Kozain was a one in a million research assistant. He collected, ordered, searched, photocopied and discussed the ideas.

My appreciation to Biodun Jeyifo, Lokangaka Losambe and Clive Wake for their support.

To Ros and Saul Teukolsky for flying me over to the bookshops, for the flowers and for being my family and best friends.

The institutional support of the University of Cape Town and the staff of the Centre for African Studies enabled the research.

The author wishes to thank *Wasafiri* for permission to reproduce a version of her paper 'Liberated Repressions' as Chapter One.

The financial assistance of the Centre for Science Development (Human Sciences Research Council, South Africa) towards this research is acknowledged. The opinions and conclusions are the author's.

As always, Adam and Sara Cooper are present.

1

SEEING WITH A THIRD EYE

In this book I focus on three magical realist writers of West Africa: Syl Cheney-Coker (Sierra Leone), Ben Okri (Nigeria) and Kojo Laing (Ghana). I argue that their fictions are characterized by the powerful, restless reincarnations of myth into magic and history into the universal. They are writers on the margins, inhabiting borders.

Why 'seeing with a third eye'?

Magical realism strives, with greater or lesser success, to capture the paradox of the unity of opposites; it contests polarities such as history versus magic, the pre-colonial past versus the post-industrial present and life versus death. Capturing such boundaries between spaces is to exist in a third space, in the fertile interstices between these extremes of time or space:

> And then suddenly, out of the centre of my forehead, an eye opened, and
> I saw this light to be the brightest, most beautiful thing in the world.
>   (Ben Okri, *The Famished Road*)[1]

But there is also a third space of another kind, a theoretical position that might be called a 'reconstituted Marxism'; a middle ground, between Marxism and post-modernist theory. This is a space that retains the central recognition that power relations underlie texts, and from which one can continue to ask materialist questions such as 'who benefits?'; 'In whose interests does this tale work or this device operate?' But it is also a space in which the problem of reducing everything to class issues is acknowledged; it accepts that metaphors such as 'base' and 'superstructure' are too rigid when attempting to construct the complex and global cultural networks into which we are all woven. This approach re-examines the concept of humanism and its relationship to power and oppression. It is a position that recognizes individuals as gendered, racially constituted, unevenly privileged subjects, playing out many-layered lives that are both structurally determined and also idiosyncratically forged. Such a project can 'reintegrate' the postmodern concern for 'liminality, diversity, multivalency', with the 'historical explanatory force of

Marxism'.[2] The middle ground between the two, however, cannot be some nebulous compromise, but must rather be holistic, seeking totalities, recognizing that global social, political and economic forces fundamentally affect human lives and creativity, but retaining the humility to accept that knowledge of those structures and systems is always mediated, debatable and partial.

Holistic explanations have, rather, gone out of fashion. A champion of the totality is Fredric Jameson, who in his *Postmodernism or, The Cultural Logic of Late Capitalism*, declares war on the 'war on totality', on the 'so many people' who are 'scandalized' by his attempts to 'map a totality'. He insists that

> the positing of global characterizations and hypotheses, the abstraction from the 'blooming, buzzing confusion' of immediacy, was always a radical intervention in the here and now and the promise of resistance to its blind fatalities.[3]

Jameson undertakes a Marxist analysis of postmodernism, which he understands as having emerged at a particular stage of capitalism, and to be logically the nature of culture at that moment of late capitalism. In Chapter 3, I enlarge on his analysis of this moment; here I wish to emphasize his retention of the notion of 'mode of production' within his attempts to celebrate some of postmodernism's new freedoms. Jameson insists uncompromisingly that:

> Despite the delirium of some of [postmodernism's] celebrants and apologists . . . a truly new culture could only emerge through the collective struggle to create a new social system.[4]

Homi Bhabha resolutely refuses Jameson's 'third space of representation', refuses the possibility of a Marxism which forges a new position, which is neither the old, reductionist Marxism, nor freewheeling postmodernism. He dismisses this enterprise:

> We have, by now, learnt that this appeal to a 'thirdness' in the structure of dialectical thought is both an acknowledgment of the disjunctive cultural 'signs' of these (postmodern) times, and a symptom of Jameson's inability to move beyond the binary dialectic of inside and outside, base and superstructure.[5]

Bhabha sees Jameson as 'constrained' by 'the concept of class'.[6] But is it not Bhabha who is constrained and limited in his refusal to acknowledge the global and systemic historical realities which motivate his political and intellectual stance?

Bhabha, however, also wishes to participate in social reconstruction. In *The Location of Culture*, he insists that 'the interest in postmodernism' should not be simply negative, restricted to the exposure of the interests motivating the stories

2

that powerful white, imperialist men have peddled as universal. It should not, in his words, be 'limited to a celebration of the fragmentation of the "grand narratives" of postenlightenment rationalism'.[7] For Bhabha, the 'wider significance of the postmodern condition' lies in the spaces that open up when the limits of ethnocentric ideas are exposed, spaces that can be seized by 'a range of other dissonant, even dissident histories and voices – women, the colonized, minority groups, the bearers of policed sexualities'.[8] Such spaces may be border interstices, the 'micropolitics' to which Jameson himself refers when he describes 'the emergence of this whole range of small-group, nonclass political practices' as a 'profoundly postmodern phenomenon'.[9]

It is true that within these rich and diverse spaces that have opened up, the once-colonized have re-written history in ways that will become clear in the chapters that follow. However, I think that it is also true that these new, interstitial spaces that have emerged in postmodernity can only be fully conceptualized within an understanding of oppression, of interests and of the social totality. 'Seeing with a third eye' is my attempt to grasp these totalities, without reducing political or artistic complexities. It is the belief that systems of oppression continue to determine history and also that life is complex and paradoxical, mysterious and idiosyncratic; it is the certainty that if life is thus, art is doubly so.

If seeing the nature of systems of oppression is retained as a goal, then the ethical drive to transform those systems comes into play. Furthermore, I believe these ethics are based on a philosophy of humanism. Michele Barrett suggests that the assumption that ' "humanist" is a derogatory term . . . is historically a great injustice, in that it ignores the immensely progressive role that humanism . . . has played'. Barrett provides examples of this progressive role, such as opposition to religious fundamentalism or resistance to anti-abortion campaigns in the USA. Specifically, in regard to apartheid South Africa, she questions:

> How does one apply an anti-humanist position to South African politics, where the strongest card the black majority has to play, in the politico-moral arena, is an argument based on 'human rights' and 'equality' and other equally liberal humanist ideas?[10]

These examples link the brand of humanism that Barrett is excavating to an ethics that enable it to be progressive, and which distinguish it from the Eurocentric, liberal humanism that sought to universalize, and thereby to justify the dominant interests of white men and Western capital. Rather, Barrett's ethics are based on the perception of power and how power operates, and on the moral purpose of human intervention. Postmodernism has emphasized the inextricable relationship between knowledge and power while rejecting humanism. This leads to the question as to how, for example, Foucault can maintain an anti-humanistic position – seeking to define and expose the operation of power in terms of its own neutral, self-activating dynamics – when his subject matter is oppressed and

3

marginalized groups. Foucault's seminal works on those defined as insane or criminal surely depend on 'the reader's familiarity with and commitment to the modern ideals of autonomy, reciprocity, dignity and human rights'.[11]

If I am someone who is attempting to make an intervention within the arena of cultural politics, by trying to discern the complex grids of power and oppression, then who am I? If postmodernism has taught us anything, it has been to interrogate the positioning of the commentator; to be self-aware about what is refracted, reflected and rejected by our particular eyes, when we speak, read or write.

In general, white women do not fare well in African fiction.[12] In Chinua Achebe's *Anthills of the Savannah*, one of the main characters had in his past been married to a white woman. The marriage was never consummated in the six months it lasted. The cause of this unnatural situation is unambiguously represented as the white woman's psychological deficiencies. Such a depiction in literature is never merely idiosyncratic. Achebe is writing here in the tradition of Ayi Kwei Armah, building on the motif of white female sexuality as frigid, white women as dangerous and destructive to black men. Negative depictions of white women abound in African writing. This is the milieu within which I have to write.

Most black writers assert the beauty and dignity of their cultural heritage's, in opposition to the corrosive, distorting racism that has permeated Western culture. Alice Walker writes from her 'Mother's Gardens'[13] and Kwame Anthony Appiah in his 'Father's House'[14]. My childhood and schooling in the parochial small town mediocrity of white, Jewish Port Elizabeth were typical of the mean, racist society at large. I cannot write a beautiful book 'From the Balcony of my Parents' Flat', overlooking a segregated beach. But I do have a story to tell which is also the story of realization and resistance which is common to many white South Africans; a refusal to accept white fascists as 'my' people and to assume the responsibility for them that guilt assumes; at the same time, I accept the fact that I am privileged and have gained from apartheid's bounty reserved for 'whites only'.

A field of daffodils may assist in creating an image for my refusal of self-hatred as well as the recognition of the cruel and exploitative reality of cultural imperialism and of racism that I am trying to describe. The following is an extract from Jamaica Kincaid's novel, *Lucy*:

> Mariah, mistaking what was happening to me for joy at seeing daffodils for the first time, reached out to hug me, but I moved away, and in doing that I seemed to get my voice back. I said, 'Mariah, do you realize that at ten years of age I had to learn by heart a long poem about some flowers I would not see in real life until I was nineteen?'
>
> As soon as I said this, I felt sorry that I had cast her beloved daffodils in a scene she had never considered, a scene of conquered and conquests; a scene of brutes masquerading as angels and angels portrayed as brutes. This woman who hardly knew me loved me, and she wanted me to love this thing – a grove brimming over with daffodils in bloom – that she

loved also. Her eyes sank back in her head as if they were protecting themselves, as if they were taking a rest after some unexpected hard work. It wasn't her fault. It wasn't my fault. But nothing could change the fact that where she saw beautiful flowers I saw sorrow and bitterness. The same thing could cause us to shed tears, but those tears would not taste the same. We walked home in silence. I was glad to have at last seen what a wretched daffodil looked like.[15]

Through the passionate voice of Lucy, the young West Indian *au pair* to the white American Mariah, Kincaid captures the imperialist gaze that denigrates local landscapes and substitutes absurd images of European climes, meadows, lambkins and daffodils, thereby undermining the dignity and self-respect of colonized people. These are the selfsame daffodils that Ngugi wa Thiong'o decries in a place far from Lucy's grove.[16] His tears taste the same.

Kincaid is writing her resistance to the imagery. Lucy is no passive victim of her history; the daffodils have shrivelled under her gaze as surely as if she had indeed fulfilled her fantasy of killing them with 'an enormous scythe'.[17] However – and here I wish to liberate my own repressed emotions with an observation that I would have retained a guilty silence about, were I writing this still from the balcony of the Port Elizabeth flat – Kincaid has linked her articulate resistance to domination with an image of the white woman as gauche and uncomprehending, loving the black girl she hardly knows, stupidly showing off a torture chamber as if it were a field of beauty, structurally incapable of perception of suffering. And again, Mariah is not an idiosyncratic creation of an individual author. She is another wax model in the infamous hall, along with Aidoo's Marija, Armah's Aimee and Achebe's Lou Cranford.

Kincaid constructs Mariah out of the tensions that have arisen between white, Western feminism and black women. The accusation from some black, Third World women is that 'Western feminism' is merely a particular and quite self-indulgent interest. Chandra Talpade Mohanty has highlighted the erroneous assumption that all women are

> an already constituted and coherent group with identical interests and desires, regardless of class, ethnic or racial location, [implying] a notion of gender or sexual difference or even patriarchy . . . can be applied universally and cross-culturally.[18]

This critique is valid. In a 'world system dominated by the West' this distorted universalization leads to licence on the part of some Western feminists to produce 'a composite, singular "third-world woman" – an image which appears arbitrarily constructed but nevertheless carries with it the authorizing signature of western humanist discourse'.[19]

However, the false universalizing assumptions of 'Western feminism' have also

5

been recognized by a great number of feminists working within First World contexts. Thus Barrett and Phillips point to 'the gulf between feminist theory of the 1970s and the 1990s'.[20] Likewise, Mohanty later recognizes that:

> Since the 1970s, there have been key paradigm shifts in western feminist theory. These shifts can be traced to political, historical, methodological and philosophical developments in our understanding of questions of power, struggle and social transformation.[21]

In short, 1970s feminism has been contested 'by a politics of difference (the charge that the specificity of black women's experience and the racism of white feminists had been ignored)'.[22]

However, a generalized Western feminism, defined as culturally imperialistic, survives, not least of all because Western women guiltily accept and reinforce the universalized stereotype. Here, for example, is Julia Watson's highly questionable concurrence with Buchi Emecheta's equally essentializing and generalizing categories of Western and African women as homogeneous wholes:

> For Emecheta, colonization, and particularly the neocolonization of African countries, creates macropolitical issues that are obscured or distorted by a preoccupation with sexual politics at the micropolitical level. While indifference to social responsibility might be entertained by educated Western women, African women, situated in networks of family responsibility, must resist it.[23]

While few would deny the fundamental priority of the struggles for food, shelter and safety, it does not follow that all Third World women are engaged in that struggle, or that all Western women are privileged. Emecheta could not have failed to notice the tragic straits of homeless men and women of all colours living in cardboard on the freezing streets of London in winter. Does anyone have the right to weigh up other people's life's joys and burdens against a pre-constructed and one-dimensional political hierarchy?

While this earlier feminism constructed a Manichean-like[24] gender opposition between men (evil) and women (good), the danger is that the subsequent recognition of difference between women can lead to a new polarity of race – black women as good and white women as evil. Manicheism takes a single, overriding duality as the founding classification for the world. Its classic text is Abdul R. JanMohamed's *Manichean Aesthetics. The Politics of Literature in Colonial Africa*, in which the primordial divide is between 'the physically and culturally different worlds of the colonizer and the colonized, which are both engaged in a manichean conflict'.[25] This is a paradigm which, in my view, simplifies social and historical complexities to the point of distortion. Because, however, it carries a core of analytical validity, it is compelling and has influenced a great deal of postcolonial writing.

As an alternative, I propose the concept of 'nomadic identity', a term taken from Sidonie Smith who writes about two white women in the colonial context, Beryl Markham and Isak Dineson. The latter has received Western acclaim with the film popularization of her *Out of Africa*, but not even the magnificent Meryl Streep could neutralize the vehement bitterness and hostility among African writers like Ngugi wa Thiong'o, who are enraged by Dinesen's patronizing racism. Ngugi makes some very telling and valid criticisms in this regard, criticisms which Sidonie Smith shares.[26] However, she is aware that Dinesen and Markham, in addition to being white and implicated in colonizer ideology and culture, are also oppressed women who used the colonies as 'an arena of resistance'. They could do this because

> far from the European center's hold, they could as white women break through the borderland of female embodiment and achieve a mobility of autobiographical script unavailable to them in the 'home' country.[27]

Smith explores 'the complications of colonized place, gender, and race in the politics of self-representation'[28] and ultimately, in her awareness of the similarities and also fundamental differences in the ways these two white women conceptualize African women, Smith observes that we are positioned 'complexly and relationally in consciousness, behavioral practices, and politics'. She rejects

> any simplistic or romanticized notion of 'marginality', recognizing instead that positions of marginalities and centralities are nomadic, that each of us, multiply positioned in discursive fields, inhabits margins and centers. Thus the call for reading the other woman requires that we consider the multiplicity of differences between one woman and another, the multiplicity of differences within each of us.[29]

Another rich, multi-layered reading which exemplifies the nature of nomadic identity is Suzanne Chester's analysis of Marguerite Duras. Duras is not only white in the colonies (French Indochina) and female, she is also poor; to be a poor-white in the colonial context is to carry a particular burden of suffering and concealment, humiliation and secrecy. Duras wrote her autobiography, *The Sea Wall*, in the 1950s and Chester demonstrates the challenge to Manichean fixity in her description of the causes and effects of Duras' re-write of this autobiography, more than thirty years later, when it was transformed into *The Lover*.

Duras' protagonist in the early work is a victim, her body 'the site of domination by both colonizer and colonized' and symbolic of 'the marginalized position of the lower-class, white colonial woman'.[30] In 1984, a mature Duras refuses this victimized, powerless character and 'radically transforms the subordinate status of the female protagonist of *The Sea Wall*'.[31] In terms of gender struggle, this is a liberating advance on the earlier text. But the device Duras uses to achieve this liberation relies on distorted racial stereotypes. In *The Lover*, the central male figure

7

is metamorphosed from the European Mr Jo into the Chinese 'man from Cholon'. The depiction of this man, moreover, as his namelessness already indicates, exhibits many of the typical features of Orientalism, so articulately described by Edward Said. Chester illustrates how Duras feminizes, eroticizes and exoticizes the 'man from Cholon' within a 'representation of the Orient as an ontological and unchanging essence'.[32] Thus Duras' 'exploitation of Orientalist discourse is instrumental in the textual transformation of the subordinate status of the poor white woman in French colonial patriarchal society'.[33] The man has had to become emasculated, weakened, metaphorically castrated, in order for the woman to become powerful.

Chester does not exonerate Duras' racism in the context of her new found feminism:

> [Duras] reinscribes a variety of Orientalist/colonialist themes in order to transform her own marginalized position as Other and to achieve a position of power and dominance in relation to her Chinese lover. Through her participation in colonialist politics in service to a 'white' female subjectivity, Duras engages in textual strategies that have disturbing implications for the politics of women's autobiography.[34]

Chester's recognition of these 'disturbing implications' is critical if Western feminism is to throw off its reputation for racism and inability to incorporate a historical understanding of imperialism. Equally, Duras' story contests a one-dimensional Manichean framework that divides the world into colonizer and colonized, which cannot incorporate her struggles against poverty and patriarchy, and which denies the complexity of the multiple identities she assumes and the deviousness of many of the devices available to enable her to move between them.

Chester explicitly distances herself from JanMohamed's Manichean allegory in her conviction that 'the factors of gender and class problematize the relationship of the colonizer to the colonized'.[35] Because JanMohamed's analysis relies on an absolute opposition between colonizer and colonized, it cannot engage with the multi-faceted network of factors and forces that constitute complex lives. In these examples, gender positioning set up contradictions in the white woman writer, that challenged the fixed opposition between subject and object of JanMohamed's Manichean allegory.

If these white women acted out a kind of nomadic identity, then so do the magical realist writers, who traverse many varied terrains, both culturally and politically, as we shall see. In fact, we are all travellers across a network of changing, nomadic identities. This network is neither random nor one-dimensional. It can be woven from the complex social, cultural and economic histories from which we emerge, and can incorporate any number of psychological, personal and idiosyncratic factors.

There are, however, limitations in working solely within a paradigm of identity, be it Manichean or nomadic. First, at the core of the identity paradigm is the assumption that people passively and inevitably represent their one or their many roles. They speak as a white, or a woman or a Jew or a worker, or as a complex combination of many of these. The paradigm of identity suggests that we are structurally disabled from moving beyond our own experience. But there can be no mechanistic equation between a person's identities and their politics, no easy assumption that, for example, white, middle class women will necessarily hold certain views.

In establishing identity, only hindsight is appropriate; when views are expressed, evidence for their genesis can be sought from the author's particular social, political, economic and personal circumstances. Ngugi's reading or Smith's, stand or fall on the evidence of Dineson's text, not on her identity as a white woman. In addition, the concept of nomadic identity contributes to the demise of theory and thereby of analysis. Sylvia Walby emphasizes that, with the attempt to move away from the old universalizing and essentializing categories of 'patriarchy' or 'universal women' comes the potential for the denial of the 'possibility of causality and macro-social concepts'. She suggests that

> rather than abandoning the modernist project of explaining the world, we should be developing the concepts and theories to explain gender, ethnicity and class. Not only is the concept of 'woman' essential to grasp the gendered nature of the social world, but so is that of 'patriarchy' in order that we do not lose sight of the power relations involved.[36]

The necessity of not losing sight of the power relations involved brings us back to the challenge of holistic vision. And in terms of this vision, how can we incorporate the possibility of the intervention of the individual, within a recognition of those structures of power that determine us? Or, as Robert Young puts it, in *White Mythologies* (his analysis of the key writings of postcolonial intellectuals such as Edward Said, Gayatri Spivak and Homi Bhabha) when he points to the problem

> of how Said [for example] separates himself from the coercive structures of knowledge that he is describing. What method can he use to analyse his object that escapes the terms of his own critique?[37]

The exposure of the structures of power as merely the stories that self-interested and powerful people told the world, as if these stories were universally true, underpins the more radical spectrum of postmodernists. If postmodernism can be allowed a core, it is that the authority and assumed primacy of 'the West' is what is being uncovered. With the postmodern, 'we are witnessing the dissolution of "the West" '.[38] However, is the mantle of authoritative storytelling merely inherited by non-Western commentators? Is blackness the badge of legitimacy, within the old identity politics of polarized racial difference? From where do postcolonial intellectuals, on their part, derive their authority?

9

At times Gayatri Spivak, one of the most celebrated of the postcolonial intellectuals, vehemently contests the homogenization of speaking as any one identity:

> The question of 'speaking as' involves a distancing from oneself. The moment I have to think of the ways in which I will speak as an Indian, or as a feminist, the ways in which I will speak as a woman, what I am doing is trying to generalize myself, make myself a representative, trying to distance myself from some kind of inchoate speaking as such. There are many subject positions which one must inhabit; one is not just one thing.[39]

Even more recently, in exposing 'the fraud at the heart of identity politics', Spivak has written that

> all over the world today identity politics (that is to say, a separation in the name of the undifferentiated identity of religion, nation, or subnation) is big news and almost everywhere bad news.[40]

She has in these terms addressed the abject and apologetic position of some white males that she teaches:

> I will have in an undergraduate class, let's say, a young white male student, politically-correct, who will say: 'I am only a bourgeois white male, I can't speak'. In that situation . . . I say to them: 'Why not develop a certain degree of rage against the history that has written such an abject script for you that you are silenced?' Then you begin to investigate what it is that silences you, rather than take this very deterministic position – since my skin colour is this, since my sex is this, I cannot speak. I call these things . . . somewhat derisively, chromatism: basing everything on skin color – 'I am white, I can't speak' – and genitalism: depending on what kind of genitals you have, you can or cannot speak in certain situations.[41]

Spivak, moreover, acknowledges that the white male dilemma is shared by other privileged speakers, including herself as 'an infinitely privileged person' when she thinks 'in terms of the much larger female constituency in the world'. She concedes that even she sometimes compares herself 'to my white male students, who complain that they can no longer speak'.[42]

What this suggests is that, through an intellectual process of study, through the awareness of the exploitative role that others who have similar backgrounds to you have played, you can edit the script prepared for you and speak another role, one that understands power and oppression, even where you are powerful, even if you have not been oppressed. In this vein Spivak quite tentatively proposes that one must unlearn one's privilege 'so that, not only does one become able to listen to that other constituency, but one learns to speak in such a way that one will be taken seriously by that other constituency'.[43]

But again, from what source does the progressive intellectual derive the knowledge, the power and the legitimacy to be authoritative, given the subaltern's silenced voice? Or, in Spivak's terms, how does one 'earn the right to criticise'? In other words, Spivak's prime issue is not the silenced voice of the progressive white male, but her now-famous statement that 'the subaltern cannot speak'. If the subaltern is understood primarily as black, underclass and female, how can she find a voice or, more to the point for us here, can anyone speak for her, and if so how and in what language? It is here that the contradictions with the enlightened stances above begin to show. Spivak becomes significantly speechless in answer to this question, put to her as – 'What are you trying to set up? A new speaking place?':

> I have no idea what I'm trying to say about this particular problem. I don't have a very specific answer yet. I don't see my way clear, because I don't think one can deny history quite so easily. This is a very difficult undertaking, and it also seems to me that I'll probably not succeed in it.[44]

Of course one cannot escape history so easily. We have to search for explanations that are historical and that incorporate the individual commentator, but that are larger than issues of identity, of origins or of chance. Spivak seems unable to frame such explanations and tends to revert to the legitimacy of speaking as a Third World woman after all. She insists that the white men 'will of course not speak in the same way about the Third World material'.[45] This suggests that Spivak's white male student will not speak the same as some unnamed authoritative voice. The implication is that an insider, a Third World person (herself?), will speak differently and somewhat more authoritatively. This is questionable and contradicts Spivak's earlier vehemence against identity politics. It is an example of the fact that

> although Spivak constantly attempts to undo the homogeneity of the signifier 'Third World Woman', by announcing her position as investigator so insistently, she runs the inevitable risk of presenting herself as the representative of that very 'Third World Woman'.[46]

Young describes how Sartre, in his introduction to Fanon's *The Wretched of the Earth*, experiences 'the discomfiture felt by a European reading [it]'.[47] In a slightly different context Young refers again to the 'discomfiture' experienced in reading Spivak's dense, complex and shifting texts.[48] Although Young is not in the case of Spivak referring directly to the response of the European reader, the repetition of the term 'discomfiture' raises Sartre's observation as European reader and links, even if unconsciously, to Young's own responses as European critic of a radical, Third World text. It is precisely this 'discomfiture' of which Spivak is gleefully aware and mercilessly exploits when assuming the role of speaking as an insider, a black, colonized, subaltern, Third World woman:

Subordinate people use this also; and we are not without a sense of irony: we use it. I talk a lot, right? And when I get very excited I interrupt people; and I am making a joke, but in fact it is never perceived as a joke unless I tell them. I will quite often say, 'You know, in my culture it shows interest and respect if someone interrupts': and immediately there are these very pious faces, and people allow me to interrupt. It is not as if we don't perceive the homogenization; we exploit it, why not?[49]

I think there are very good reasons for 'why not'. It promotes the very homogenization that Spivak elsewhere so vehemently contests. It is not by chance that here we have the use of 'we' for the subordinate, in opposition to the earlier admission of privilege.

Spivak attempts to resolve this contradiction between being privileged and simultaneously being representative of an homogenized Third World woman. This she does by creating a concept of subalternity that is stretched to incorporate not only the oppressed underclasses, but also those radical intellectuals who align themselves 'with the subaltern as a strategy for "bringing hegemonic historiography to crisis" '.[50] No amount of emphasis regarding the discontinuity between 'the two forms of subalternity' can erase the questionable blurring.

In summary, all these different, contradictory stances taken up by Spivak can co-exist only very uneasily. She is self-conscious about her own privileges, yet speaks as a Third World woman and fervently rejects speaking as any one identity. She encourages white males to speak out and promotes discomfiture in them when they do. All of this results in a mixture of strategies such as becoming inarticulate, or blurring both her own speaking voice and the definition of what actually comprises a subaltern position.

What I am writing here is my own, personal refusal of discomfiture, of having a caricatured pious face and in so doing, to sketch out a Third Eye framework within which to work.

The fact of the matter is that neither Said, Spivak, nor Young himself satisfactorily answers the question of where they themselves speak from and derive authoritativeness. Young has correctly emphasized that 'the problem of history becomes indissociable from the role of the investigator'.[51] What is his role as investigator in this instance? He is a Fellow and Tutor in English at Wadham College, Oxford. Perhaps he is one of Spivak's white males, resisting the abject script with which he has been saddled? How can we stop the futile cycle where Young questions where Spivak derives the authority to speak and I question where Young does and you question where I do?

Arising out of, and moving beyond, our nomadic identities, I believe that the individual can analyse and oppose the inequalities arising out of structural power relations within the humanistic framework that I outlined earlier on in this chapter.

What is the relationship between power, humanism and my explorations around the question of the role and authority of the commentator? Surreptitiously emerging from the work of Said and Spivak is the recognition of the possibilities inherent in intellectual work of developing beyond the determining forces of one's background and of making a progressive intervention. Young is critical of this position and yet his own work articulately enacts how a white, middle class male can, through painstaking research, depict postcolonial power struggles.

Robert Young's *White Mythologies* is based on his belief in the desirability of the demise of the authoritativeness of the West in the context of a recognition of the exploitativeness of imperialism and a support for Third World struggles. His postmodernism is precisely linked to a radical postcolonialism that deconstructs the Eurocentricity of bogus humanism. However, his fervent opposition to this type of humanism makes him shy away from acknowledging that his own speaking position is established by means of his intellect, his own compassionate humanity and his ethics, which defy seeing the world in terms of the interests of white, Western capitalism.

Tzvetan Todorov was asked to comment on the contributions to the special issue of the journal *Critical Enquiry* on the relationship between 'race' and writing. He is aware that 'what has been presented as universality has in fact been a fair description of white males in a few Western European countries'. He insists, however, that this fact should not result in the very dangerous denunciation of 'the very idea of shared humanity'. He rejects as 'excessively pessimistic' the view of JanMohamed that one (meaning the Colonizer) can only comprehend the Other if he (literally male) negates his own being. Todorov affirms that

> We are not only separated by cultural difference; we are also united by a common human identity, and it is this which renders possible communication, dialogue, and, in the final analysis, the comprehension of Otherness – it is possible precisely because Otherness is never radical.[52]

He rejects Henry Gates Jr's proposition that black writing must find black indigenous theories of criticism to analyse it, a common proposition among black African critics who contest the ability of white critics such as myself to assess their work.

Lucy and Mariah's story does not terminate in the embattled grove of daffodils. Near the end of the book, Mariah invites Lucy to eat with her. Mariah has suffered. Her identity has shifted. Her husband has left her and she has had to face the difficulties of being a woman alone. She has a gift for Lucy:

> As a present, she gave me a notebook she had bought in Italy a long time before. . . . The cover was of leather, dyed blood red, and the pages were white and smooth like milk. Around the time I was leaving her for the life I now led, I had said to her that my life stretched out ahead of me like a book of blank pages. As she gave me the book, she reminded me of that; and in the way so typical of her, the way that I had come to love, she spoke of women, journals, and, of course, history. When we said good-bye, I did not know if I would ever see her again.[53]

The book is empty because it holds the potential to write any number of stories. They may not meet again because their histories are disparate; but again they may, and even if they do not, Lucy will write her stories facilitated by Mariah's gift. Lucy's stories will emerge from her life and her life springs from many sources – her time and place, her courage and her luck. More than that, we should not dare to predict. As for me, I think that I too have inherited empty books full of unpredictable potential, along with all the other inheritances and enrichments, both innocent and guilty, that I have tried to inscribe in the book that follows.

The goal of the third eye is to have the confidence to perceive the system and the humility to recognize that the vision of structure is mediated by the eye, in complex, but not altogether random ways. It is to dream of a better life and to embrace art and literature as part of this dream. It is to embrace the uniqueness of the fictional dream's poetry, language and logic.

2

'SACRED NAMES INTO PROFANE SPACES'

Magical realism

. . . sacred names into profane spaces – brothels or magical realist novels.[1]

Magical realism. Writers reject the label; many readers, mostly in Europe and North America, are fascinated by its overtones of exotic otherness. Part of its allure is its elusiveness, which enables it to be all things. Is it a mode, a genre, style, a politics? Is it only applicable to those parts of the world that have undergone colonialism of one kind or another? Given the looseness and scepticism surrounding the term, why retain it?

The concept of magical realism continues in usage because, midst all the confusion, it retains explanatory value. A grouping of African novels has emerged out of the historical and cultural conditions of Africa, which is heir to the cultural traditions of Africa, both oral and written, and to the traditions of the Latin American brand of magical realism. In order to chart the positioning of these writers – of Laing, Okri and Cheney-Coker – the contexts, milieus and histories out of which they emerge must be established. The four interlinked questions of this chapter, precede examination of magical realism in its African incarnation in the next chapter. First, what are the socio-economic conditions that have given rise to magical realism? Second, what is the social positioning of magical realist writers? Third, arising out of this social positioning, what are some of the common characteristics of these writers and the politics associated with their magical realism? Finally, what are some of the fictional characteristics of this mode of writing?

Magical realism thrives on transition, on the process of change, borders and ambiguity. Such zones occur where burgeoning capitalist development mingles with older pre-capitalist modes in postcolonial societies, and where there is the syncretizing of cultures as creolized communities are created. Linking socio-economic conditions and the rise of cultural forms is dangerous if applied too crudely and literally. Nonetheless, at the heart of the emergence of magical realism in the Third World is the fact that these countries encountered Western capitalism, technology and education haphazardly.[2] Communications – road and rail – were set up where raw materials required transportation; elsewhere areas remained isolated and only indirectly transformed by new economies. Cities grew wildly from rural origins, and families were divided between members who were Western-educated and those who remained inserted in pre-colonial economies and ways of seeing the world, with any number of positions in between these extremes. This social patchwork, dizzying in its cacophony of design, is the cloth from which the fictional magical carpet is cut, mapping not the limitless vistas of fantasy, but rather the new historical realities of those patchwork societies.

Fredric Jameson and Perry Anderson connect the development of capitalism and the rise of magical realism. Jameson suggests that 'magic realism depends on a content which betrays the overlap or the coexistence of pre-capitalist with nascent capitalist or technological features'. In other words, 'the articulated superposition of whole layers of the past within the present . . . is the formal precondition for the emergence of this new narrative style'. It is, then, 'as a formal mode . . . constitutively dependent on a type of historical raw material in which disjunction is structurally present'.[3] This is what Salman Rushdie means when he says of Marquez (and we could say of some of Rushdie's fiction itself) that the 'source of his fabulism' is that he has elevated 'the village world-view above the urban one' and that his magical realism 'deals with what Naipaul has called "half-made" societies, in which the impossibly old struggles against the appallingly new'.[4]

What are these traces of older pre-capitalist modes? They are the seam that is mined for the magical raw material itself. Magical realism has very often been seen as steeped in the beliefs, the point of view, of an indigenous, peasant class, like the Indians of South America or the Aborigines in Australia.[5] Fredric Jameson, for example, describes how magical realism came to be understood 'as a kind of narrative raw material derived essentially from peasant society, drawing in sophisticated ways on the world of village or even tribal myth'.[6] The magic has also been seen as spun randomly from the writer's creative imaginings. Chanady points out, for example, that in Marquez's *One Hundred Years of Solitude* 'there are many supernatural motifs such as flying carpets and levitation' that have absolutely no 'connection with an indigenous world-view'.[7] In other words, the magical is defined as the fictional device of the supernatural, taken from any source that the writer chooses, sycretized with a developed realistic, historical perspective. However, this pre-capitalist worldview is still a critical inspirational source.

But Western educated and well travelled writers of magical realism are not themselves inserted within these indigenous, pre-technological cultures that provide their inspiration. Although connected to such communities by their own history, such writers are separated from them by their class, despite claims they may make for an 'authenticity' derived from a unity with indigenous culture. Garcia Marquez, for example, describes 'a world of omens, premonitions, cures and superstitions that is authentically ours, truly Latin American'.[8] But in proclaiming uncomplicated ownership of this world of magic, Marquez claims too much. He is 'native' only in a substantially qualified sense. A far more realistic observation is that

Latin American literature was not developed by the Mayans, Incas
Aztecs, writing about a world familiar to them. Although magic realism
frequently considered as an authentic expression of Latin America, t
practitioners of the mode were strongly influenced by the consideration
of the New World as marvellous.[9]

As Jean Franco puts it, 'the Indian is just as strange to a Latin American as an
Armenian'.[10]

It is this contradiction that is the very heart of the magnetic pull of the magical
realist novel. Magical realist writers have an urge to demonstrate, capture and celebrate ways of being and of seeing that are uncontaminated by European
domination. But at the same time, such authors are inevitably a hybrid mixture, of
which European culture is a fundamental part.

If the societies about which magical realists write are various and mixed in their
economies and cultures, then their populations are also hybrid and heterogeneous,
constantly undergoing transformation. Gerald Martin has suggested that:

> The most cursory glance at Latin America's typical cultural expressions
> in the twentieth century would suggest that within each Latin American
> two mythical beings are always at war, an original Spaniard (or
> Portuguese, or Frenchman) and an original Indian (or Negro, especially
> in Brazil, Cuba and Haiti).

This means that

> A Latin American must face the fact that s/he is both part of and the
> product of many cultures, but *at least two*: hence the proliferation of
> concepts like bi-culturalism, transculturation, the neobaroque, or
> Magical Realism, as codes for the social reality and cultural expression of
> the colonized Mestizo continent.[11]

Such Latin American writers share much in common with postcolonial writing in
general. As Boehmer notes:

> The proliferation of postcolonial migrant writing in English has become
> so closely linked to the runaway success of magic realism that the two
> developments appear almost inextricable. The reasons for the borrowing
> are easy to see. Postcolonial writers in English share with their South
> American counterparts like Gabriel Garcia Marquez and Isabel Allende
> a view from the fringe of dominant European cultures and an interest in
> the syncretism produced by colonization. Drawing on the special effects
> of magic realism, postcolonial writers in English are able to express their
> view of a world fissured, distorted, and made incredible by cultural
> displacement.[12]

In other words, these postcolonial, culturally displaced migrants, who write magical realist novels, or who celebrate these fictions in their criticism, share some common features. Specifically, these writers are quite distant from the mass of poor, illiterate peasants and workers that populate their countries of origin. These urban intellectuals, who produce the bulk of the literature and culture of their countries, share this in common despite their own differences and those of their countries' histories. For example, Timothy Brennan quotes Rushdie as writing that he

> recognized a deeper affinity with that small country in a continent (Central America) upon which I had never set foot. I grew daily more interested in its affairs, because, after all, I was myself the child of a successful revolt against a great power, my consciousness the product of the triumph of the Indian revolution. It was perhaps also true that those of us who did not have our origins in the countries of the mighty West, or North, had something in common – not, certainly, anything as simplistic as a unified 'third world' outlook, but at least some knowledge of what weakness was like, some awareness of the view from underneath, and of how it felt to be there, on the bottom, looking up at the descending heel.[13]

But how can Salman Rushdie describe his vistas as panning out from underneath, from weakness, from 'a view from underneath', given that he is a second generation Cambridge graduate? Why does he pose the existence of 'something in common' with other Third World countries, something as powerful as a wretched place beneath the 'descending heel', and simultaneously retreat from such an identification with the disclaimer that he has nothing 'as simplistic as a unified "third world" outlook'?

Aijaz Ahmad takes a different view. He appears to reject generalizations about postcolonialism, about whole worlds, about how 'difference between the first world and the third is absolutised as an Otherness'. He interrogates the way in which 'the enormous cultural heterogeneity of social formations within the so-called Third World is submerged'.[14] He insists, in relation to Asia, Africa and Latin America, that

> These various countries, from the three continents, have been assimilated into the global structure of capitalism not as a single cultural ensemble but highly differentially, each establishing its own circuits of (unequal) exchange with the metropolis, each acquiring its own very distinct class formations. Circuits of exchange among them are rudimentary at best; an average Nigerian who is literate about his own country would know infinitely more about England and the United States than about any country of Asia or Latin America or indeed about most countries of Africa. The kind of circuits that bind the cultural complexes of the advanced capitalist countries simply do not exist among countries of backward capitalism, and capitalism itself, which is dominant but not

altogether universalized, does not yet have the same power of homogeni-
sation in its cultural logic in most of these countries, *except among the urban
bourgeoisie.*[15]

Ahmad is here appropriately insisting on difference and specificity. He accepts,
however, that what he says about the fundamental cultural differences between
Third World countries does not altogether apply to the urban bourgeoisie of these
various countries. Given that he later states, in a different context, that it is 'the
urban intelligentsia which produces most of the written texts', he would need to
accept the possibility that a degree of generalization is valid in the context of
culture and in relation to that social stratum of urban intellectuals.[16] While, in
economic terms, it is no longer possible to talk sweepingly about the natures of the
First and the Third Worlds, or of postcolonial societies, it remains true that the war
against the cultural hegemony of the First World continues not only to dominate
the literary strategies, images, languages and forms of postcolonial intellectuals,
but in fundamental ways to define them as a group.

Arif Dirlik is also dubious about generalizations with reference to postcolonials.
In his essay, 'The Postcolonial Aura: Third World Criticism in the Age of Global
Capitalism', he suggests that it is 'misleading' to classify together as 'postcolonial'
intellectuals who differ as widely politically as, for example, Edward Said, Gayatri
Spivak, Homi Bhabha and Kwame Anthony Appiah.[17] However, Dirlik goes on to
make stinging generalizations about the positioning of all of those 'Third World
intellectuals, who have arrived in First World Academe'.[18] He contests not so
much classification *per se*, but rather the particular concept of hybrid in-betweeness.
He implies that whatever their differing politics, such intellectuals share a 'postcolonial discourse' that is 'an expression not so much of agony over identity, as it
often appears, but of newfound power'.[19] It is this power that he sees as playing a
critical role 'in the resolution of contradictions presented by hybridity'.[20] Having
overtly rejected the lumping together of very different thinkers, Dirlik covertly
unites them by stating 'bluntly' that:

> postcoloniality is designed to *avoid* making sense of the current crisis and,
> in the process, to cover up the origins of postcolonial intellectuals in a
> global capitalism of which they are not so much victims as beneficia-
> ries.[21]

Obviously, the social position of relative privilege that characterizes these
writers determines, at least to some extent, the nature of their politics – the ambiguity of being both opposed to cultural imperialism and also aloof from any
organized political engagement, of being implicated in the outlooks of ordinary
people back home and also alienated from them culturally and distanced from
them by privilege and global experience.

Timothy Brennan's book on Salman Rushdie attempts to capture the nature of
these 'Third World cosmopolitans'. He explains that he began his book

by looking at a group of literary celebrities from the Third World who all seemed to share something. Originally, this included Mario Vargas Llosa, Derek Walcott, Salman Rushdie, Isabel Allende, Gabriel Garcia Marquez, Bharati Mukherjee, and a few others – a group I would come to call 'Third-World cosmopolitans'.[22]

Brennan attributes the idea of the 'cosmopolitan intellectual' to Antonio Gramsci for whom it was a derogatory term – a cosmopolitan was 'the enemy', a decadent sell-out, 'poised against the vital work of creating "national culture"'.[23] For Gramsci ' "the cosmopolitan" – almost always negative in usage – implied a superficial or 'picturesque' attachment to a cultural miscellany . . . '.[24] This resulted in a 'challenge to national culture'.[25]

A continuing ambiguity to nationalism, national culture and the call to national liberation remains a defining feature of such cosmopolitans, even though circumstances have changed radically since Gramsci wrote. These changes have included the migration of writers to the metropolitan centres:

> These immigrations – in the United States of Mukherjee and the Britain of Rushdie, for example – have in a sense muted the national question, not only because they have happened in the wake of (and partly as a result of) formal independence, but because they have been motivated by economic and cultural opportunity or flight from repression. In that way they deny the old pattern of need to create a national mythos in the country of origin.[26]

By moving away from the framework of national liberation, cosmopolitans, according to Brennan, 'violate an important Third-World rhetorical mode'.[27] The cosmopolitans' 'muted' attitude to 'the national question' is linked closely to their embrace of hybridity. This is not to say that such cosmopolitans share the same positions on the contentious political topics. But they do share 'a declaration of cultural "hybridity" – a hybridity claimed to offer certain advantages in negotiating the collisions of language, race and art'.[28] This hybridity is at the heart of the politics and the techniques of magical realism.

Salman Rushdie, for example, 'rejoices' in his 'mongrelization':

> *The Satanic Verses* celebrates hybridity, impurity, intermingling, the transformation that comes of new and unexpected combinations of human beings, cultures, ideas, politics, movies, songs. It rejoices in mongrelization and fears the absolutism of the Pure. Melange, hotch-potch, a bit of this and a bit of that is how newness enters the world. It is the great possibility that mass migration gives the world, and I have tried to embrace it. *The Satanic Verses* is for change-by-fusion, change-by-conjoining. It is a love-song to our mongrel selves.[29]

When Rushdie is not rejoicing, he writes into his fiction an awareness that there is no turning back:

> He had fallen into a torpid sleep, high above the desert sands of the Persian Gulf, and been visited in a dream by a bizarre stranger, a man with a glass skin, who rapped his knuckles mournfully against the thin, brittle membrane covering his entire body and begged Saladin to help him, to release him from the prison of his skin. Chamcha picked up a stone and began to batter at the glass. At once a latticework of blood oozed up through the cracked surface of the stranger's body, and when Chamcha tried to pick off the broken shards the other began to scream, because chunks of his flesh were coming away with the glass.[30]

Saladin is a new, hybrid instrument which will be smashed and destroyed if the futile attempt at unravelling its multiple parts is made. 'We are Hindus who have crossed the black water; we are Muslims who eat pork', says Rushdie. This makes us 'partly of the West':

> Our identity is at once plural and partial. Sometimes we feel that we straddle two cultures; at other times, that we fall between two stools. But however ambiguous and shifting this ground may be, it is not an infertile territory for a writer to occupy.[31]

Rushdie stresses that 'we are inescapably international writers at a time when the novel has never been a more international form'.[32]

Homi Bhabha is an articulate celebrant of this 'irresolvable, borderline culture of hybridity'.[33] In a chapter whose title is taken from Rushdie himself – 'How Newness Enters the World' – Bhabha celebrates *The Satanic Verses* as midwife to a new, enlightened, postcolonial way of being. What religious extremism calls blasphemous, Bhabha embraces as 'the indeterminacy of diasporic identity'. While, for him, hybridity is the new way of life, for fundamentalists 'hybridity is heresy'. The source of Rushdie's blasphemy, of his hybridity, is his 'transposition of these sacred names into profane spaces – brothels or magical realist novels'. Such 'profane spaces' are where newness is born. Rushdie's critics see his fiction as 'not simply sacrilegious, but destructive of the very cement of community',[34] Bhabha despises them for their 'phobic projections that fuel great social fears, cross frontiers, evade the normal controls, and roam loose about the city turning difference into demonism'.[35]

The profanity, then, of magical realist novels, the 'blasphemy' of Rushdie's fiction, is 'a transgressive act of cultural translation'. The life of Mohammed is hybridized in the process of being transposed 'into the melodramatic theatricality of a popular Bombay movie' creating a new form for 'Western immigrant audiences':

> If hybridity is heresy, then to blaspheme is to dream. To dream not of the past or present, nor the continuous present; it is not the nostalgic dream

of tradition, nor the Utopian dream of modern progress; it is the dream of translation as 'survival' . . . the act of living on borderlines. . . . For the migrant's survival depends, as Rushdie put it, on discovering 'how newness enters the world'. The focus is on making the linkages through the unstable elements of literature and life – the dangerous tryst with the 'untranslatable' – rather than arriving at ready-made names.[36]

The irony, according to Bhabha, is militant and insurgent and the hybrid plot, linking unstable elements, brings newness into a complex world. It is this that potentially distances these particular postcolonials from the more exclusionary ethnic strategies to which nationalist struggles are vulnerable. Magical realism at its best opposes fundamentalism and purity; it is at odds with racism, ethnicity and the quest for tap roots, origins and homogeneity; it is fiercely secular and revels in the body, the joker, laughter, liminality and the profane. I say that it can potentially do these things, when at its best, to emphasize that it does not, by definition, do them. In reality, the novels themselves are heir to many traditions, pressures and conflicting strategies and as such, tend to be an amalgam of politics and purposes, working at different times in the interests of different segments of different populations.

This brings us back to the crucial question of the relationship between magical realism and nationalism. Bhabha sees postmodernism as having created a 'new internationalism', 'the history of postcolonial migration, the narratives of cultural and political diaspora', which is in contrast to 'concepts of homogeneous national cultures'.[37] This is not to suggest that nationalism has been abandoned. Rather, Bhabha conjures up a 'third space' between 'global and national cultures'; a creative space but also a tense one, with the 'tension peculiar to borderline existences'. Bhabha gives this 'third space' image a form in the Mexican performance artist Guillermo Gomez-Pena 'who lives between Mexico City and New York' and enacts 'the new transnational world and its hybrid names'. Bhabha quotes Gomez-Pena as suggesting that:

> This new society is characterized by mass migrations and bizarre interracial relations. As a result new hybrid and transitional identities are emerging . . . . Such is the case of the crazy *Chica-riricuas*, who are the products of the Puetorican-mulatto and Chicano-mestizo parents . . . . When a *Chica-riricua* marries a Hassidic Jew their child is called *Hassidic vato loco* . . . [38]

This is a humorous image of cultural openness, tolerance and respect. But Gomez-Pena is also aware of the pitfalls of an idealized, liberal ideology of racial integration, and insists that his image is that of a chunky chowder rather than the annihilating and submerging melting pot:

> The bankrupt notion of the melting pot has been replaced by a model that is more germane to the times, that of the *menudo chowder*. According to

this model, most of the ingredients do melt, but some stubborn chunks are condemned merely to float.[39]

In other words, cosmopolitans such as Gomez-Pena have an ambiguous attitude to nationalism, notwithstanding their global affiliations and their enjoyment of the pastiche of many cultural influences. Such cosmopolitans retain an image of the 'homeland' as a bulwark against the cultural arrogance and racism of the global metropoles in which they live. The melting pot, in contrast, is a Eurocentric image, the cultural take-over of a great, gelatinous soup. The chunks in the chowder are Bhabha's cautionary note to Julia Kristeva that she 'speaks perhaps too hastily of the pleasures of exile . . . without realizing how fully the shadow of the nation falls on the condition of exile'.[40]

All of this highlights the complex relationship between these migrant cosmopolitans and questions of national liberation. It accounts for Bhabha's tortured attempts to distinguish between 'national consciousness, which is not nationalism' and to describe the ' "*inter*national dimensions" ' which fall within the margins of the nation-space'.[41] Brennan sees such tensions as replicated in ambiguity about the West:

By stressing the global nature of everyday life . . . they [the cosmopolitans] consciously allude to the centre/periphery conflicts raised by decolonisation, and modify them by enhancing the role of the 'West' as, alternately, foil and lure.[42]

The play between the foil and lure of the West has ensured that the question of national culture has been posed in new ways. The growth of vocal and angry ethnic minorities within the metropoles has meant that Western countries 'are being forced to account for the new composition of their collective make-up'.[43]

Not surprisingly, magical realist writers spurn the conventions of classical realism and use many of the devices and techniques that have come to be associated with postmodernism. The embrace of magic, and of the improbable and the blasphemous, has led to the excavation of Mikhail Bakhtin and the carnivalesque, of the cacophony of discordant voices and the profane body.

There is a powerful socio-economic link between the nineties and Bakhtin's post-revolutionary Russia of the thirties. Bakhtin writes within early capitalism's uneven development – a situation similar to that of the Third World in late capitalism. Bakhtin suggests that the 'polyphonic' novel – multiple points of view and the mingling of incongruous elements – could only have come about 'in the capitalist era' and most particularly in Russia, 'where it came upon an untouched multitude of diverse worlds and social groups' and where, given 'the contradictory nature of evolving social life', these different worlds were 'thrown off their ideological balance' and collided with one another. This created 'the objective preconditions . . . for the multi-leveledness and multi-voicedness of the polyphonic novel'.[44]

Bakhtin's deliberations on the novel, and on Dostoevsky and especially Rabelais, provide magnificent tools with which to analyse modern magical realism. Carnival becomes a fictional shorthand, invoking a tradition of cultural politics of resistance. In the foreword to *Rabelais and His World*, Krystyna Pomorska suggests that Bakhtin wrote in defiance of the 'official prohibition of certain kinds of laughter, irony, and satire' that was 'imposed upon the writers of Russia after the revolution'.[45] Or, as Michael Holquist suggests in the Prologue, 'grotesque realism' is a 'point-by-point inversion of categories used in the thirties to define Socialist Realism':[46]

> In the prim world of Stalinist Biedermeier, that world of lace curtains, showily displayed water carafes, and militant propriety, Bakhtin's claim that the folk not only picked their noses and farted, but enjoyed doing so, seemed particularly unregenerate.[47]

The privileged site, the ultimately symbolic space, in which this irreverent behaviour takes place is the carnival. Pomorska says that carnival is 'integral to [Bakhtin's] theory of art' and that 'the carnival principle corresponds to and is indeed a part of the novelistic principle itself'.[48] Bakhtin describes carnival in all its forms as 'sharply distinct from the serious official, ecclesiastical, feudal, and political cult forms and ceremonials', in that it 'offered a completely different, nonofficial, extraecclesiastical and extrapolitical aspect of the world'; it was 'a second life outside officialdom'.[49] It is laughter that 'gives form to carnival rituals' and which 'frees them completely from all religious and ecclesiastic dogmatism, from all mysticism and piety'. Carnival is sensuous and has a 'strong element of play'.[50] In fact, 'all the symbols of the carnival idiom are filled with this pathos of change and renewal, with the sense of the gay relativity of prevailing truths and authorities'.[51] Carnival is welded to the comic and the grotesque body, linked to fairs 'with the participation of giants, dwarfs, monsters, and trained animals'.[52] Bakhtin's carnival is 'a world of topsy-turvy, of heteroglot exuberance, of ceaseless overrunning and excess, where all is mixed, hybrid, ritually degraded and defiled'.[53]

Bakhtin's image of the senile and pregnant hag stands as a symbolic and representative symbol of all of the cacophony of carnival syncretism:

> In the famous Kerch terracotta collection we find figurines of senile pregnant hags. Moreover, the old hags are laughing. This is a typical and very strongly expressed grotesque. It is ambivalent. It is pregnant death, a death that gives birth. There is nothing completed, nothing calm and stable in the bodies of these old hags. They combine a senile, decaying and deformed flesh with the flesh of new life, conceived but as yet unformed. Life is shown in its two-fold contradictory process; it is the epitome of incompleteness. And such is precisely the grotesque concept of the body.[54]

Bakhtin's carnivalesque rompings occupy their own space and play out their dramas in their own time dimension. If space is the ritualized fair, time is neither cyclical nor linear. Bakhtin insists that 'the notion of time has also been transformed'.[55] This is so because 'the last thing one can say of the real grotesque is that it is static'. The hags embody an insistence that 'old age is pregnant, death is gestation, all that is limited, narrowly characterized, and completed is thrust into the lower stratum of the body for recasting and a new birth'.[56] Or, as Peter Stallybrass and Allon White put it:

> To complete the image of grotesque realism one must add that it is always in process, its is always *becoming*, it is a mobile and hybrid creature, disproportionate, exorbitant, outgrowing all limits, obscenely decentred and off-balance, a figural and symbolic resource for parodic exaggeration and inversion.[57]

It is in this tradition of grotesque carnival, of supernatural realism, that Marquez creates his central figure of Melquiades in *One Hundred Years of Solitude*, 'a heavy gypsy with an untamed beard and sparrow hands' and unnatural powers.[58] The novel begins with the gypsies and their 'dances and music' which

> sowed a panic of uproarious joy through the streets, with parrots painted all colours reciting Italian arias, and a hen who laid a hundred golden eggs to the sound of a tambourine, and a trained monkey who read minds.[59]

There is a 'tumult' of 'acrobats with gold-capped teeth and jugglers with six arms'.[60] These powerful images of ambivalent festivity and laughter, of paradoxical bodily revulsion and celebration, of reconstructions of human shapes and forms, normality and aberration, recur fundamentally and very significantly in the magical narratives of Syl Cheney-Coker and especially of Ben Okri, as we shall see in the chapters which follow. But for the moment one must resist the lure of the mesmerizing fairground and ask some hard questions of the political nature of the carnivalesque, and by extension, of magical realism itself.

Although the transgression of borders can be a directed journey, it can also become a roller coaster ride across liminal spaces, going only back to the point of departure – part of postmodernism's exuberant focus on boundaries and 'gargantuan incertitude of the whole'.[61] Such aversion to totality, to the system and structure of social life, is a blind spot. Seeing with a third eye entails celebrating the rich, sensuous irreverence of carnival, revelling in the riotous imagination, in the truths of mysteries and imponderables. But it also entails a vision that can perceive oppression and can focus on systems of exploitation.

A generation before Homi Bhabha, Mikhail Bakhtin warned of the futility of seeking in Dostoevsky's world 'a *systemically monologic*, even if dialectical, *philosophical finalization*' and this 'not because the author has failed in his attempts to achieve it, but because it did not enter into his design'.[62] In true postmodern mode, Bakhtin described the 'labyrinth of the polyphonic novel' in which whoever enters loses their way and 'fails to hear the whole behind the individual voices':

> Everyone interprets in his own way Dostoevsky's ultimate word, but all equally interpret it as a *single* word, a *single* voice, a *single* accent, and therein lies their fundamental mistake. The unity of the polyphonic novel – a unity standing above the word, above the voice, above the accent – has yet to be discovered.[63]

Here Bakhtin appears both to reject the whole – the totality – and simultaneously to retain it as mystically indescribable and still to be revealed. The unity that stands above the word, above the joke, is surely Feudalism and the plundering of the Church, Stalinism and the betrayal of the ideals for which the Russian Revolution was fought. Bakhtin's purpose is the championing of ordinary people and their rights and culture. He rejects the cultural authoritarianism of his own time by bringing on laughter and parody. The repressiveness of the regime in which Bakhtin had to live and work was responsible for the mask and the cacophony of voices.

'A unity above the voice', or possibly within the voice itself, is an authority that is only possible when fiction has a sense of the structure, of the system whose politics mediate it. Bakhtin revels in devices such as the mask and the loophole and these can certainly be tools of subversion and resistance. But if these devices develop fractured autonomy, the mask ultimately becomes a smokescreen and the loophole an escape – a retreat, rather than a weapon in the cultural arsenal. It is on Bakhtin's fear of totality that I wish to concentrate, rather than on his idealization of 'the low', or the fact that the carnival was sanctioned transgression and as such, its rebelliousness domesticated.

Stallybrass and White, who themselves think holistically, suggest 'against the populist element in Bakhtin' that the fair should be seen 'as a point of economic and cultural intersection'; if it was the 'site of opposition to official ideologies', then 'it was also the means by which emergent mercantile interests could stimulate new desires'.[64] In fact,

> one could even mount the precise contrary argument to Bakhtin: that the fair, far from being the privileged site of popular symbolic opposition to hierarchies, was in fact a kind of educative spectacle, a relay for the diffusion of the cosmopolitan values of the 'centre' (particularly the capital and the new urban centres of production) throughout the provinces and the lower orders.[65]

If the fair played a complex and ambiguous role on the domestic social soil, it also played a potentially reactionary role as regards gender and imperialism. The inverse of the image of the regenerative, pregnant hag is a terror of the powerful woman and her fecundity. Moreover, the fair was 'a crucial point of intersection between the imperialist spoils of the nation-state and the European citizen'. Increasingly from the sixteenth century, the fair's 'monsters' (Siamese twins, a calf with a pig's head) were supplemented by a display of the exotic – the marketable wonders of the colonized world. These included 'a midget from the West Indies', a 'great Zulu', and a savage Tonga known as 'the black cannibal', who would 'eat raw meat and dance the war dance'.[66]

History flowed through the carnival – imperialism, gender and class struggles all played out their dramas within the fairground, and laughter, aberrance and debauchery were the languages of the script. This is Stallybrass and White's point when they insist that 'Bakhtin simplified the paradoxical, contradictory space of the market and the fair as a place-beyond-place, a pure outside'. Such simplification is a distortion because 'the fair, like the marketplace, is neither pure nor outside. The fair is at the crossroads, situated at the intersection of economic and cultural forces, goods and travellers, commodities and commerce'. By avoiding this social totality, 'Bakhtin succumbs to that separation of the festive and the commercial which is distinctive of capitalist rationality as it emerged in the Renaissance'.[67]

However, Stallybrass and White do not reject the politics of the carnival and of grotesque realism out of hand. They demonstrate concretely that ambiguity and instability within a cultural system becomes a danger zone that is unpredictable – 'there was never a guarantee that the "low" spectator would not find his or her own radical identity in the "low" spectacle of the fair'. Hybridity is radical in a context where 'a dominant ideology . . . has already set the terms, designating what is high and low'.[68] It is a situation where, as Terry Eagleton puts it,

> birth and death, high and low, destruction and renewal are sent packing with their tails in each other's mouths. Absolutely nothing escapes this great spasm of satire: no signifier is too solemn to be blasphemously invaded, dismantled and turned against itself. The grotesque is intrinsically double-faced, an immense semiotic switchboard through which codes are read backwards and messages scrambled into their antithesis.[69]

This hybridity could, potentially 'unsettle "given" social positions and interrogate the rules of inclusion, exclusion and domination which structured the social ensemble' because 'in the fair, the place of high and low, inside and outside, was never a simple given'.[70] This perhaps accounts for the fact that the most successful of the attempts to apply Bakhtin occurs precisely within the kind of fictions that I am exploring, fictions that

> focus upon cultures which still have a strong repertoire of carnivalesque practices, such as Latin America, or upon literatures produced in a colonial or neo-colonial context where the political difference between the dominant and subordinate culture is particularly charged.[71]

Ultimately the question remains that which Eagleton recalls Walter Benjamin asking of the surrealists, with their ' "magical" uses of language' – 'Can their intoxicating liberation be politically directed?'[72] Stallybrass and White, in their conclusion, seem to answer with some doubt: 'only a challenge to the hierarchy of *sites* of discourse, which usually comes from groups and classes "situated" by the dominant in low or marginal positions, carries the promise of politically transformative power'.[73]

It would, however, be rash to dismiss the migrant cosmopolitans and their global carnivals as apolitical, or even as hedonistic. In attempting to refine the nature of the politics of cosmopolitanism further, we must question the relationship between postcolonialism and postmodernism.

As we saw in Chapter 1, Robert Young's *White Mythologies. Writing History and the West*, captures the politics of cosmopolitan postcolonialism within a postmodern era. He emphasizes that 'deconstruction involves the decentralization and decolonization of European thought'. His answer to what it is that deconstruction deconstructs is 'the concept, the authority, and assumed primacy of, the category of "the West" '. Postmodernism then 'becomes a certain self-consciousness about a culture's own historical relativity' – it results in 'the loss of the sense of an absoluteness of any Western account of History'.[74] This necessary re-writing is pitted against what Biodun Jeyifo calls '*the imperialism of representation*', a struggle which 'has continued as a central problematic of post-colonial discourse'.[75] Jeyifo includes 'the most important theorists and critics of post-colonial writings in the Third World' in this 'vast project of demythologization' of the 'residue of colonialist myths and their more *neo-colonial* re-codings'.[76] Cosmopolitan writers turn around formulations of Western leftists like Eagleton, Anderson and Jameson when they characterize postmodernist culture itself as the commodity worship of First World society in the advanced stages of industrial capitalism.[77] Far from characterizing Western late capitalism as a homogeneous sprawl contrasting with the fertile and potentially revolutionary unevenness of, say, the Latin American life that Anderson and Jameson romantically depict, they insist on the presence of the colonial past within the very heart of the First World, manifested in the existence and forcefulness of its Third World cosmopolitans.

It is not clear, however, that this seizure of a space at the heart of the Sovereign West has been effected through an activist politics in the interests of the oppressed. Such ambiguities surrounding the politics of migrant postcolonialism are at the root of a slippage in Bhabha's argument between his own position and that of the underclasses of the Third World. Bhabha, extraordinarily, lumps together all the 'wandering peoples who will not be contained within the *Heim* of the national culture and its unisonant discourse'. These wanderers are 'colonials, postcolonials, migrants, minorities'. But there are dangerous political implications when the term 'migrant' doubles for both the romantic image of a successful, talented, well travelled and sophisticated cosmopolitan writer-intellectual, and for 'a Turkish worker in Germany', 'Marx's reserve army of migrant labour'.[78] Such a slippage between the two uses of 'migrant' is structural to the ambiguous social and political insertions of cosmopolitanism. Border interstices may be fertile spaces for artistic creation but these nooks and crannies are also privileged and comfortable spaces, a planet away from the poverty and oppression of migrant workers. Ahmad points out that there are words other than 'migrant' that invite a similar slippage, 'words like "exile" or "diaspora" – words which have centuries of pain and dispossession inscribed in them'. He resents the assumption of an exile identity on the part of cosmopolitans who have left 'home' voluntarily and who bear no real resemblance to either the migrant worker or the genuine diasporic who has 'to choose between death, prison or exile'.[79]

What has emerged, then, is a debate with regard to the nature of postcolonial cultural politics. Magical realists are postcolonials who avail themselves most forcefully of the devices of postmodernism, of pastiche, irony, parody and intertextuality; they are alternatively recognized as oppositional to cultural imperialism, but also as reactionaries, who perpetuate the retention of the Western stereotype of the exotic Other. In other words, magical realism and its associated styles and devices is alternatively characterized as a transgressive mechanism that parodies Authority, the Establishment and the Law, and also as the opposite of all of these, as a domain of play, desire and fantasy for the Rich and Powerful.

Aijaz Ahmad and Arif Dirlik emphasize the privileged position of the Third World intellectual, who arrives 'in the metropolitan country to join not the working classes but the professional middle strata, hence to forge a kind of rhetoric which submerges the class question and speaks of migrancy as an ontological condition, more or less'.[80] They despise these 'Third World intellectuals' who 'represent the undifferentiated colonized Other' without recognizing their own privileged position, 'without much examining of their own presence in that [metropolitan university] institution, except perhaps in the characteristically postmodernist mode of ironic pleasure in observing the duplicities and multiplicities of one's own persona'.[81] Bhabha exemplifies for Ahmad such a Third World intellectual: 'it takes a very modern, very affluent, very uprooted kind of intellectual to debunk both the idea of "progress" and the sense of a "long past" ':

> Those who live within the consequences of that 'long past', good and bad, and in places where a majority of the population has been denied access to such benefits of 'modernity' as hospitals or better health insurance or even basic literacy, can hardly afford the terms of such thought.[82]

This leads Ahmad to a critique of Bhabha's 'exorbitant celebration of Salman Rushdie' in his *Nation and Narration*. But in this critique, Ahmad himself collapses social categories – Rushdie, workers, immigrants, art, poetry and magical realism are, according to Ahmad, 'assembled in the manner of a postmodern pastiche':

> The bastion of Englishness crumbles at the sight of immigrants and factory workers. The great Whitmanesque sensorium of America is exchanged for a Warhol blowup, a Kruger installation, or Mapplethorpe's

naked bodies. 'Magical Realism', after the Latin American boom, becomes the literary language of the emergent post-colonial world.

Ahmad sees Rushdie's irony as destabilizing 'not only the object of irony but also its author', trapping him in 'linguistic quicksand':

> as if the truth of each utterance were conditioned by the existence of its opposite, and Rushdie seems forever to be taking back with one hand what he has given with the other . . . he makes statements, but he does not believe in them; the fictive and the real coexist but do not correspond.[83]

It is represented as a corrosive irony, damaging not only to its object but to its cynical author. 'Rushdie has given us Laughter which laughs, unfortunately, much too often'.[84] Such laughter and irony may be a smokescreen for a lack of political seriousness or compassion for the lives of ordinary people. Ahmad sums up what, for him, is missing in Rushdie's writing:

> the dailiness of lives lived under oppression, and the human bonding – of resistance, of decency, of innumerable heroisms of both ordinary and extraordinary kinds – which makes it possible for large numbers of people to look each other in the eye, without guilt, with affection and soli-darity and humour, and makes life, even under oppression, endurable and frequently joyous. Of that other kind of life his fictions, right up to *The Satanic Verses*, seem to be largely ignorant.[85]

This critique of an irony, which allows a destructive ambiguity to enter and to wreak havoc with the novel's sense of purpose, will echo through later chapters in some of my own deliberations on the West African magical realists.

Jean Franco's critique of the politics of the Third World intelligentsia in general, and of the magical realism of the literati of Latin America specifically, reinforces Ahmad's position. Franco describes the unevenness of capitalist devel-opment in Latin America, where capitalism was 'articulated with the hacienda and the mine, both of which disciplined the work force not only through direct repres-sion but also by using the paternalistic discourse of the Church'. Also, the institution of the family 'coexisted with plantation and mining enclaves'. The result was that economic modernization harnessed the good services of church and family, reinforcing pre-capitalist ways of thinking. These ways of thinking were 'archaic', but also became a weapon of resistance for indigenous people:

> Thus, the belief systems of the indigenous blacks, and women were *of necessity* archaic, for no other options were open to them. At the same time, this very anachronism provided them with 'regions of refuge', with traditions, moral rights, and spiritual bonds to particular territories (often

organized around devotion to saints) that could be explosive when the state encroached on them.[86]

Franco distinguishes between the conditions and beliefs of these oppressed people and those of the literary intelligentsia, 'a secular group, empowered by writing and therefore isolated from the culture of the majority of the population'.[87] She is critical of what she sees as this literati's appropriation of those 'archaic' beliefs to further their own reputations:

> The rich heterogeneity that formerly had to be subordinated as irrational began to be proudly displayed by Latin American writers as proof of cultural vitality. Writers like Asturias, Arquedas, Carpentier, Roa Bastos, and Rulfo undertook the recycling of ancient legends, traditional cultures, and archaic ways of life. . . . As the literary intelligentsia discovered the utopian elements in popular culture, it also discovered in that very carnivalesque pluralism the claim on metropolitan attention that had so long eluded it.[88]

In other words, these writers 'discovered the shock value of catachresis and juxtaposition in which those once embarrassing heterogeneous elements became positive devices for defamiliarization'.[89] Far from opposing cultural imperialism by immersing their fictions in local beliefs, symbols and philosophies, Franco's position suggests that magical realist writers reinforce this imperialism by peddling the exoticism and otherness of indigenous cultures to a metropole greedy for escapism. The exotic, moreover, is simply the flip-side of racism, which conceptualizes Third World people as weird, uncivilized and stupid. In this situation

> the Third World becomes the place of the unconscious, the rich source of fantasy and legend recycled by the intelligentsia, for which heterogeneity is no longer a ghostly, dragging chain but material that can be loosened from any territorial context and juxtaposed in ways that provide a constant frisson of pleasure.[90]

Many of the issues surrounding postcolonial writing, its politics, its method of study, and the terminology of its language, pose difficult questions. Ahmad's and Franco's critiques expose the shallowness of a hybridity set in opposition to the recognition of totality, as sometimes seems to be the position in Bhabha's writing. Bhabha's delight in the infinite possibilities of syncretization works against the reconstruction of the ways in which systems of exploitation occur. It is true that the cosmopolitan opposition to holistic thinking – to understanding how systems of oppression work – lays such writers open to becoming exploitative themselves. While Franco may be harsh in her judgement, her point about the slide into exoticism is well taken, and is a particular vulnerability of magical realism.

It seems to me that if this debate on the politics of magical realism has revealed anything clearly, it is the *instability* of the outcomes of these fictions. Whereas fiction embedded in myth, and particularly in the foundational myth of the nation, is bonded to a cyclical view of time, to a privileging of the recurrent over the historical linear, to the universal over the particular, magical realism can go, and is pulled, in many different ways, with varying consequences with regard to its politics.

Moreover, has the critique from the left found an appropriate aesthetic language to deal with celebration and experimentation, with the unpredictable, funny and sensual, with that which is irrationally terrifying and painful, and which challenges the pre-knowledge of the contours of the totality? This brings us to the question of what the fictional language is – what are the techniques and devices which set the imagination on fire? If magical realism can be characterized as arising from particular socio-economic circumstances, and if it can been seen to be participating in the cultural politics of postcolonialism, then it also has to be understood as a set of devices that makes its politics possible, and enables its writers to reflect upon, and mediate, history.

Hybridity, the celebration of 'mongrelism' as opposed to ethnic certainties, has been shown to be a fundamental aspect of magical realist writing. A syncretism between paradoxical dimensions of life and death, historical reality and magic, science and religion, characterizes the plots, themes and narrative structures of magical realist novels. In other words, urban and rural, Western and indigenous, black, white and Mestizo – this cultural, economic and political cacophony is the amphitheatre in which magical realist fictions are performed. The plots of these fictions deal with issues of borders, change, mixing and syncretizing. And they do so, and this point is critical, in order to expose what they see as a more deep and true reality than conventional realist techniques would bring to view.

Magical realism attempts to capture reality by way of a depiction of life's many dimensions, seen and unseen, visible and invisible, rational and mysterious. In the process, such writers walk a political tightrope between capturing this reality and providing precisely the exotic escape from reality desired by some of their Western readership.

This readership is facilitated, moreover, by a familiarity with many of the devices of postmodernism. Irony, parody, disruption and pastiche, when in the hands of consummate cosmopolitans like Rushdie or Marquez, turn into strategies that both invite Western appropriation and also contest imperialism. The thread that binds the politics and the techniques of this genre is tension, danger and ambiguity, threads that often tighten around the novels and produce raw marks on their narrative structures.

If the here and now of history is syncretized with the mysterious and the magical, then time and space are potentially transformed within the hybrid, magical realist plot. Edwin Williamson suggests that 'magical realism undermined a sense of linear progress, deepening the mystery of historical time'.[91] Carlos Fuentes describes 'linear, positivistic time' as 'a denial of half our being, of our past, a denial of many things that define us as a polycultural and multiracial society in Latin America'.[92] Geoff Hancock describes how history is 'not linear' in magical realism, how it is 'fragmented, disrupted, secretive, a fabrication'. He notes that 'precise dates mingle with the mythic qualities of a place', but misses the point by simply concluding that 'time becomes distorted'.[93] While this distortion can occur, what magical realism aims for is an even more true perception of the complexities of the history chosen for scrutiny, by means of the 'exact dates' of the plot and by means of the supernatural devices. Kumkum Sangari captures the complexity of the magical realist time ideal in her *The Politics of the Possible*. For her, 'the absence of a single linear time need not be read as the absence of a historical consciousness, but rather as the operation of a different kind of historical consciousness'. In other words, 'the play of linear time with circular time' enables magical realism 'to generate and manage various kinds of alignments, tensions, and discontinuities between sequential and nonsequential time'.[94] Time itself is hybrid. Magical realist time tries to be neither the linear time of history, nor the circular time of myth. Time

is poised in a liminal space and in an in-between time, which having broken out of the binary opposition between circular and linear, gives a third space and a different time the chance to emerge.[95]

What is this 'liminal space' that Sangari couples with her 'in-between time'? It is what Robert Wilson calls 'a third kind of space' that ideally unfolds in magic realist narratives. It is, according to him, neither the real place that can be found on any map, nor the space in fantasy of the boundless imagination. The mystical third space returns in many guises. Wilson enlarges on his assertion that 'in magic realism space is hybrid (opposite and conflicting properties are co-present)'.[96] It is a space in which the recognizable external world co-exists with what Wilson describes as the 'abnormal, experientially impossible and empirically unverifiable'.[97] He suggests that we 'consider this tentative hypothesis: magic realism is the name that one currently gives to the fictional space created by the dual inscription of incompatible geometries'.[98]

If 'hybrid' is the keyword for the magical realist plot, then 'ironic' is the keyword for its author's point of view. It is an irony that is compromised, contradicted and sometimes corrosive in the fiction. What is always the case, however, is that it is neither possible nor appropriate for magical realist writers to present in an unmediated, undistanced way, the pre-scientific view of the world that some of their characters may hold. The gulf between the peasant's and the writer's point of view is a critical space where the negotiations between magic and realism take place. The magic will only work if it is afforded dignity. This dignity can only evolve if there is a lack of patronization, which is itself dependent on genuine faith in, and respect for, the beliefs portrayed. This is in tension with the almost inevitable, simultaneous scepticism of Western educated writers who assume an ironic distance from the lack of a 'scientific' understanding. This they do paradoxically while celebrating the so-called authenticity of superstition.

In other words, the writer must have ironic distance from the magical worldview or else the realism will be compromised. However, the writer must at the same time have a deep respect for the magic, or else it evaporates into mere folk belief or total fantasy, separated from the real instead of syncretized with it. James Higgens both makes and misses this point when he observes that Marquez's ' "magical realism" is counterbalanced by an ironic, irreverent tone which subverts the very legend it is propagating'.[99] The legend, that so-called authentic world of omens and superstitions, is not the magical realism which is 'counterbalanced' or contrasted by the irony and irreverence. The magical realism is born precisely out of that perilous and fragile embrace between the superstitious beliefs and the ironic distance.

Amaryll Beatrice Chanady battles with this fundamental point. She states that 'what the magical realist does . . . is to present a worldview that is radically different from ours as equally valid'. She insists that the author should be 'reticent', should refuse to judge the veracity, the authenticity of the characters' worldview, and she gives this reticence as a criterion defining the very existence of magical realism:

> If the narrator stressed the exclusive validity of his rational worldview, he would relegate the supernatural to a secondary mode of being (the unreliable imagination of a character), and thus the juxtaposition of two mutually exclusive logical codes, which is essential to magical realism, would become a hierarchy.[100]

Throughout her book Chanady emphasizes the possibility of, and necessity for, 'authorial reticence' which 'naturalizes the supernatural' and refuses 'to analyse the perspective that differs from our normal view of reality'.[101] This reticence 'serves the purpose mainly of preventing the reader from questioning the narrated events, as no attention is drawn to the strangeness of the worldview'.[102] At the same time, and contradictorily, Chanady seems aware of, but unable to cope with, 'the simple fact' that the magical realist author 'is an educated and literary man [sic] who lives in an age which clearly distinguishes between reality and fantasy'. Therefore this writer's adoption of 'the worldview of an unreliable focalizer who believes in magic is invariably ambiguous'.[103]Again later, 'obviously, a narrator who adopts the point of view of superstitious or hallucinating characters is not considered reliable'. However Chanady continues to insist that 'a narrator who describes his world ironically destroys the validity of the characters' perspectives' and the magical realism in the process.[104] I have been suggesting that it is precisely the mix of authorial reticence with authorial irony that is a defining feature of the magical realist text.

This is not to suggest that the mix is a smooth, untroubled merging between irony and faith. There is tension between the scepticism of Western educated writers who assume an ironic distance from the lack of a 'scientific' understanding on the part of the 'uneducated' and their simultaneous celebration of the so-called authenticity of superstition, a celebration that is vulnerable to degeneration into the exotic.

Mention of the exotic brings us back to the question of the politics of narrative. If magical realism is as much a set of formal devices and strategies as a way of seeing the world, what can the nature of narrativity itself illustrate about this genre? The study of narrative is predicated on the proposition that, like language, narrative structure is not neutral. The ways in which the form of a story is artificially constructed out of life's maelstrom, the method in which it is told, by whom and with what authority, contribute to the deepest political and philosophical preoccupations of the novel. In Hayden White's words, narrative involves 'choices with distinct ideological and even specifically political implications'.[105] It is 'far from being merely a form of discourse that can be filled with different contents' because it 'already possesses a content prior to any given actualization of it in speech or writing'.[106] White makes the fundamental link between narrativity as 'the impulse to moralize reality' and authoritativeness. The masses of events that characterize an historical moment are organized into a story for a purpose. This purpose is moral, social and linked in to a relationship with a legal order of authority, which either reinforces or opposes the morality the story espouses. White is struck by the 'frequency with which narrativity . . . presupposes the existence of a legal system against or on behalf of which the typical agents of a narrative account militate'. This raises for him the suspicion that narrative broadly defined 'has to do with the topics of law, legality, legitimacy, or, more generally, *authority*'.[107]

Thus the organizing principle that dictates the form of a story is political, and it is this political, moralizing force that provides the content of the narrative form. White suggests that in the situation 'where there is ambiguity or ambivalence regarding the status of the legal system', this ambiguity towards the social system and its legitimacy results in a lack of the basis for 'closure of a story one might wish to tell about a past'.[108] This crisis of authority at the heart of the nation character-izes postcolonial societies and produces the conditions for the ambivalence of the magical realist narrative point of view. The search for a way to represent the enor-mity of colonialism and its aftermath unites postcolonial fiction writers, even as the routes they choose to follow divide them into different tendencies. They travel together in their ambiguous relationship with social and legal structures, be these of the metropolitan societies to which they have migrated, or of a corrupt ruling class in alliance with metropolitan capital, at home.

The content of the narrative form of magical realism can be approached by way of looking at the nature of the plot structure as well as at the locus of the narrative point of view, both of which we have already touched upon.

It is quite centrally by way of the plot that the chaos of life is organized into a story and it is via the plot that moralizing is conducted. White's description of how fantasies, daydreams, mystery and history come together in the plot has a partic-ular resonance for magical realism. White argues that the moment a writer attempts 'to represent the meaning of historical events', he or she symbolizes them, 'because historicality itself is both a reality and a mystery':

All narratives display this mystery and at the same time foreclose any inclination to despair over the failure to solve it by revealing what might be called its form in 'plot' and its content in the meaning with which the plot endows what would otherwise be only mere event.[109]

It is, in other words, through rendering events meaningful, making them symbolic of wider and deeper processes, that plots endow stories with the ability to represent history and overcome the mystery of the historically unknowable. Later, White broadens this function of the plot by suggesting that there is a parallel between the way in which 'a unity of plot is imposed upon the superficial chaos of story elements' and the possibility that 'a unity of meaning can be imposed upon the chaos of history'. In this way

> Narrativity not only represents but justifies, by virtue of its universality, a dream of how ideal community might be achieved. Not exactly a dream, rather more of a daydream, a wish-fulfilling fantasy that, like all such fantasies, is grounded in the real conditions of the dreamer's life but goes beyond these to the imagining of how, in spite of these conditions, things might be otherwise.[110]

Magical realists inscribe the chaos of history not by way of unity, but by means of plots that syncretize uneven and contradictory forces. Utopia, recurrent in magical realist dreams, as we will see in West African writing, stands for the possibility that such unity might ultimately be achieved in societies where this currently appears only as a slight hope. This is so because the societies in such writing are in transition, uneven, the product of different cultures, stages of economic development and undergoing transformation. The function of the magical realist plot is to represent history by symbolizing these mixtures as meaningful.

The form of magical realist plots, however different their contents may be, is this syncretism of disparate elements. The genesis of this bonding is the interplay of the history of cruelty and imperialist oppression as well as the celebration of indigenous culture and beliefs, especially those which contradict a modern, 'Western' 'scientific' view of reality. It is a utopian imagining of a society that is simultaneously modernizing and also returning to an original, nurturing source.

In the ideal magical realist plot, there is no gothic subtext, no dark space of the unconscious, no suppressed libidinous attic space, in which a madwoman is concealed. The mysterious, sensuous, unknown and unknowable are not in the subtext, as in realist writing, but rather share the fictional space with history.[111] The alternative histories, the mysteries, dreams, pain, bewilderments and nightmare labyrinths, struggle to be visibly inscribed within the text's surfaces. This cacophony is viewed through the lens of the ambiguously ironic gaze of the creator of the magical realist plot. Searching for authoritative textual weight demands sleuth work by the critic. Characters cannot be assumed to hold the opinions of their authors; omniscient narrators are not as trustworthy as was once thought; and the text has even been known to turn tables on the author and have a last word.

3

AN ENDLESS FOREST OF TERRIBLE CREATURES

Magical realism in West Africa

> [The dwarfs] related the story of how they were the last members of a race of dwarf children who had been trapped in a grove by an evil spirit, which had once been a beautiful woman who had consorted with the devil. By so doing she had sold her soul to him, and promised him all the children of the region. Teaming up together, the children had found a way out of the grove, and discovered the herbs that could prolong life, shorten the forms of people, and allow them to be in several places at the same time.
>
> (Syl Cheney-Coker, 1990, p. 205.)

African writers tend to reject the label of magical realism. One reason for this perhaps is that it implies the slavish imitation of Latin America. It suggests a denial, in other words, of local knowledge and beliefs, language and rhetoric; it seems to perpetuate imperialist notions that nothing new, intellectually or spiritually, originated in Africa. But, as I argued in the previous chapter, local context is of central importance in magical realist writing. Marquez was deeply influenced by the worldviews and ways of life of the mixed populations of African, Indian and Spanish descent of his tropical Caribbean zone of Columbia.[1] Salman Rushdie's fictions can only be partially appreciated without a deep knowledge of India's religions and attendant politics. Likewise, the West African novels which will be considered in the chapters which follow are moulded and constructed out of West African cultural and religious heritages.

To search for local knowledge, however, carries, on the one hand, the danger of essentialism, overtones of a static, homogeneous African authenticity. On the other hand, an African postmodernist like V.Y. Mudimbe warns us that Africa has itself been invented by Western discourse, denying the possibility of any terms with which to describe the continent's past other than those contaminated by the very forces we wish to remove from the centre of the stage.

I will not, therefore, be attempting to recover some pristine past. Writers are shaped by, and select from, multiple traditions, including those received locally, in a quite narrowly defined geographical sense, as well as through contact, both within the continent, and also within the globe; their legacies come from diverse sources and are put towards new aesthetic enterprises, whose origins cannot be easily unravelled.

37

Why would we wish to unravel them? In other words, if a core question of this chapter is, what is the nature of some of the West African spiritual and literary traditions that are selected, mediated and transformed into modern African fictions, then a prior question is: what is the purpose of investigating these traditions, especially given that this whole zone is surrounded by minefields? Or, as Eileen Julien puts it: 'Those elements in African novels . . . may well derive from African oral traditions. But then we must ask ourselves, What is the usefulness of this judgement . . . ?'[2] She answers her own question by insisting that the elements of oral traditions that are present in modern fiction are clues to the particular purpose to which the writer is putting the work. They are strategic devices, called upon to serve particular functions – 'They solve or help to solve a formal or aesthetic problem that the writer faces'.[3] I would emphasize *the politics* of those choices, but Julien is correct in insisting that writers are 'conscious and crafty' – the inclusion of oral references is not involuntarily linked to an African essence, to the writer's fixed roots, not created 'without the complicity or knowledge of the author'.[4]

This approach leads to an understanding that the oral tradition, along with written textual influences, is part of the cross referencing that has come to be known as intertextuality. In other words, 'The exchanges, allusions, and self-reference that we take for granted among written texts exist across modes of language and narrative art as well'.[5] When Cheney-Coker refers in my interview with him to the work of Amos Tutuola (to which I will be referring again later) this is because he has elected to adapt a Tutuolan story to suit his own purposes; he does not have to have Yoruba background to do so.[6] Tutuola has, of course, himself selected from what he has to hand. Writers are influenced by other writers, who have themselves been influenced by the traditions of their own particular families, groups and regions, as well as by those of other writers. If there is a predominance of Yoruba reference in what follows, that is because there has been more written about the Yoruba, ethnographically and in cultural studies, than most other groups, and this in turn has made available certain images and forms, stories and devices to non-Yoruba writers. And in all of this cross referencing of old and new stories, anonymous tales and renowned and celebrated contemporary cultural heroes, Booker and Nobel prize winners, there is the politics of renunciation of the perceived stranglehold of Western cultural origins.

This cultural politics helps to explain, as I argued in Chapter 2, that a critical, although not obligatory, component of magical realism, was the inspiration writers actively chose to derive from their interpretations of the worldviews of indigenous people – of those deemed to live within a pre-industrial, and hence pre-colonial, way of life. Many consequences flowed from this attempt on the part of a literati that had greater or lesser links with those people and that way of life, but who were never seamlessly unified with them. These consequences were deemed to be aesthetic and political. In order to investigate the aesthetics and politics of the particular brands of West African magical realist novels that I am scrutinizing, the nature of that inspiration apparently derived from the oral traditions, from the tales, the rhetoric, the conventions and poetry of Africa, has to be part of that investigation, however, fraught the terminology, however dangerous the generalizations. This chapter has to be taken together with the previous one, in which the more global picture was sketched out.

What all this should also clarify is that it is almost irrelevant that the writers under discussion hive from very different backgrounds. It is, of course, true that Nigeria's nationhood was artificially constructed by the British, and Soyinka's Yoruba and Achebe's Igbo backgrounds differ in fundamental ways. And where are Okri's roots to be found, given that his family migrated from one side of the country to the other? Different again is the past in Kojo Laing's Ghana, to say nothing of Cheney-Coker's Sierra Leone, which has a unique history entangled with the mutations forged by slavery. What is shared, however, is precisely a cultural milieu of borrowing, reading, and cross referencing; of Yoruba, Igbo, Akan or any other proverbs, tales or poetry; what is in common is a militant appropriation of devices, tools, narrative structures and poetic images, that will serve the purpose of proving that literature and art are not the preserve of the West, and that writing is not the sole form of literature.

To sum up, cultural and religious traditions are dynamic and mutated and transformed themselves, both prior to and also after, colonialism. Varied interpretations of what constituted these traditions of West Africa have contributed to forging contemporary African writing. This writing is itself diverse, consisting of many styles and politics, including a distinctive magical realist mode. In this situation, there are both pitfalls and possibilities in looking at the adaptation of the cultural past in modern fiction. Two writers – D.O. Fagunwa and Amos Tutuola – are widely recognized as straddling indigenous oral traditions and the literary experiments associated with recent West African magical realism and an examination of their writing will be particularly illuminating. This chapter will also explore the more dominant and familiar paths through oral traditions that have been taken by some contemporary, non-magical realist African writers. Of particular interest is Chinua Achebe's novel, *Anthills of the Savannah*. This will provide the point of departure for an examination of magical realist writing.

When Kojo Laing enlists rabbits and pineapples, along with fighting men, in Major Gentl's war, in his *Major Gentl and the Achimoto Wars*, he is invoking an indigenous belief in the crossovers between humans and animals, spirits and people, the animate and inanimate, the dead and the live:

> Amassed on the home army's side were the thousands of fighting men and women, the sparrows, the crows, the camel's six cousins that had suddenly appeared, goats, hundreds of rabbits, termites, the train engines, the snakes, two rivers diverted into the army with their intelligent water power, belligerent bananas, pineapples . . . [7]

The disrespect for boundaries happily occurs in a futuristic novel, set in the year 2020 and includes computers, which along with 'rats and Romans, elephants and lizards', comprise the army of 'the other side'.[8] African writers very often adhere to this animism, incorporate spirits, ancestors and talking animals, in stories, both adapted folktales and newly invented yarns, in order to express their passions, their aesthetics and their politics. The stories, encompassing a transgression of boundaries, lies at the heart of the adaptation of the past. It is no coincidence that this adaptation should occur most forcefully in West Africa, although it is not restricted to it. Here British colonialism, with its policy of indirect rule, made a far more superficial inroad into the way of life it found there, than was the case in many other parts of Africa. Ama Ata Aidoo, for example, says in an interview:

> I come from a people who told stories. When I was growing up in the village we had a man who was a good story teller. And my mother 'talks' stories and sings songs.[9]

Or Chinua Achebe, who explains that 'I have always been fond of stories and intrigued by language – first Igbo, spoken with such eloquence by the old men of the village . . . '.[10]

Contemporary African writers, almost without exception, incorporate elements from the oral tradition, ranging from using the stories to illustrate moral points, to echoing the worldviews of the stories, to incorporating narrative devices and strategies into their fictions, along with all the other traditions and influences which have moulded them, and which they select and transform.

What are some of the spiritual beliefs that drive the stories and continue to inspire contemporary writers? In the first English translation of the complete sacred texts of Ifa, the editors attempt to capture the spiritual basis of Ifa. The predictions undertaken by the *babalawas* are predicated on the goal of bringing the energies of the individual 'client' into harmony with the rest of the universe.[11] What underlies this 'treatment' is the view that humanity is part of every life form and energy that makes up the complex organism of the universe. The *orisa*, of which there are over four hundred, 'are the less-than-God, more-than-human physical representations of these various energy sources who, in Yoruba mythology, were originally sent to live on earth': the energy of the ocean, trees, sea and sky, for instance.[12] The *odus* are the sacred stories of Ifa, passed through the oral tradition, stories which are specially cast by the *babalawas* for a client to correct the loss of harmony, manifesting in a problem such as infertility, physical or mental illness, or other ill fortune.[13]

The specifics of the Yoruba Ifa Oracle reverberate with other African contexts. Most important is that belief in the existence of living forces in all the dimensions of material life and also within death, forces which are seen to comprise an intricate and indivisible mosaic of the universe. This religious belief, sometimes referred to as 'animism', contests the divide between the human and the divine, the animate and inanimate, objects and humans. As Margaret Thompson Drewal puts it, in relation to the Yoruba, but more broadly applicable:

In Yoruba thought, the otherworldly domain (*orun*) coexists with the phenomenal world of people, animals, plants, and things (*aye*). *Orun* includes a pantheon of uncountable deities (*orisa*), the ancestors (*osi, egun*), and spirits both helpful and harmful. The world and the otherworld are always in close proximity, and both human and other spirits travel back and forth between the two.[14]

This mosaic, however, is not an harmonious and seamless unity. The spirits, gods and mysterious forces which inhabit the world can be threatening and destructive, necessitating containment and propitiation. Andrew Apter, in his *Black Critics and Kings* summarizes *orisa* worship as sacrifice to the deities 'in return for requested services'. The purpose of the rituals associated with this worship is

> to harness the power which rages in the outside world by transporting it from the surrounding bush into the center of the town, where it can purify the community and revitalize the king. Thus contained, controlled, and incorporated into the community, the powers of the outside world – personified by the *orisa* – replenish the body politic with fertile women, abundant crops, and a strong, healthy king.[15]

While 'the outside menace' changes historically and includes, in addition to the more metaphysical and intangible threats, slave raids, attacks by neighbours and, more recently, 'the federal government, oscillating between civil and military regimes', it is symbolically and mythically characterized by Apter as 'the bush'. The wild forces of this untamed forest must be confronted and domesticated.

The bush, as a symbolic site, is crucial to the texts which are considered in the chapters that follow. Contemporary writers approach the dangerous forest by way of the representational power of the word. Traditionally, this was the spoken word. Beliefs were acted out, verbalized, ritualized and passed on through the oral tradition, which continues to play a fundamental part in cultures across the continent, albeit transformed and syncretized through writing. Stories describe the deities, the spirits and hazards, old and new, and provide guidance and moral lessons for younger generations.

Apter returns to this theme later in his book, linking the journey from bush to town to the symbolic rites of passage that are at the heart of ritual:

> The passage from bush to town, however, is more metaphysical than physical; it crosses the most fundamental boundaries of space, life, and experience. Even as a literary topos in Yoruba novels, the bush is the place of ghosts, demons, monsters, even inverted societies which only the most powerful hunters and heroes can survive. It is also the habitat of dangerous animals and special plants used by herbalists to make *juju* medicines. In ritual, the bush shrine is off-limits to the uninvited and uninitiated. It is the domain of powers which dwell in ponds, streams,

41

hills, and trees, but which roam freely and capriciously. The bush is wild, dangerous, uncultivated – it intrudes on farms and has to be cut back. In a deeper sense it represents the void, the unknown, the other side of social life – bad death, estrangement, unbounded space, unpredictability, chaos. The ritual passage from bush to town is clearly transformative.[16]

These ritual journeys into the threatening and mysterious forest, whose forces must be confronted and conquered, form the basis of D.O. Fagunwa's *The Forest of a Thousand Daemons* and of the tales of Amos Tutuola, a West African writer who has been characterized by E.N. Obiechina as representing a transitional phase 'from a purely oral narrative tradition to a purely literary narrative tradition'.[17] In this liminal position at the crossroads, Tutuola and Fagunwa will have much to tell us about the nature of the adaptation of the past, along with their tales of quests and journeys, spirits and medicines, hymns and conversions.

Tutuola is perhaps the most enigmatic of all African writers, posing dilemmas for Nigerian writers and critics alike. Unschooled in the elite English-style educational system, Tutuola has prolifically produced books which might be called mutated folk tales, rendered in what has been called 'Yoruba English'[18] and arising as much out of the modern town, where Tutuola was based, as out of the rural culture. Tutuola was deeply influenced by Fagunwa, who wrote his stories in Yoruba, and 'published at least nine books between 1948 and 1951, the years immediately preceding the publication of Tutuola's first two works'.[19] Both structured their epic tales around intrepid heroes, who venture into the unknown, questing, searching for cures, for knowledge, for power. They depart from the safe and orderly village or town and cross the literal and symbolic boundary into the bush, the wild forest, which is, as Fagunwa puts it (as translated by Wole Soyinka), 'the home of every vicious beast on earth, and the dwelling of every kind of feathered freak. Ah, a most evil forest . . . ; it is the very abode of ghommids'.[20] Their stories appear seamlessly to integrate the power of magic and of the spirits and deities with Christian injunctions and Bunyanesque allegory. For example, Fagunwa's hero, Akara-ogun, comes to realize that his charms and spells would only work if he 'reckon[s] with God'. He has been captured by a horrible creature with a hunched back, the limbs of a man, fins of fish, a tail and enormous red eyes.[21] He prays thus:

> O God, do assist me in this. Forbid it that I become meat for this creature; forbid it that he use my skull for a bugle. Let me not perish in this forest; forbid it that from this spot I become a voyager to heaven: let me not die the death of a fowl; forbid it that this man devour me as a cat devours mice. Let the masquerader worship the mask for as long as he pleases, he must return to render account to you; let the follower of Sango serve and serve Sango, he must render account to you; let the devotee of Oya bow to Oya, he must return in the end to you and render accounts. The Moslems worship you as Anabi, the Christians offer you every minute of

their existence. I implore you rescue me, I cannot alone save myself, God Almighty, save me from my plight![22]

A quite recent story by Tutuola, *The Witch-Herbalist of the Remote Town* (1981), is similarly pervaded by Christian morality. The hero is traversing the wilds, armed with a juju ring which makes him invisible, in order to find the powerful female healer to cure his wife's barrenness. The strange and magical assembly of this mother-witch slides into a Church service with songs from the Gospel Hymn Book:

> Then she told us to sit back on our seats. But I wondered greatly that all of the songs which we sang were from the Gospel Hymn Book. Although the people called her Witch-Mother, she did not pray to the witches but to the God Almighty. It was not idols, gods, images or witches that they worshipped in this Hall of Assembly.[23]

The cures may be magical, but the morality is Christian and consists of strait-laced warnings against rejecting traditionally established modes of behaviour. For example, the bald lady whose hair is returned to her is warned that when she returns to her town 'she must not provoke the men of her town with her beauty'[24] and the one-eared *abiku* ('born and die baby') woman is warned to break all her ties with the spirit world as the price for two normal ears.[25]

What are the implications for the old gods when, for example, they follow in the footsteps of Christ, like Tutuola's River God and Goddess, and walk on water? What mutations have the old ointments and charms, juju and sacrifices undergone when questing heroes are armed not only with magical juju rings, but also with guns, as is Fagunwa's Akara-ogun, and where the magic can only come to life when offered up in prayer to God?

Bernth Lindfors insists that the ghost world in Tutuola's *My Life in the Bush of Ghosts*, 'is an African ghost world', derived 'almost exclusively from indigenous sources',[26] and goes to some lengths to indicate that the image of television in Tutuola's 'Television-handed Ghostess' is African in origin with roots in divination rather than Western electronic technology, especially given that Tutuola had never seen a television in operation:

> Certainly Tutuola must have been familiar with the magical practices and divination lore of his own tribe. And since we have reliable evidence that he created the television-handed ghostess without ever having seen a tele-vision set in operation, it is no doubt safe to assume that his fabrication of the ghostess's transcendental hand was inspired more by the Yoruba folk belief in the ability of professional diviners to magically tune in on a distant spirit world than it was by Western electronic technology. Tutuola was still operating entirely within a traditional African metaphysical system.[27]

Lindfors concludes, emphatically, that Tutuola 'does not spew forth white culture. He may be a literary freak but he must be recognized as a thoroughly African one'.[28] This comment highlights the pitfalls of taking an indigenous view too far. Lindfors himself, in an earlier paper on Tutuola, seems to recognize that the distinction between so-called white or African culture is an impossible one. For example, Tutuola's version of the fish man with the red eyes, obviously derived from Fagunwa's described earlier, has the eyes electrically operated and over thirty horns, fanning out like umbrellas. Lindfors comments that:

> The umbrella-like horns and the electrically operated eyes are arresting images. Tutuola frequently surprises his readers with such comparisons. An angry king has 'hot steam . . . rushing out of his mouth as a big boiler'. Rolling skulls sound like 'a thousand petrol drums . . . pushing along a hard road'. Many other contrivances of modern civilization – bombs, razor blades, cigarettes, sandpaper, telephones, floodlights, football fields – are scattered in similes throughout the narrative. No doubt Tutuola saw nothing odd or inappropriate about including modern civilization in the palm-wine drinkard's world of experience.[29]

Lindfors concludes, that 'by keeping one foot in the old world and one in the new while translating oral art into literary art, Tutuola bridges two traditions. Herein lies his originality'.[30] This is, I think, a much truer characterization than one that attempts to prove that, notwithstanding the language of television and electricity, images and worldview are uncontaminated and purely indigenous African.

Tutuola's television does not represent the intrusion of a Western scientific worldview; the River Gods are strengthened by absorbing Christ's attributes; certainly, the supernatural myths of Christianity are not incompatible with an indigenous worldview, as they are steeped in the same paradigm of supernatural power and miraculous cures and feats. The point is that there is no perception here of the transformation of cultures into hybrid newness. These devotees and storytellers have not been torn from their societies in the manner of those modern writers whose village is now global. They have not distanced themselves from their belief in the supernatural, and therefore do not need to qualify their depictions with the irony of the magical realist. Their fiction is mythical, supernatural, allegorical and epic; it is not the fiction of magical realism.

This retention of older values, notwithstanding the trappings of modernity, tallies with Drewal's insistence that an uncomplicated accommodation and absorption of the new occurs in the ordinary lives of ordinary people. She explains that 'sometimes individuals apply established rituals to new situations or create new rituals that partake of old ideologies'. For example, a Yoruba king, although Christian, 'consulted a priestess in charge of the deity of his forebears, who prepared medicine to protect him on his journey'. Furthermore

When he arrived at his destination, he told his son-in-law that the first thing he had to do was to go to the center of London (which he perceived to be St Paul's Cathedral) to pay homage to its founding father. The king explained to me that it would be dangerous for him to enter another king's domain without paying proper respect. Reportedly, his son-in-law warned him to be careful because the London police would not understand what he was trying to do.[31]

Further examples are the masks that are the basic tools for ancestor worship and ritual transformation, and which have found new components such as 'a World War II gas mask' which 'becomes the spirit's face, or plastic dolls become spiritual accoutrements'. Similarly, in cosmopolitan Lagos 'masks became posh and elaborate, made of imported damask, brocade, and velveteen'.[32] Drewal concludes by reiterating that ritual is neither one-dimensional nor authoritarian. Rules 'such as they were, were often averted and broken; new ones were invented'.[33] Ritual is not restricted to a cyclical, primordial time. Its symbolic journeys embody movement and change. Yoruba rituals are characterized as

> plural, fragmentary, experimental, even idiosyncratic and quirky – the ritual burning of the foam bed pillows, the disruptive fighting, the commandeering, the ruses, the millionaires walking in solemn solidarity behind Sote in nonverbal discourse with the pickpockets, the Christian elite sacrificing to the deities to dialogue with Catholicism.[34]

Andrew Apter, likewise, in 'focusing on indigenous forms of knowledge and understanding which structure and restructure the Yoruba world', insists that 'the Yoruba are not ruled by timeless traditions' and that they make their history 'in different idioms and registers and from multiple perspectives'.[35] Apter goes on to insist that, while unquestionably the *orisa* cults were weakened by colonial Christianity, they also widened their horizons 'to embrace the wider structures and contradictions of indirect rule'. However, 'the genius of "paganism" lies within its oppositional logic' which 'confronts and appropriates the outside world to control it from within its kingdoms and cults'.[36] In other words, missionaries, colonial officials and their followers 'entered the Yoruba universe of power relations' rather than displacing it. They became the threatening forces, the mysterious bush, the danger; 'all the more reason to regulate their powers by traditional, time-honoured, ritual means'.[37]

Apter demonstrates the uncomplicated accommodation of new technology with old customs, by way of a pair of photographs which carry the caption 'a hotel manager sacrificing a dog to Ogun to protect his new Peugeot 504 against thieves. His former car was stolen'. The photographs depict the dog being beheaded in the yard in front of the modern hotel building and the new car. The participants in the ritual are serious – committed to the sacrifice. They do not appear self-conscious in the photograph and, if Apter is to be believed, they are not struck by the traditional and the Western elements side-by-side in the ritual appeasement of an old God to protect a new Peugeot 504.

What Drewal and Apter are emphasizing is that, in the everyday perceptions of those ordinary people who sacrificed a dog to appease Ogun and protect the Peugeot, as well as of Fagunwa and Tutuola, the impact of Western culture is more superficial than many observers have believed. Apter and Drewal are saying, in other words, that the local and traditional have simply soaked up new images and incorporated them into indigenous customs, rituals and beliefs, that change occurs on African terms, rather than following old models of culture clash and European cultural domination.

What Drewal and Apter are describing, however, may be true for the person in the West African street or village. But in their wish to contest imperialist assumptions that history began with European influences in Africa, in their admirable desire to expose the European master text as mere postscript to a more fundamental and indigenous story, I think they go too far. They appear to be denying the real changes in mindset and philosophy, ideology and language that modernity has brought and which filters quite far down. Apter and Drewer paradoxically themselves freeze Africa into the mould of its own traditions, even as these are characterized as dynamic and changing. What they are saying, however, and this point is crucial to our purposes, most certainly does not apply to the Western educated West African literati, who write modern African fiction.

When Okri writes about a similar car washing ritual incident in *The Famished Road*, as we shall see, it is presented with all its contradictions and inherent peculiarities – the perspective of an intellectual writer who has been exposed to global culture. It is telling that Apter rejects the concept of the hybrid, which will be so significant in defining magical realism. In what Apter terms 'rewriting paganism', indigenous spirituality is translated into 'the colonizing language of the church'. What emerges is so grounded in local custom that Apter insists that 'to consider the result a hybrid is wrong, since the very opposition between Christian and "pagan" is itself a product of the missionary mind'.[38] According to Apter, for people living in the urban melange of Lagos (and elsewhere in the Third World), mutations arising in different religious and cultural traditions are the norm of everyday reality.

To consider the result a 'hybrid' is not only the 'product of the missionary mind', however; it also is the point of view of many Westernized West Africans who understand and confront, but also live out these spiritual and cultural amalgamations. This point is fundamental. A degree of distance, coupled with the perception of some of their funny and dizzying combinations, results precisely in the ironic point of view that is part the definition of a magical realist writing. Okri says as much in his latest novel, *Dangerous Love*, through the fictional character, Omovo. The omniscient narrator describes the young and still developing artist that Omovo is, as looking through a book of African art:

> He looked at reproductions of sculptings, mysterious monoliths, jujus, masquerades and serene bronze busts. But he studied them with too

much familiarity, for African art seemed to him to be everywhere. He saw the terrifying shapes, the evil-fighting forms, and the ritual powers as being part of things, part of an order. They were in him. *It was only later that he would learn to see them with estranged eyes, see them for the first time and be startled into the true realm of his artistic richness.*[39]

Tutuola, then, stands at the border of West African magical realist fiction writing, and does not enter the heart of this country. The metaphor is considered, given that Tutuola, for all the adventurousness of his heroes and the riotousness of the extraordinary places and creatures within his forests and uncleared bush, retains an unambiguous set of boundaries between the village and that bush, and even within the bush, between different species and monsters. Chinua Achebe points this out:

> here in this most unlikely of places, this jungle where everything seems possible and lawlessness might have seemed quite natural, there is yet a law of jurisdiction which sets a limit to the activity of even the most unpredictable of its rampaging demons. Because no monster however powerful is allowed a free run of the place, anarchy is held at bay and a traveller who perseveres can progress from one completed task to the domain of another and in the end achieve the creative, moral purpose in the extra-ordinary but by no means arbitrary universe of Tutuola's story.[40]

Obiechina reinforces this point with his observation that 'within the seemingly amorphous structure of Tutuola's universe, there are clearly defined boundaries'. These are:

> as fully demarcated as modern national boundaries and a good deal more rigid since the folk-tale world, having no provision for the visaed traveller, has no means of admitting him from the outside except on terms of hostility. Within the Tutuolan jungle, therefore, the inhabitants, whether they are human trees or human animals or even spirit beings, know the extent of their own territory and do not violate the territorial integrity of their neighbours.[41]

The Tutuolan world 'shows clearly defined geographical and national boundaries and racial differences'.[42] Perhaps the most significant Tutuolan boundary, the one that structures all the others, is the conservative moral code which results in the punishment of those who infringe it. As Obiechina observes, 'obedience to parents and elders by children is a cardinal virtue' and therefore 'the whole story of *Simbi* is an extended moral treatise on the theme of parental obedience'.[43]

This conservatism is further illustrated by Viktor Beilis, in his comparison between Rabelais, as interpreted by Bakhtin, and Tutuola. While similarities have been noted between Tutuolan and Rabelaisian popular culture, Beilis suggests that, while the term 'carnival culture' as coined by Bakhtin 'would not be out of place' in relation to Tutuola's work, there is a fundamental difference between them. He suggests that the content of Tutuola's work is 'much more archaic than any "carnival culture"'. Rather than 'carnival', Tutuola's writing is 'ritual' culture.[44] It is 'archaic' is that it is steeped in the old ways and traditions: 'the mother culture of . . . Tutuola is more archaic because it belongs to a tribal society'.[45]

Bakhtin and Tutuola, according to Beilis, have very different politics. Tutuola, for all his innovativeness and challenge to the establishment in his unstandardized tongue, tells tales in the tradition of warning and conserving. The stories within *The Palm-Wine Drinkard* conspire to reform the lazy and degenerate drinkard. Thus 'the comic often proves to be sinister and threatening' because ritual (or myth) operates:

> with the sole aim of restoring or establishing order, that is, to ensure normal functioning of society in general and its separate representatives in particular. Ritual is a law-governed, hyperbolized (almost grotesque) deformation, but it is engaged not in self-ascertainment but rather it is a moment for establishing stability, eternity, that is, order, norms, rather their violation.[46]

Indeed, although stories may adopt the trappings of Western civilization their ultimate purpose is to bring people back into line, often through the language of a Christian sermon. For example, there is the famous story of Tutuola's 'beautiful "complete" gentleman' from *The Palm-Wine Drinkard*. Lindfors believes that this could have been derived from two versions of an original tale, published in English in 1929.[47] In Tutuola's story there was once a beautiful but rebellious lady who refused to choose a husband or to marry her father's choice for her – 'this lady was very beautiful as an angel but no man could convince her for marriage'.[48] She soon learns her lesson. She becomes obsessed by a 'fine or complete gentleman' at the market and she follows him 'inside an endless forest in which only all the terrible creatures were living'.[49] The ominous warning in the text reads:

DO NOT FOLLOW UNKNOWN MAN'S BEAUTY[50]

The fine gentleman turns out to be 'a curious and terrible creature'.[51] Once in the forest, he begins 'to return the hired parts of his body to the owners'[52] until he is reduced to a skull and holds the woman captive. The point is not made subtly: 'When the lady saw that she remained with only Skull, she began to say that her father had been telling her to marry a man, but she did not listen to or believe him'.[53] She has learnt her lesson, marries the drinkard, who saves her along his own road to reform and redemption. The price a woman pays for rebelling against custom is exacted. There is no ironic distancing from the indigenous worldview, its injunctions and prohibitions. As Lindfors says of *The Palm-Wine Drinkard*'s structure – there is 'no dramatic irony'.[54]

Ironic distancing is a crucial feature of the magical realist narrative point of view. Magical realist writers strive towards incorporating indigenous knowledge in new terms, in order to interrogate tradition and to herald change. Thus upholding the indigenous as a justification in itself for returning to ancient values and customs, without ironic distancing, is inimical to magical realism. Rather, such a position will tend to promote the fiction of cultural nationalism, which employs myth and legend, deities and spirits, rituals, proverbs and injunctions. This is in distinction to one of magical realism's defining features – its hybridity that contests boundaries and violates them.

It is obvious that only a writer who has travelled away from indigenous ways of life and belief can develop this ironic distancing. In their comprehensive retention of belief in magic and in the penalties inherent in disobeying its rules, writers and storytellers like Fagunwa and Tutuola cannot write within the magical realist mode. But they have inspired and influenced such writers who do write magical realist fictions. Overtones of the story of the Perfect Gentleman whose true nature is ultimately revealed appear in both Cheney-Coker's *The Last Harmattan of Alusine Dunbar* as well as Okri's *The Famished Road*,[55] and Kojo Laing's heroic travellers appear to enter a Tutuolan landscape in *The Woman of the Aeroplanes*.

However, going back for a moment to the Drinkard's chastened wife, who had been so horribly disillusioned by her 'beautiful, perfect' gentleman, or to Simbi, who learns to obey her parents, we have to acknowledge that one of the most powerful moral urges in these stories is to control women and to prevent them from contesting patriarchy. The depiction of women, in *both* the carnivalesque and the indigenous traditions, is ambiguous and contradictory. Bakhtin's pregnant hag may be a transgressive, hybrid image that defies the boundaries between life and death, youth and age, but it is also a conventional, stereotypical image of woman as witch, combined with the feared and supernatural power of fecundity, with a womb that is alive with invisible forces and unpredictable in its potential. The images of woman as witch, mother and whore perfectly co-exist in their similarity as archetypes and in their contradictoriness in embodying man's ambivalence. The woman's body, wrested from her private ownership and barometer of the social and natural condition of the cosmos, is a universal symbol that cuts across past and present, African ritual and European transgression.

V.Y. Mudimbe illustrates magnificently such paradoxes and ambivalences about woman's simultaneous power and powerlessness in Luba stories. The woman's womb 'as a fecund body' stands at the crossroads between life and death, nature and culture.[56] It does this because she is both child of an ancestor and mother of her child.[57] This is the root of the ambivalence towards the woman's body: 'In effect, the ambiguity of the woman is there at the outset of all the stories: genitrix, yet eternally second; threshold of culture, yet reduced to the works of nature. This system claims to formulate itself since the foundation of myths'.[58]

Mudimbe recognizes that, in affording women a vast mythical power at odds with their relative powerlessness, the 'real human being with feelings and fears' is elided, and also that this 'patrilineal discipline' silences is its own insecurities – the vulnerability of 'its own solidity'.[59] Apter reinforces Mudimbe's point with regard to the Yoruba of West Africa. He highlights the antithetical sides co-existing within the Yoruba goddess, Yemoja, her priestesses and 'Yoruba women in general'. Women cool and comfort, calm and assuage the hot, tough power of men. Women, as beautiful and fertile, uphold 'the virtues of sexual reproduction'; 'hidden witchcraft, however, explains death, disease, and infertility'.[60] Both witchcraft and fertility, then, 'constitute irreducible antinomies of female power'. Yemoja's status as fertility goddess 'is compounded and confounded by her status as a witch'.[61]

Mother and witch, hag and whore, women are to be found at unstable places – the crossroads, or the marketplace – where spirits mingle with humans, where strangers find entry points into villages, where threatening bush encounters civilized trade:

> The market is a transient place, at once the domain of women and the worldly domain of spirits, the place where they enter 'the world' to mingle freely with mortals. 'The mothers,' by definition, also have this ability; they are mortals who have access to the otherworld. It is in their supernatural capacity, reflected in the power of transformation, that women are considered the 'owners of two bodies' . . . and the 'owners of the world'. . . . They control the world; they control the market. Indeed the market is a microcosm of the world, for the Yoruba concept of *aiye* implies the phenomenal world that any number of spirits, by assuming human or animal form, can penetrate.[62]

This description reverberates in the fiction of Kojo Laing, with his splitting, doubling and mingling of spirits and humans, and likewise in that of Ben Okri.

At the same time there is the recognition that, for all their ambiguous positioning, 'the sanction of the mothers' as embodied in the ritual performance of Gelede 'has the performative power to marshall the forces in the Yoruba cosmos for society's well-being'. It is, in other words a mechanism to maintain social control by criticizing antisocial individuals and deeds.[63] This potentially transgressive power erodes patriarchy by counterposing the reality of social subordination to the patriarchal order. An image that sums up these contradictions, one that recurs in the literature and especially in the magical realist fiction, is that of the *abiku* baby. This is the wilful spirit child, who masquerades as human baby, only to recurrently 'die' and be re-born, causing grief and mischief among the living. Fecundity is compromised; the woman's power is qualified. A mother weeps for a natural baby while through the gateway of her body the world of the spirits find entry; her body and its issue is a commentary on the health of the human condition. The *abiku* baby is the protagonist in Okri's *The Famished Road* and is central to the plot of Cheney-Coker's *The Last Harmattan of Alusine Dunbar*.

In conclusion, and leading to the final section of this chapter, I will say a last word on Tutuola. This relates to a refinement of the assessment of the Tutuolan tradition as conservative. There are many different modes and genres within the oral tradition itself, some of which are more open to transformation than others. Eileen Julien makes the point that epic tends to be patriarchal and 'tied to nationalistic agendas and military might', while fable is 'a potentially subversive rather than ratifying form, premised on magical possibilities or the fantastic'.[64] At the end of the book, she returns to this point and enlarges on 'a trend in contemporary fiction toward "magical realism" as a response to contemporary political and economic realities', and she suggests that these novels 'participate in a tradition of fable'. However, while she suggests that the fable has an affinity with the Bakhtinian outlook, she recognizes that the fable has had itself to be transformed in these modern fictions:[65]

> In each novel, the representatives of power are portrayed through a deprecating, minimalizing caricature, through grotesque physical appetites and bodily deformations that serve to expose their puniness and puerility, to mock the authority, political or economic, that they represent. *In addition, the principled, knowable worlds that characterize fable and other forms of romance have become in these novels worlds of discontinuity, arbitrariness and excess.*[66]

In this sense, Tutuola's fables may truly be the ancestors of the West African magical realists, but, as illustrated, those fables have to undergo crucial mutations, in both their narrative strategies and their politics, before they emerge as contemporary magical realist novels. This underlines Julien's appropriate and repeated warning against essentializing the indigenous culture and recognizing the limits that identifying such ancestry carries. These magical realist novels must be read 'not as a natural derivation of an oral tradition but as a meaningful reappropriation of an oral narrative genre'.[67]

The distinction between epic and nationalist myth-making, on the one hand, and fable and magical realism, on the other hand, reverberates with the nature of distinctions that I will attempt to explore in the rest of the chapter.

In Chapter 2, I sketched the postcolonial, intellectual, global travellers, who are cultural hybrids, speak with forked, ironic tongues, have ambiguous emotions about their national homelands and some of whom write magical realist novels. What I will be suggesting here is that the West African writers under consideration in this book share characteristics with that grouping, but are also distinguishable from it. This is so because of certain distinctive features of African history and the particular political and economic, cultural and aesthetic scenarios that have been played out, within that historical context.

What this has meant is that internationally known African writers, like Wole Soyinka, Chinua Achebe or Ngugi wa Thiong'o, do not tend to characterize reality in the same way as postcolonial writers and intellectuals, such as Salman

Rushdie, Gabriel Garcia Marquez, Edward Said or Gyatri Spivak. African countries became independent more recently than many other former colonies. Africa is still grappling with forging new nations, new national identities, a process made more difficult by the arbitrariness of colonial borders. As Reed Dasenbrock has pointed out, in Africa 'where European powers created states without any regard for traditional borders or tribal enmities, a national consciousness has seemed an urgent need'.[68] This distinctive African situation has been summed up by Kwame Anthony Appiah, who suggests that there is a 'particular constellation of problems and projects' that are 'not often found outside Africa'. These are:

> a recent colonial history, a multiplicity of diverse sub-national indigenous traditions, a foreign language whose metropolitan culture has traditionally defined the 'natives' by their race as inferior, a literary culture still very much in the making.[69]

Writers like Chinua Achebe and Wole Soyinka, Ngugi wa Thiong'o and Ayi Kwei Armah have all dedicated themselves to building such national cultures, within their concerted critiques of the corruption and betrayals of the class of African leaders that emerged after independence. They have all, from different political standpoints, and through varied fictional strategies and styles, described the disillusionments of post-independence African politics. They have all, in those different ways, attempted to offer hopeful alternatives to the betrayals and corruptions. If Ngugi calls on workers and peasants to represent this hope, and if Armah and Soyinka, each in his own way, call on a benevolent elite of healers or interpreters to do so, they all rely heavily on their interpretations, modifications and reconstructions of indigenous beliefs and myths, in order to contribute towards the creation of new national cultures. If Ngugi and Soyinka are in exile, it is because they risk imprisonment, or even execution, if they return home.

In other words, out of a brave, concerted and consistent critique of the corrupt state, there has often emerged within African fiction, an unambiguous commitment and dedication to the nationalist project of political reform. National cultural strategies have been adopted with political and aesthetic consequences. If Bakhtin has been excavated as the father of the voluntary migrant postcolonial, who celebrates carnival laughter and the grotesque body, then Fanon remains hallowed as the ancestor of the African intellectual, who sees that the work of national liberation is still incomplete.

I think, in other words, that there is a far greater unity between quite different African writers than has often been understood. Perhaps this has not been widely recognised because it is a fairly recent phenomenon. For example, there have been quite dramatic changes in the writing of Wole Soyinka, who is often frozen in an earlier phase of his career when he rejected ethnic and nationalist strategies in favour of a concerted cosmopolitanism. This is the phase in which he was known as the oppositional force to the politics of negritude with his notorious 'tigritude', his caricature of the absurdity of a tiger displaying its spots. This has changed, as I show elsewhere.[70] This trend in Africa towards more nationalistic projects of recovery can be seen also in the writing of Sembene Ousmane, by simply comparing his politics in *God's Bits of Wood* with the position in *The Last of the Empire*. Likewise, this same transformation can be traced from Ngugi's *Petals of Blood* to his *Matagari*.[71] It helps account for the mythology that comprehensively re-writes history in Armah's *Two Thousand Seasons* and *The Healers* after the powerful and demonic disillusionment with Nkrumah's Ghana in *The Beautyful Ones Are Not Yet Born*.

Thus while the 'giants' of African writing – Wole Soyinka, Ngugi wa Thiong'o, Chinua Achebe and Ayi Kwei Armah – differ significantly from each other, they are also similar in certain fundamental ways that relate to the national question. I will be demonstrating this here, when I examine Achebe's most recent novel later on in this chapter.

Anthony Arnove makes this point when he links Ngugi and Achebe:

> Ngugi can quite accurately be described as a Kenyan cultural nationalist, whose goal, like Achebe's, is 'forming the foundations of a truly national literature and culture, a truly national sensibility' through his writing, with all the attendant 'pitfalls of national consciousness' that project entails.[72]

This positioning of Ngugi along with Soyinka and Achebe is controversial. Far more accepted is Neil Lazarus's distinction between, on the one hand, Ngugi and Sembene Ousmane as radical socialist writers, and on the other hand Achebe, Soyinka and Armah, who retain as their central focus 'the situation of intellectuals and other members of the political elite'.[73] For Lazarus, the big divide emerged out of these writers' distinctively different political attitudes in the face of revolutionary anti-imperialist movements in places like Guinea-Bissau, Angola and Mozambique. Ngugi's *Petals of Blood* is described as 'definitive of the new politically committed writing that has emerged in Africa since 1970'.[74] But, notwithstanding all such undeniable differences, the internationally known African writers have become focused on recapturing a local national culture based on a constructed pre-colonial past, expressing an ever-increasing disillusionment with current political realities in their countries. As cultural nationalists, these writers attempt to excavate an African mythology, uncontaminated by Western influences. They attempt, in other words, to decolonize their cultures. This wish to decolonize stands in contrast to the cosmopolitan tendency, described in the previous chapter, to revel in a mongrelism born out of cultural mingling. It is a difference that Ashcroft, Griffiths and Tiffin note when they contrast cultural politics committed to the ' "decolonizing" [of] the culture' with that of the acceptance of cultural syncreticity as a valuable and inescapable feature of all postcolonial societies and, indeed, as 'the source of their peculiar strength'.[75]

I am all too aware of the dangers inherent in the binary of African decolonizers versus postcolonial cosmopolitans from elsewhere in the world that experienced colonialism. If, however, this binary is understood rather as a tendency, as itself a border admitting of traffic, then it is useful as a mechanism of classification. It is useful particularly in identifying the difference between the West African magical realist writers examined in this study, and those, like Marquez and Rushdie, from elsewhere in the world. The crucial difference is that the African writers hive from this context of the political struggles linked to the nationalist project of decoloniza-tion, albeit that they transform it in certain fundamental ways.

That these different postcolonial tendencies exist has been identified, if not applied to the African situation in quite these terms. Elleke Boehmer, for example, notes the Western preference for migrant over what she describes as the 'more specifically national' writers.[76] Likewise, Biodun Jeyifo observes that

> the writers and theorists of the second formation – cosmopolitan, hybrid, exilic, diasporic, interstitial post-coloniality – enjoy far greater visibility and acclaim in the academies, journals and media of the metropolitan First World countries than the post-coloniality of the more nationalistic, counter-hegemonic expression.[77]

Aijaz Ahmad clarifies a similar complex distinction when he identifies 'two moments', which he labels poststructuralism and Third-Worldism. Ahmad explains that 'questions of empire, colony, nations, migrancy, post-coloniality, and so on' have been posed 'from the 1960s onwards – first under the insignia of certain varieties of Third-Worldist nationalism and then, more recently and in more obviously poststructuralist ways, *against* the categories of nation and nation-alism'.[78] He suggests that 'anti-colonial nationalism was a tremendous historical force until about the mid 1970s' and that 'this force declined sharply in the succeeding years'.[79] His 'two moments' are unambiguously 'for or against nation-alism' and he insists that they 'remain discrete and epiphenomenal, even though the more outlandish of the poststructuralists have tried to combine them'.[80] For Ahmad their organic link is historical in the sense that 'the precise terms in which this shift away from cultural nationalism has taken place would be unintelligible without taking into account the ascendancy of poststructuralism'.[81]

However, I am suggesting that Ahmad's two moments are *simultaneously* oper-ating and furthermore that cultural nationalism is the dominant moment in African writing, while Ahmad's poststructuralism – Brennan's cosmopolitanism, Bhabha's magical realism – has been the more potent trend among black writers originally from elsewhere in the once-colonized world.

Ahmad is highly critical of both 'moments'. Arguing from a Marxist perspec-tive, he asserts that 'both Third-Worldist cultural nationalism and the more recently fashionable postmodernisms offer false knowledges of real facts'.[82] The Third-Worldists are problematic because 'the ideology of cultural nationalism . . . lends itself much too easily to parochialism, inverse racism and indigenist obscu-rantism',[83] while postmodernism does not critique nationalism because of its suppression of questions of gender and class, but debunks '*all* efforts to speak of origins, collectivities, determinate historical projects'.[84]

Brennan also implies that there is another politico-cultural 'tendency' which contrasts with that of cosmopolitan writers. This is a minority of nationalist and politically radical writing, 'what Barbara Harlow has called "resistance literature", the literature of the independence movements'. 'Resistance literature' supposedly engages overtly in political struggles which 'privilege the vision of the oppressed and argue that process lies in organising from below';[85] this is in contrast to writers like Rushdie, Vargas Llosa, Mukherjee and Allende, who reject the view of the centrality of the masses 'although they are deeply aware of it. To a great extent their work is specifically addressed to it, and against it'.[86] Not surprisingly, given his romanticization of 'resistance literature', Brennan ends his book on a note of disillusionment with the politics of cosmopolitans such as Rushdie. He suggests that ' "discipline", "organization", "people" . . . are words that the cosmopolitan sensibility refuses to take seriously'. What Cabral and Fanon (and Brennan implies, writers of combative protest, decolonizing fiction) know and insisted upon 'was the necessity of national struggle. That is a point of view Rushdie shares in theory, but which he cannot bring himself to fictionalise'.[87] Thus Brennan links an insistence on 'national culture' with 'a decisive valorisation of "the people" '[88] as character-izing this alternative vision to the cosmopolitan. But this is fundamentally to mis-read the political similarities and pitfalls shared by this class of literati all of whom have, as Ahmad has shown, an ambiguous relationship with the oppressed, all of whom are separated from the mass of poor people in their countries of origin by their privileges.

Stuart Hall throws further light on these postcolonial tendencies in questioning 'what is happening to cultural identity in late-modernity? Specifically, how are national cultural identities being affected or displaced by the process of globaliza-tion?'[89] Hall describes how globalization does not simply result in a weakening of local, national affiliations. With ever more intricate and intertwined networks joining the world together, there is a simultaneous resistance to cultural homoge-nization and a revival of interest in the local and the ethnic. As a tentative conclusion, and echoing my earlier distinctions, Hall suggests that the 'general impact' of globalization 'remains contradictory':

> Some identities gravitate towards . . . 'Tradition', attempting to restore their former purity and recover the unities and certainties which are felt as being lost. Others accept that identity is subject to the play of history, politics, representation and difference, so that they are unlikely ever again to be unitary or 'pure' . . . .[90]

Hall goes on to enlarge upon these two different directions taken by considera-tion of identity in postmodernity. That which Brennan calls cosmopolitan, Hall describes as 'identity formations which cut across and intersect natural frontiers, and which are composed of people who have been *dispersed* forever from their homelands':

The difference is that they are not and will never be *unified* in the old sense, because they are irrevocably the product of several interlocking histories and cultures, belong at one and the same time to several 'homes' (and to no one particular 'home'). People belonging to such *cultures of hybridity* have had to renounce the dream or ambition of rediscovering any kind of 'lost' cultural purity, or ethnic absolutism.[91]

This situation he contrasts with 'equally powerful attempts to reconstruct puri-fied identities, to restore coherence, "closure" and Tradition, in the face of hybridity and diversity'.[92] This 'reaffirmation of cultural "roots" has long been one of the most powerful sources of counter-identification amongst many Third World and post-colonial societies and regions'.[93]Hall concludes that 'the trend towards "global homogenization", then, is matched by a powerful revival of "ethnicity", sometimes of the more hybrid or symbolic varieties, but also frequently of the exclusive or "essentialist" varieties'.[94] What I have been identi-fying in modern African fiction, and have described elsewhere,[95] is precisely this powerful revival of ethnicity by way of excavating the past.

Nevertheless, it is important to qualify this critique with the point that, in a colo-nial and postcolonial context, nationalism is politically complex. Ahmad recognizes that 'some nationalist practices are progressive; others are not'.[96] Moreover, he suggests that the 'fall of cultural nationalism' is related to the turning away 'from activist kinds of politics', a politics with which he obviously identifies.[97] This results in Ahmad's acknowledgement that 'nationalism is no unitary thing', and that

> so many different kinds of ideologies and political practices have invoked the nationalist claim that it is always very hard to think of nationalism at the level of theoretical abstraction alone, without weaving into this abstraction the experience of particular nationalisms and distinguishing between progressive and retrograde kinds of practices.[98]

Ultimately, Stuart Hall is far more uncompromising in his rejection of the ideology of a national culture than Ahmad. He isolates and discusses five main elements of the 'narrative of the national culture'. There is first the *narrative of the nation*, by which Hall means the 'stories, images, landscapes, scenarios, historical events, national symbols and rituals which stand for . . . the shared experiences, sorrows, and triumphs and disasters which give meaning to the nation'. There is second 'the emphasis on *origins, continuity, tradition and timelessness*' and third *the inven-tion of tradition*. A fourth feature 'is that of a *foundational myth*'. Hall explains the use of the term 'myth' because 'as was the case with many African nations which emerged after decolonization, what preceded colonization was not "one nation, one people", but many different tribal cultures and societies'. Fifth, 'national iden-tity is also often symbolically grounded on the idea of a *pure, original people or "folk"*'.[99] All of these elements work to deny differences 'in terms of class, gender or race' as 'a national culture seeks to unify them into one cultural identity, to represent them all as belonging to the same great national family'.[100] Equally pertinent is Hall's comment that national culture

> constructs identities which are ambiguously placed between past and future. It straddles the temptation to return to former glories and the drive to go forwards ever deeper into modernity. Sometimes national cultures are tempted to turn the clock back, to retreat defensively to that 'lost time' when the nation was 'great', and to restore past identities. This is the regressive, the anachronistic, element in the national cultural story. But often this very return to the past conceals a struggle to mobilize 'the people' to purify their ranks, to expel the 'others' who threaten their identity, and to gird their loins for a new march forwards.[101]

Isidore Okpewho agrees that there has been a strong tradition of African nationalist myth-making. Okpewho is himself deeply committed to the cultural nationalist project. In direct opposition to Stuart Hall's critique of myth in association with nation and culture, Okpewho approvingly defines myth 'as a creative resource from which the larger cultural values are derivative'.[102] The link between myth and national reconstruction is made unambiguously. Halfway through his study, Okpewho explains the relationship between myth, as this creative resource and 'the oral tradition and culture':

> Up until the last two decades, distinguished European historians and social scientists contended that, in view of the absence of written records in tropical Africa dating from the pre-colonial past, the African could not be said to have any history of account or even a sense of it; the history of African nations could therefore only be traced from their colonial or commercial contacts with Europe . . . African historians have reacted with just pique against this gross misapprehension of their origins. In doing so they have put considerable emphasis . . . on the evidence provided by their oral traditions as proof positive of a past that dates well before the European violation of their cultural integrities. African creative writers have equally felt the urge to exorcise this cultural embarrassment.[103]

This exorcism of cultural embarrassment motivates Okpewho's own work, enabling him to describe those writers who engage in the preservation of the 'virile oral narrative tradition' as experiencing 'the sheer joy of wading in the lush legacies of the race'.[104]

In other words, and bringing us back to the earlier part of this chapter, the strategic selection of elements of the oral tradition in contemporary African fiction, forms part of a very particular tradition. In addition to being the local knowledge, or wisdom, used by postcolonial magical realists quite generally, it is also, within the African context, harnessed to the particular tradition of cultural politics of decolonization and national reconstruction.

However, what must be emphasized, as a caution against false polarities, is the rather obvious reality that the well known African writers, like Ngugi, Soyinka or Achebe, are as at home in London or Paris as any of their cosmopolitan counterparts, and have also selectively appropriated global intellectual and aesthetic traditions, along with the local. In other words, the strategic rejection of hybridity does not make a Soyinka or an Armah any less of a complex mixture of syncretized parts than a Rushdie or a Marquez.

Another way of putting this, is that Africa and its writers and intellectuals have not been isolated from global developments and networks, that the past which is excavated is, in fact, constructed, within new contexts and with vastly new tools for the job. This point has been emphasized by Arjun Appadurai, whose book focuses on the 'cultural dimensions of globalisation' which is its subtitle. He suggests that:

> primordia (whether of language or skin color or neighborhood or kinship) have become globalized. That is, sentiments, whose greatest force is in their ability to ignite intimacy into a political state and turn locality into a staging ground for identity, have become spread over vast and irregular spaces as groups move yet stay linked to one another through sophisticated media capabilities. This is not to deny that such primordia are often the product of invented traditions . . . but to emphasize that because of the disjunctive and unstable interplay of commerce, media, national policies, and consumer fantasies, ethnicity, once a genie contained in the bottle of some sort of locality (however large), has now become a global force, forever slipping in and through the cracks between states and borders.[105]

Soyinka, Achebe, Ngugi and others, operate on a world stage. Their strategies for mobilizing support for their positions are as much the myths of the past as the networks of the present and future. If primordia are circulated globally, then they too undergo change, become hybridized and can only be contrasted with the mongrel politics of Bhabha's migrants with great nuance and subtlety. It is because the genie is abroad that magical realism is beginning to articulate its desires and goals in Africa.

Party to inherited traditions, open to global influences and scepticism, the West African magical realists also offer antinomies, embrace hybrid transformations and, at the same time, wish to participate in the project of national healing. In these endeavours they represent a departure from the dominant and more familiar magical realist traditions of Latin America, but also they represent something new in African fiction. In the final part of this chapter, I will flesh out the nature of the more dominant African tradition, by way of an analysis of Chinua Achebe's recent novel, *Anthills of the Savannah*. This should help us to understand both the context and the newness of the writers examined in later chapters.

Anthills of the Savannah was published in 1987, two decades after Achebe's previous novel, *A Man of the People*. Its setting is the same one as twenty years earlier, a Nigeria, thinly veiled as the fictional Kangan, still bedevilled by rulers who are selfish and corrupt megalomaniacs, and by poverty, which is as much spiritual as material. The novel searches for solutions. Like Soyinka's *The Interpreters*, whose structure this novel resembles, the plot focuses on a group of talented, Western educated and well travelled literati – Ikem, Chris and Beatrice – who become dis-illusioned with the country's chaos and struggle to bring about reform. The solution to the country's, and indeed the continent's, degeneration is couched in a patchwork of many parts, including ideas, stories and writing itself, the creation of a written record, not unlike the role played by the oral tradition, but now the written stories, the modern fiction, the *Anthills of the Savannah* fictional myth itself, as new epic for national recovery.

Ikem, a newspaper editor, and Chris, initially in government, fall foul of the ruling establishment, and both die. Ultimately, an alliance of ordinary people and the enlightened elite, led by Beatrice and symbolized by Elewa's baby, born after its father, Ikem, has died, carry the hope for the future and bear testimony to the fail-ures of the past. Beatrice, Ikem, Chris and the village elder, appear to be different voices and viewpoints, 'witnesses' to events. Stories and accounts, old and new, written and oral, would appear to indicate that Achebe is availing himself of some of those devices and techniques that are associated with the cosmopolitans. This is deceptive. These many voices that include oral tales, hymns, riddles and nursery rhymes as a web of subtexts, excavate founding narratives as part of a project of regenerative national cultural myth-making.

This nationalist project helps to explain how Achebe has recovered his voice after the twenty year silence. The question is not, I think, why Achebe maintained such a long silence; it is rather, what enabled him to write fiction again? The answer lies, I think, in his new-found ability to resolve the contradictions of the postcolonial cacophony, to construct a bridge across the gulf that has often been observed existing between his novels set in the past and those played out in modern Nigeria.

C.L. Innes and others have referred to 'the gap between the contemporary and the traditional novels' which suggests that 'Achebe saw little organic continuity between past and present'. This changed with *Anthills of the Savannah* where 'the traditional is seen to be living and continued in new and viable forms in the present'.[106] How does this resolution relate to our concerns regarding cultural nationalism?

In a wonderfully suggestive paper Gareth Griffiths questions 'Chinua Achebe: When Did You Last See Your Father?' Griffiths suggests that there is an absent novel 'in the interstices of the existing fictions'. The period that Achebe leaves out, in between his novels of the past and of the more recent present, is that of 'Nwoye/Issac's maturity', the time of his father. Griffiths quotes Achebe as saying quite overtly that 'the middle story in the Okonkwo trilogy . . . never got written'.[107] Most significantly, what is absent is not the figure of Nwoye/Isaac but a full account of the period of transition from traditional society to the post-colonial, Christianized world; of the interrelationship with the surviving traditional elements.[108]

As Griffiths explains, and crucially for us, what Achebe does not face is the moment of 'the interface of the two cultures, of the two systems of artistic patronage they generate, *and of the production of the hybridized poetics this implies*'.[109] Griffiths concludes that Achebe had difficulty in confronting 'the hybridized consequences of the personal "betrayals" of those transitional figures who straddle the period of cultural onslaught and change'. To have dealt with that period Achebe would have had to question boundaries and dualities in a way that would have called some of his absolutes into fundamental question.[110] He dealt with this difficulty by simply omitting the middle story in the Okonkwo trilogy. I think that the same dilemma faced him again in the later postcolonial/postmodern period where questions of how to portray the hybrid, global nature of modern Nigerian life silenced him for two decades. Now Achebe is ready to confront 'the cross-roads of different eras':

> the members of my generation are living, you might say at the cross-roads of different eras. This is a very powerful place in African mythology. The cross-roads is where things meet: where spirits meet human beings, where water meets land, where the sky meets the horizon.[111]

This resonates powerfully with Bhabha's borders, interstitial spaces and hybrid celebrations. However, Achebe's crossroads are ultimately traversed by Tutuolan heroes who respect boundaries and do not infringe old customs; his is the way of the sacred mythical past, where the spirits commune with mortals about ancient wisdoms. It is only now, two decades later, that a literary path, a tradition, has been blazed by other writers, enabling Achebe to cross over, but not as a migrant, embracing a chequered reality, but as an epic traveller on an archetypal journey, bearing gifts from the past. In other words, this novel has been facilitated by the decolonizing literary fictional solutions of Achebe's colleagues, both writers and critics, who have provided an aesthetic and political milieu, absent when the younger Achebe first produced his fictions. This accounts not only for the recovered voice, but also for the enormous emphasis on the literary milieu, built into the novel itself:

> Whereas the earlier novels exposed or explored the dichotomy between African oral and European literary cultures, *Anthills of the Savannah* is far more concerned with the African, literary culture that has grown up since Achebe's first novel was published in 1958.[112]

The journey towards the future has to go by way of the past, back to rural Abazon, which stands symbolically for the pre-colonial traditions and ancient wisdoms. The wise old elder of Abazon does insist that traditions do have to change:

> We do not fully understand the ways of today yet but we are learning. A dancing masquerade in my town used to say: 'It is true I do not hear English but when they say *Catch am* nobody tells me to take myself off as fast as I can'. . . .
>
> 'So we are ready to learn new things and mend our old, useless ways. If you cross the Great River to marry a wife you must be ready for the risk of night journey by canoe . . . '[113]

However, this change has to be played out on what is conceptualized as 'traditional' African terms, which involves dipping into the spiritual reservoir from the past: 'The choice of Abazon as sanctuary came quite naturally'. And going there after Ikem's murder, given that it had been his native province, became 'something of a pilgrimage'.[114] This pilgrimage begins with Ikem's tract, his *Hymn to the Sun*, which he 'composes' in the language of the Bible, of legend, of archetypal Gods, Mortals and Nature. It begins with the ancient human lament over the terrible drought. This drought will ultimately lead to the founding of Abazon and the Hymn must be understood in the light of the repetition of the seasons of Suffering. Abazon is currently again suffering from such a drought and a delegation has come to the city to plead for assistance from the national government. Will this drought and the crisis spiralling out of it, lead once again to the formation of a new society, this time a new nation?

> Great Carrier of Sacrifice to the Almighty: Single Eye of God! Why have you brought this on us? What hideous abomination forbidden and forbidden and forbidden again seven times have we committed or else condoned, what error that no reparation can hope to erase?[115]

The blazing, relentless sun and drought that kills all natural life seems to be an inexplicable Suffering visited upon the human condition – 'No-one could say why the Great Carrier of Sacrifice to the Almighty was doing this to the world, except that it had happened before, long, long ago in legend'.[116] Current political atrocities are linked to this ancient time of the sun and to male power, as we will see in a moment. In the ancient, afflicted time:

> The trees had become hydra-headed bronze statues so ancient that only blunt residual features remained on their faces, like anthills surviving to tell the new grass of the savannah about last year's brush fires.[117]

The tree, like the anthills, going deep into the earth and into time, become the wisdom and witnesses of the present. This point is emphasized – 'And now the times had come round again out of story-land'.[118] The ritual journey that has to be undertaken is back to the traditions and spirituality of the past.

It is true that the founding of Abazon is far from idealized in the Hymn. The brutal and violent realities of the pre-colonial past are given uncompromisingly. However, Abazon is revered as having learnt from the lessons of that past. This is a wisdom that the intellectuals, who have trained in Britain and lost their 'roots', have to learn, by way of a baptism of violent modern experience, and with the help of Abazon. As is quite typical of myth, the modern politics loses its reality and becomes the archetypal Suffering, through which the elite are able to reach their human 'essences'. This healing is facilitated by Ikem's reincarnation as a disciple of Agwu, the god of healers so reminiscent of his counterparts in Ayi Kwei Armah's novel, entitled *The Healers*, whose task it is to bring people back to the ancient ways of the past.

What makes myth inappropriate, in my view, as a language of history or politics is its linkage of the social to the organic – that is to natural phenomena like the seasons, to natural disasters like droughts and earthquakes, and related to this, its bondage to the recurrent and universal time of the seasons, of the cycles of birth and death. In *Anthills of the Savannah* the social and the natural worlds are very precisely given as reflections of each other. This is so by way of two major mythical motifs. The first is Africa as the young and strong tree of David Diop's poem; the second is the Sun and the Water as male and female principles, respectively and these as linked in the novel to the country's problems and their solutions. This Hymn to the Sun tells the tale of the founding of Abazon; it describes male power run rampant in the form of the burning sun; it introduces the hardy, surviving tree that invokes both Africa and the desirability of slow growth, of reform rather than revolution, based on the example of the growth patterns of the tree. It reinforces the circular time of myth as tales return out of storyland with messages for our times. David Diop provides the myth with an image and links it to the modern storytellers of Africa. The poem echoes symbolically through the novel:

> Africa tell me Africa
> Is this you this back that is bent
> This back that breaks under the weight of humiliation
> This back trembling with red scars
> And saying yes to the whip under the midday sun
> But a grave voice answers me
> Impetuous son, that tree young and strong
> That tree there
> In splendid loneliness amidst white and faded flowers
> That is Africa your Africa
> That grows again patiently obstinately
> And its fruit gradually acquire
> The bitter taste of liberty.[119]

The slow, piecemeal and undramatic change is exemplified by the tree of Africa. David Diop was a Westernized poet, alienated from his past and using his poetry to construct a mythical, unified Africa through which he could create a home. The poem homogenizes the continent as an African whole, and unifies Africans and African-Americans within the imagery of slavery and 'the whip under the midday sun'. The politics is bonded to nature. The strongest tree is slow growing, patient and obstinate. Only after many seasons will the young tree be ready to bear fruit. The tree that bears too soon endangers its growth. We must wait for the fruit of liberty.

The Hymn, the Poem and then the Speech – Ikem begins his speech to the university students, crucially, with the story out of the oral tradition, as told by the wise elder of Abazon, the story of 'The Tortoise and the Leopard', confirming the role of this elder, of Abazon and the oral tradition, as the receptacle of wisdom.[120] Chris is linked to Ikem and becomes his disciple. Initially, he is in danger of becoming co-opted by the corrupt government which he serves at the opening of the novel. Instead he becomes transformed by Ikem's 'religion' with his Hymn to the Sun as the holy book. On Chris's now archetypal journey of self and political discovery along the Great North Road to Abazon, 'the ensuing knowledge seeped through every pore in his skin into the core of his being continuing the transformation, already in process, of the man he was'.[121]

Beatrice also has a pilgrimage to make, as a woman and an intellectual, a journey which will weave into, and ultimately weave together, the mythical strands. She is summoned by His Excellency, Sam, the corrupt President, to the palace for a 'small private dinner'. This catastrophic evening is a turning point, propelling Beatrice back into the past and forcing her, like Ikem, to reconnect with tradition, from which Christianity and her stunningly successful English education had alienated her. She will become the goddess of water, the cool Idemili, antidote to the scorching sun of unchecked male political power. This mythical role of woman, as we saw earlier in this chapter, is a traditional way of conceptualizing intrinsic differences within the sexes, based on indigenous folklore. Achebe tells us about Idemili, through whom Beatrice is going to find her roots:

> In the beginning Power rampaged through our world, naked. So the Almighty, looking at his creation through the round undying eye of the Sun, saw and pondered and finally decided to send his daughter, Idemili, to bear witness to the moral nature of authority by wrapping around Power's rude waist a loincloth of peace and modesty.
> She came down in the resplendent Pillar of Water, remembered now in legend only . . . .[122]

Beatrice, although destined to play the part of Idemili, cannot herself tell the story because she 'did not know these traditions and legends of her people because they played but little part in her upbringing'. However, despite this Christian upbringing, Beatrice has a 'vague sense . . . of being two different people'. Ikem, who comes closest to Achebe's voice in the novel, also 'came close to sensing the village priestess' side of her nature, and again in patriarchal fashion, it is Ikem who 'knew it better than Beatrice herself'. Chris, who is not quite as perceptive, only senses Beatrice's power through the other familiar stereotype – that of the fatal woman: Beatrice 'almost sucked him into fatal depths'.[123]

In the pages following, Beatrice reconnects with her African roots and becomes alert to sounds and sights previously hidden from her, including her manner of dressing, which is part of her awakening to her African past, to the negritude tradition of cultural nationalism where African food, dress, skin colour and so on serve as a symbolic shorthand of resistance to Western cultural imperialism. She

> changed into a long, loose dress of blue *adire* embroidered in elaborate white patterns at the neck, chest, sleeves and hem. As she looked at herself in her bedroom mirror and liked what she saw, she thought: We can safely leave grey drabness in female attire to the family of lizards and visiting American journalists.[124]

From here on Beatrice assumes the priestess role more and more powerfully. The portrayal of Chris and Beatrice's lovemaking is in terms of the stereotype of woman as fatal priestess in her temple. As he comes inside her:

> she uttered a strangled cry that was not just a cry but also a command or a password into her temple. From there she took charge of him leading him by the hand silently through heaving groves mottled in subdued yellow sunlight, treading dry leaves underfoot till they came to streams of clear blue water. More than once he had slipped on the steep banks and she had pulled him up and back with such power and authority as he had never seen her exercise before. Clearly this was her grove and these her own peculiar rites over which she held absolute power. Priestess or goddess herself? No matter. But would he be found worthy? Would he survive? This unending, excruciating joyfulness in the crossroads of laughter and tears. Yes, I must, oh yes I must, yes, oh yes, yes, oh yes. I must, must, must. Oh holy priestess, hold me now. I am slipping, slipping, slipping. And now he was not just slipping but falling, crumbling into himself.
>
> Just as he was going to plead for mercy she screamed an order: 'OK!' and he exploded into stars and floated through fluffy white clouds and began a long and slow and weightless falling and sinking into deep, blue sleep.
>
> When he woke like a child cradled in her arms and breasts her eyes watching anxiously over him, he asked languorously if she slept. 'Priestesses don't sleep'.[125]

The familiar combination of fatal Priestess and Mother unites with the archetypal gender polarity as the heat of the man is tempered by the feminine coolness.

Beatrice is ultimately the anthill that survives. By the end, she is immortal, cast as she is into the mould of the divine. She is 'immobile as a goddess in her shrine'.[126] Chris and Ikem both die tragically, products of the evil society. However, Ikem's woman, Elewa, bears his baby and it is the priestess Beatrice, who officiates over its symbolic naming ceremony. This ceremony stands for the forging of a new mythical ritual, designed to replenish the spiritual poverty of the nation at large. The band of people who end the novel at the naming, represent a new alliance. Beatrice is priestess, Elewa, Ikem's bereaved widow, is Mother and the hope of the nation is vested in the woman's fertility.

Far from wishing to construct Bakhtin's polyglot world, or to become Bhabha's migrant, traversing the crossroads into new territories, the nationalist dilemma is how to incorporate the many voices into one homogeneous voice of the nation. Nationalism and heterogeneity are terms in radical contradiction. Achebe will have Beatrice find a way, through the ritual of collective memory, of incorporating all those voices. The many voices, however, do leave cracks on this avowedly seamless decolonizing project. The discordant cosmopolitan voice refuses to be entirely silenced – Beatrice, the inspiration of the European Dante, retains her European name, for all her return to her roots.

Thus I am suggesting that Achebe conceives of himself as an activist whose story contributes to the national culture by building on ancient wisdoms and traditions, by constructing a myth, by writing an epic tale. This is a politico-literary solution, inscribed in the book itself. It is the work of the enlightened intellectual who can transform ideas into written records, which will stand as documentation against the crimes of the regime. This is common to African decolonizing writing. It is the structural core of its plots – of Soyinka's proudly resurgent Ogun, on his white horse, in his *Isara*, of Armah's healers and seers, of Ngugi's godly guerrillas, permanently enlisted in the freedom army hidden in the sacred grove of the forest.

In conclusion, West African magical realists share the West African history and culture that gave rise to the dominant tradition that I have been discussing in this chapter, while arising from their own distinctive historical situations which are in many ways akin to those of the cosmopolitan magical realists. No-one exemplifies their stance better than Kwame Anthony Appiah, whose *In My Father's House* illuminates many of the enigmas and tensions of living at the crossroads. His description of the sculpture of the 'Yoruba Man with a Bicycle' captures both cosmopolitan hybridity and also cultural nationalism. James Baldwin, Appiah tells us approvingly, had this to say about the sculpture:

> This is something. This has got to be contemporary. He's really going to town. It's very jaunty, very authoritative. His errand might prove to be impossible. He is challenging something – or something has challenged him. He's grounded in immediate reality by the bicycle. . . . He's apparently a very proud and silent man. He's dressed sort of polyglot. Nothing looks like it fits him too well.[127]

Appiah, however, goes on to say that this sculpture, and pieces like it, are 'produced for the West', are made 'for Western tourists and other collectors'.[128] If African art collectors 'want African art, they would often rather have a "genuinely" traditional piece: by which I mean a piece that they believe to be made precolonially, or at least in a style and by methods that were already established precolonially'.[129] This appears to set up a polarity between authentically African collectors and American tourists. But then Appiah goes on to retrieve the image, which clearly expresses something of his own cultural hybridity – his father was a Ghanaian statesman and brother-in-law of the King and his mother, Peggy Cripps, daughter of a British aristocrat. This retrieval he accomplishes by stating that 'it matters little who is was made *for*':

> The 'Man with a Bicycle' is produced by someone who does not care that the bicycle is the Whiteman's invention – it is not there to be Other to the Yoruba Self; it is there because someone cared for its solidity; it is there because it will take us further than our feet will take us; it is there because machines are now as African as novelists.[130]

Tutuola places his men and women on bicycles, or arms them with guns, bibles and juju rings; he happily orchestrates his images of spirits in the ancient jungle by adorning and embellishing them with electric eyes or umbrella horns; it is the Ghanaian Appiah, with his Western education, who peers at the image through the long end of the binoculars, distancing it in the moment that he embraces its possibilities. 'Yoruba Man with a Bicycle' is an appropriate symbolic gateway to the chapters which follow.

4

'OUT OF THE CENTRE OF MY FOREHEAD, AN EYE OPENED'

Ben Okri's *The Famished Road*

And then suddenly, out of the centre of my forehead, an eye opened, and I saw this light to be the brightest, most beautiful thing in the world. It was terribly hot, but it did not burn. It was fearfully radiant, but it did not blind. As the light came closer, I became more afraid. Then my fear turned. The light went into the new eye and into my brain and roved around my spirit and moved in my veins and circulated in my blood and lodged itself in my heart. And my heart burned with a searing agony, as if it were being burnt to ashes within me. As I began to scream the pain reached its climax and a cool feeling of divine dew spread through me, making the reverse journey of the brilliant light, cooling its flaming passages, till it got back to the centre of my forehead, where it lingered, the feeling of a kiss for ever imprinted, a mystery and a riddle that not even the dead can answer.

(p. 229)[1]

Ben Okri's hope and goal in *The Famished Road* is to see with a new 'third eye'. Does this eye perceive paradox – heat that does not burn, a dazzling light that does not blind? Can it see the connections, the syncretisms, the kaleidoscope of possibilities? Does it comprehend history in the language of magic and of dreams? Its range attempts to span this world, the previous one and the one to come.

The Famished Road was first published in 1991 and won the Booker Prize of that year. Okri had lived in England since 1978, leaving Nigeria for a university education abroad when he finished secondary school at the age of nineteen.[2] This is somewhat unusual among African writers, many of whom tended to travel to the West somewhat later in their lives, retaining stronger home bases in the countries of their origins. But at the same time as being much more acculturated by the West than some of his fellow Nigerian writers, Okri's work remains steeped in indigenous images and West African oral culture, as well as in his sense of the transformations, degradations and poverty of his native Lagos. As Biodun Jeyifo puts it, with reference to Omovo, the main character of Okri's second novel, *The Landscapes Within*, but with relevance to *The Famished Road*:

through his art and ruminations he sets down in a personal diary . . . the disintegrative chaos in his family, the neighbourhood slum, and the whole country. This may indeed be the quintessential contribution of Okri's fiction to the novelistic delineation of the present predicament of our society; a mostly unsentimental depiction of how the youthful generation of post-Civil War Nigeria came of age through an embittering experience which leaves them lost and floundering in a world they cannot comprehend.[3]

Set at the historical moment just prior to Nigerian independence, *The Famished Road* is situated primarily within three sites. There is the wild forest, in which the spirits, witches, monsters and ghosts find dark and dense safe-cover. Then there is the road, which clears and encroaches on this bush and brings Western technology and 'progress', while exposing and thereby annihilating the hiding spirits. Thriving on the borders between road and bush is Madame Koto's bar, through which pass new politicians and old witches, electricity and ghosts, a gramophone, a motor car and malevolent *abiku* spirits.

All this might imply that there is a linear progression in the plot and in the novel's structure, as burgeoning progress moves along its constructed road, cutting away the bush and pushing the border constantly backwards. And indeed the bar does perpetually change and metamorphose as the relations between the road and the bush – between the past, the present and future – realign themselves. However, we will see that Okri abolishes the neat polarities and linear movement – of the past and future, of the modern and the old – in the very process of their erection.

All of this is not to suggest that *The Famished Road* has a full and busy plot. If Cheney-Coker's novel is going to be hard to pin down in the next chapter because of the vastness of its epic canvas, then Okri's is elusive because of its insubstantiality. Not much happens. What does transpire seems familiar and repetitive, as though one is living through many versions of the same dream or nightmare.

Azaro, the main character through whose eyes the bulk of the novel unfolds, as an *abiku* baby, has an ambiguous existence. *Abiku* babies torment their mothers by being spirits in the guise of babies, spirits who repeatedly are born, only to die and return to the spirit world. He may have decided to stay in the world of the living, but he is perpetually vulnerable to the call, and even to the threat, of his companions in the spirit world, who wish him to return.

The novel is set in the historical reality of Nigeria at a very specific moment – independence looms, along with the construction of modern communications, of roads and cars, photography and electricity. Azaro lives with his poverty stricken parents in Nigeria on the eve of independence. Their lives are touched destructively by the corrupt political parties who use dishonest, ruthless and violent means to try to win support. However, the story is simultaneously situated in the world of the dream, of the nightmare, of the dead, of those waiting to be born, and crucially, linking up with the circularity of time, of those *abiku* babies, with their repeated deaths and re-births.

Azaro has restless feet and traverses between bush and road, bar and forest, spirit and human world, seeking knowledge and understanding of the bewildering changes he encounters, of the poverty in which his family lives, of the spiritual dimension from which he comes and to whose call to return he is so vulnerable. Situated as it is within a variant of Tutuola's bush, teeming with spirits and hazards and heroic journeys, does *The Famished Road* replicate Tutuola's conservative moral code? In other words, as Ato Quayson asks with reference to Okri, can 'indigenous beliefs such as those to do with spirits . . . be transferred into literature without carrying with them the moral particularities of the belief-systems which were their foundations in the first place'?[4]

I would like to attempt to answer that question in the first instance by looking at the role of the oral tradition in the novel and the symbolic meaning of the road that gives the novel its title. This will lead to an examination of the theme of hybridity in *The Famished Road*, a hybridity that stands in contrast to the tendency to conservatism in traditional folklore. This theme takes us to the site of Madame Koto's bar, where spirits and politicians mingle, and to the question of burgeoning Nigerian independence politics. It also brings us to the mythical *Madame* herself and to questioning the nature of gender portrayals in the novel. Throughout the discussion it will be obvious that Okri's authorial viewpoint is elusive, that he offers a mixed message and takes an ambiguous stance. The narrative's many points of view will also be examined in this light. Finally I will touch on Okri's sequel to this novel, entitled *Songs of Enchantment* and will, in the process and in conclusion, revisit the issue of gender.

It is a mistake to assume too readily that the road of the title of Okri's novel is a colonial symbol of Western intrusion and technology. At the outset of the novel this road passes through the ancient world of the spirits and is conceptualized within traditional mythology. Azaro's father, as storyteller, tells him that *his* father (Azaro's grandfather) is

> head-priest of our shrine, Priest of the God of Roads. Anyone who wants
> a special sacrifice for their journeys, undertakings, births, funerals, what-
> ever, goes to him. All human beings travel the same road.
>
> (p. 70)

Azaro's father, in the mode of hiving back to past values, emphasizes that 'our old people are very powerful in spirit' and sadly that 'We are forgetting these powers. Now, all the power that people have is selfishness, money, and politics' (p. 70).

The story that Dad tells, however, is about the greed and restlessness of long ago, that resulted in the creation of a monster – the insatiable King of the Road: ' "Once upon a time", Dad began suddenly, "there was a giant whom they called the King of the Road" '. This giant 'used to be one of the terrible monsters of the Forest and there were many like him' – that is to say, he originated from deep within the bush's own greed and insatiabilities. Then 'Man' [sic] came along and the forest began to shrink and 'when the giant couldn't find enough animals to eat, he changed from the forest to the roads that men travel' (p. 258).

Okri emphasizes that the famished monster of the road is not the obvious symbol of either the greed of colonialism or the new brand of politicians. Although these are its more modern manifestations, the greed is universal and ancient – 'people believed that he had lived for thousands of years and that nothing could kill him and that he could never die' (p. 259). The story continues to describe how the monster wreaks terrible havoc, including devouring the various delegations sent to reason and bargain with him. Indeed, he is so hungry and so monstrous as to have even eaten himself until only his stomach, melted by the rain, remains 'growling from under the ground'. The ending of Dad's story reiterates the universality of the danger of being exposed to the monster of insatiability, and proffers a warning:

> What had happened was that the King of the Road had become part of all the roads in this world. He is still hungry, and he will always be hungry. This is why there are so many accidents in the world.
>
> And to this day some people still put a small amount of food on the road before they travel, so that the King of the Road will eat their sacrifice and let them travel safely. But some of our wise people say that there are other reasons. Some say people make sacrifices to the road to remember that the monster is still there and that he can rise at any time and start to eat up human beings again. Others say that it is a form of prayer that his type should never come back again to terrify our lives. That is why a small boy like you must be very careful how you wander about in this world.
>
> (p. 261)

This is the quite familiar Tutuolan myth of origins and warnings, set in the long past of 'our great-great-great grandfather' (p. 260), and cautioning against unbridled innovation and exploration. This story stresses the power of the past and of the stories and wisdom contained in it, as guides to behaviour in the present:

> On many of those nights in my childhood hour, Mum told me stories of aquamarine beginnings. Under the white eye of the moon, under the indigo sky, in the golden lights of survival in our little room, I listened to the wisdom of the old songs which Dad rendered in his cracked fighting voice. Mesmerized by the cobalt shadows, the paradoxical ultramarine air, and the silver glances of the dead, I listened to the hard images of joy. I listened also to the songs of work and harvest and the secrets of heroes.
>
> Outside, the wind of recurrence blew gently over the earth.
>
> (p. 183)

These are the old stories, the proverbs and myths, the tales of origins and warnings, of human well-being linked to the recurrence of the seasons and the conservation of custom; these are the stories that discourage change, foster purity in aquamarine origins and work against newness entering the world.

Dad has other stories to tell. He has a nightmare, which he relates to Azaro and which must have autobiographical overtones for Okri, who emigrated to London at a tender age. Dad firstly dreams a continent into existence. The inhabitants of this continent are 'not like us. They are white. Bushmen' (p. 436), unwelcoming, and insisting that they have been there 'since time immemorial'; consequently, Dad dreams them away (p. 437). Then later he dreams that he is on 'a strange island':

> The people treated me roughly. They were also white. Unfriendly people. Unfriendly to me, at least. I lived among them for many years. I couldn't find my way out. I was trapped there on that small island. I found it difficult to live there. They were afraid of me because of my different colour. As for me, I began to lose weight. I had to shrink the continent in me to accommodate myself to the small island.
>
> (p. 437)

Eventually, presumably as part of the degrading process of accommodation, Dad 'looked into the mirror and nearly died of astonishment when I saw that I had turned white'. His shame and humiliation reach a pinnacle in 'a big city on the island' where everything is cold and icy and where 'ice turned my hair white' when Azaro appears as a young man to buy a newspaper from his shrunken, icy white father, who is a news-vendor – 'when you gave me the money it burned my hand' (p. 437). This is reminiscent of the embarrassment when Azaro sees him as the nightsoil man, and the lesson about race is unambiguous – the familiar warning about not straying from one's own people and culture.

Mum has a similar story about whites, for all its apparent plot differences with Dad's tale. This time, the whites come to Africa, an Africa, which is more advanced in all spheres of knowledge than the West, an Africa from which these whites come to learn. This is an Africa of the idealized negritude tradition, a homogeneous, intrinsically generous continent that shares what it has, only afterwards to be cheated and robbed. Essences, generalizations and bitterness stalk this story:

> 'When white people first came to our land,' she said, as if she were talking to the wind, 'we had already gone to the moon and all the great stars. In the olden days they used to come and learn from us. My father used to tell me that we taught them how to count. We taught them about the stars. We gave them some of our gods. We shared our knowledge with them. We welcomed them. But they forgot all this. They forgot many things. They forgot that we are all brothers and sisters and that black people are the ancestors of the human race. The second time they came they brought guns. They took our lands, burned our gods, and they carried away many of our people to become slaves across the sea. They are

greedy. They want to own the whole world and conquer the sun. Some of them believe they have killed God. Some of them worship machines. They are misusing the powers God gave all of us.'

(p. 282)

Mum's story is more nuanced towards its end, but the 'us' and 'them' polarity is not really mediated by her rather peculiar – 'they are not all bad. Learn from them, but love the world' (p. 282).

Her other story is more complex. It carries remnants of the same theme of the superiority of African, black culture over white, but it mediates this image with symbols that contradict it. It is about a degenerate misguided white man, who has to learn to be an African in order to find redemption. Mum tells how she was selling her provisions one day in the terrible heat, when she 'came to a crossroad' and saw a tortoise, coming out of the bush and crossing the road. This sets the scene as portentous, given the importance of the crossroad as a symbolic moment of choice and the road and bush as significant boundaries. The tortoise 'spoke to me' but Mum refuses to tell what it said and this afterwards becomes a riddle she sets the white man she meets on another hot day. He wants to find a way out of Africa and she wants, in return for helping him, his blue sunglasses, to protect her eyes which are red from 'the sun and the dust'. In a novel where, as we will discuss later, seeing, blindness, masks and photographs are critical, her desire for these blue sunglasses is symbolic of an acknowledgement that the white man has some-thing of value to exchange for her knowledge, for African wisdom, for the words of the tortoise, archetypal character of the oral tales of old:

> Then I asked him to tell me what the tortoise said. He stopped and thought for a long time. Then a bus went past slowly. It had a motto written on its side. The white man laughed at the motto and read it out and I said that's what the tortoise told me. 'What?' he asked. 'All things are linked,' I said. 'What has the tortoise got to do with it?' he asked. I said: 'If you don't know you will never find any road at all'. Then he gave me the blue sunglasses . . . .
>
> (p. 483)

The 'all things are linked' asserts the belief that there is no absolute divide between human and animal, animate and inanimate, life and death. The sunglasses are the masks of old syncretized with the changes brought by whites and by colonialism. They link up with the way deities or ancestral spirits, or the spirits of natural forces, are manifested through masked performances and rituals. Within the format of the riddle, what Mum is describing is precisely a modern, transformed ritual, harnessing the new technology to suit its purposes. Is the purpose, however, to create a hybrid between old and new, or do we simply have the mask of old, constructed for the same, ancient purpose, but now made out of velvet, damask or sunglasses? Let us continue the story to find out.

Another day, she meets in the market 'a strange Yoruba man' with magical powers. He asks her if she remembers him – ' "I gave you the blue sunglasses," he said':

> Then I remembered him. But it took some time, and I first had to turn and twist my mind around. He was the white man. His face and his nose and everything was exactly the same except that now he was a Yoruba man with fine marks on his face. 'I met you five hundred years ago,' he said. 'I discovered the road'. 'What was it?' I asked. Then he told me his story.
>
> (p. 483)

Here are a few significant metamorphoses and reversals. Mum is the one this time who has to learn more than one thing – to 'see' the man again through the change in the colour of his skin, to understand the riddle of time which has passed and to listen to his story as he takes over as narrator and tells a story within Mum's story within Azaro's first person narration. To make matters even more labyrinthine and postmodern, the story Okri has him tell has powerful reverberations with Camara Laye's *The Radiance of the King*. Laye's is a classic example of a story designed to resist cultural imperialism, by way of inverting its racism with a tale of the spiritual inferiority and bewilderment of the incompetent and degenerate white man, lost in the African bush, until salvation can be given by the pure, young African King.[5] It is a powerful novel, but one which retains the paradigm of essences of races, of intrinsic binaries between white and black, colonized and colonizer. It simply changes the labels of Good and Bad. This is Okri's man's story, as told by Mum:

> 'When I left you,' he began, 'I became feverish in the head and later in a fit of fury over a small thing I killed my African servant. They arrested me. I sat in a cell. Then they released me because I was a white man. Then I began to wander about the city naked. Everyone stared at me. They were shocked to see a mad white man in Africa. Then a strange little African child took to following me around. He was my only friend. All my white colleagues had deserted me. Then one day my head cleared. Five hundred years had gone past. The only way to get out of Africa was to become an African. So I changed my thinking. I changed my ways.'
>
> (p. 483)

This enables him to go back to England, a white man but one who has transformed himself, marries, has children, is successful and dies to be re-born a Yoruba businessman, presumably because of the internal adjustments he made in his previous life. This is a complete reversal of Dad's nightmare, where he has become reduced, has sold his soul, becoming a white man. The white man regains his humanity by taking on African customs, paradoxically finds his freedom and his way home back to England. When he is reborn a fine and powerful Yoruba man, who can make Mum's fishes in her basket come alive, which he does on first meeting her again, his stature has massively grown. In fact, the overtones of Christ suggest that the truths he has discovered could be the salvation of all humankind. The story ends thus:

> I said: 'But I only met you two weeks ago.' 'Time is not what you think it is,' he said, smiling. Then he left. That is the end of my story.'
> There was a long silence.
> 'Strange story,' I said.
> 'It's true,' Mum replied.
>
> (p. 484)

Note four important elements in these stories within stories. First, there is traditional wisdom and storytelling in the form of the tortoise of oral tradition, a speaking tortoise who poses a riddle, as of old, the answer to which is the philosophical cornerstone of the story, the 'All things are linked'. While this is a disruption of the Manichean polarity of Mum's earlier story as white becomes black, as teacher becomes pupil, as narrator becomes audience, it is also a continuity with the strain of negritude. This is so because the man can only, as in Laye's novel, regain his stature and self-respect through the superior humanity and wisdom of Africa. The tortoise is in the mould of the following early comment:

> These are the myths of beginnings. These are stories and moods deep in those who are seeded in rich lands, who still believe in mysteries.
>
> (p. 6)

What we must also remember, in the context of the call to decolonize by way of the pre-colonial culture, particularly of the oral tradition, is that works that invoke it, partake of its style, invent variations of it, are simultaneously speaking in a coded shorthand of opposition to cultural imperialism and the onslaught of Western forms and genres. This is a crucial battle, one that I suggested in an earlier chapter unites postcolonials culturally. The problem arises when that battle is bonded to the call for uncontaminated roots, for inclusions and exclusions that precisely characterized the imperialism that is being rejected. There is, I think, a tension in Okri, one that we will encounter in all three of the writers. On the one hand, he opposes the slavish imitation of Western forms and ideas. This gives rise to the search for a pure, pre-colonial past, linked to projects of national reconstruction. On the other hand, there is his love of change and celebration of the transformations arising out of interactions with other cultures.

With this in mind, we have to understand that, if the tortoise is the traditional wisdom, then, second and contradictorily, the blue sunglasses are more than a simple reincarnation of the ancient mask. The sunglasses are, in fact, even more than the postmodern recognition of the relativity of perception; they are a product of Western science and provide relief and comfort to Mum, whose hard days in the burning sun of the market are ameliorated by them.

There is, third, an interesting variation on the *abiku* cycle in Mum's tale, with change, death and then re-birth into a new and a better life. There is, at the same time as this change and transformation, fourth, the challenge to linear time. Here is a beautiful example of third time, when five hundred years pass in two weeks, where cycles are broken, change occurs but within a new conception of time and reincarnation. Mum insists that her strange story is true. And so it is, as it picks up on many of the major threads and tensions and philosophies of life contemplated by the novel. In our attempts to unravel these we need to return to the ambiguity surrounding the symbolic significance of the road. In fact, we must return to Dad, who tells the original story of the King of the Road, and we must return to him via the rather circuitous route of another story of the oral tradition, one told by Chinua Achebe about a fighter, who challenges his own *chi*, or, as the Igbo would have it, his own spiritual being:

> There is a story of how a proud wrestler, having thrown every challenger in the world, decides to go and wrestle in the world of spirits. There he also throws challenger after challenger, including many multiple-headed ones – so great was his prowess. At last there is no one left to fight. But the wrestler refuses to leave. The spirits beg him to go; his companion praise-singer on the flute pleads with him. But it is all in vain. *There must be somebody left; surely the famed land of spirits can do better than this*, he said. Again everyone begs him to collect his laurels and go but again he refuses. Finally his own *chi* appears, reluctant, thin as a rope. The wrestler laughs at this miserable-looking contender and moves forward contemptuously to knock him down whereupon the other lifts him clear off the ground with his little finger and smashes him to death.[6]

Achebe explains this story as a 'cautionary tale', which is mainly concerned with

> setting a limit to man's aspirations. The limit is not the sky; it is some-where much closer to earth. A sensible man will turn round at the frontiers of absolutism and head for home again.[7]

Achebe's story reverberates in Okri's. Dad, who is sick of his life of toil and poverty, of ending up carrying pails of human excrement, and of the humiliation of having his son witness him do so, decides to become a boxer and challenges increasingly deadly foes, highly reminiscent of Achebe's tale. One of them is the mysterious and sinister man in the white suit, whose unveiling as a grotesque, spirit form has overtones with yet another story, the chilling and recurrent one of Tutuola's Perfect Gentleman, referred to in the last chapter, who beguiles the proud maiden and is revealed as a skull. Dad, the 'Black Tyger', 'was absorbing monstrous punishment' (p. 472) when he tears off the fancy, dazzling clothing of his opponent, whose inhumanity is revealed:

> He had a hollow chest and a deep hole of a navel. He was so hairy, and his hair was so much like that of a bush animal that the spectators gave a shocked cry when they saw how inhuman he looked. . . . He had long thin legs, the legs of a spiderous animal.
>
> (p. 473)

He may not be Dad's *chi*, but out of his enormous energy and ego, Dad has challenged the spirit world and attempted to overcome it. What is the outcome? 'Charging his own spirit', Dad is able to release 'one of the most destructive punches' Azaro had ever seen, but

> overcome with the horror of his victory, and with fatigue, Dad sank to the ground. We tried to revive him, but we couldn't.
>
> (p. 474)

Dad's body and spirit have been rent asunder and he lies in a fearsome coma as Mum and some old witches attempt to bring him back. In this state, he 'was redreaming the world' and experiences huge insights and understandings, which are described with an intensity, but also obsessiveness that makes one fear for his sanity. Okri's perspective on Dad is, in other words, elusive. He might have escaped 'into the great realms and spaces' (p. 492) but in the meantime, Mum is driven distracted, 'waves of demented mist passed over her face' and she prays for food (p. 493). All that is clear about Dad and the outcome of his boxing bout with an evil spirit is that the message is mixed:

> His wounds had healed, his spirit had sharpened, his despair was deeper, he was a bigger man with a bigger madness.
>
> (p. 497)

Part of the new insight with which Dad awakes – and here we return to the symbol of the famished monster of the road with which we began this discussion – is to revise the tone of the original cautionary tale that he told, to revise Achebe's warning about boundaries and limits:

> In my sleep I saw many wonderful things. Our ancestors taught me many philosophies. My father, Priest of the Roads, appeared to me and said I should keep my door open. My heart must be open. My life must be open. Our road must be open. A road that is open is never hungry. Strange times are coming.
>
> (p. 497)

Is Okri modifying the original story of warning to a boy with restless feet? Or is this, rather, part of his 'bigger madness'? What he says is certainly cut down to size by Mum's response in the silence that follows Dad's passionate speech:

A long time passed in the silence that followed. Then Mum got up and laid out for Dad what food there was. He ate ravenously and when he finished he turned the plates over and looked at their undersides as if he were searching for more food.

'There's not much money in the house,' Mum said. 'You haven't been working'.

(p. 500)

Thus the force of tradition – and the warning of repercussions if ancient wisdoms are abandoned – is only a part of *The Famished Road*'s moral purpose and only part of the symbolic significance of the road. I think that in quite fundamental ways Okri parts company with the Tutuolan universe. This is the context in which to read Ato Quayson's distinction between Azaro and Tutuola's protagonists (although I disagree with his assessment of that difference):

Critics have already noted how the novel recalls the discursive schema of Amos Tutuola's work. But in Tutuola's narratives the protagonists all had heroic potential which was continually re-affirmed in the course of their adventures in the spirit realms. They have an epochal quality because they are partial inscriptions of communal values. The mythopoeic character derives strength from being a representative of a communal ethos. Azaro has none of that energetic stature.[8]

While Quayson implies a critique of Okri's character construction, I would suggest that when he moves away from that epochal, mythopoeic structure, his portrayal of Azaro potentially derives new energies and mutations. I wish, therefore, to examine some of the novel's other meanings, in the light of the question of the relationship between tradition and change, myth and magic.

Having said that we should not assume that the road is primarily the symbol of colonialism, it is true that it partly has that significance. And in that role, the road functions in the familiar way to contest the desirability of the modernization it brings – 'steadily, over days and months, the paths had been widening. Bushes were being burnt, tall grasses cleared, tree stumps uprooted'. There is the loud noise of engines and road builders. Houses take the place of trees and 'places where children used to play and hide were now full of sandpiles and rutted with house foundations' (p. 104). The trees groan as they crash down to 'the steady rhythms of axes on hard, living wood' (p. 137); this colonial, modernizing road does not, necessarily, bring progress. On one of the occasions when Azaro is abducted, he is taken along an 'endless' road and he develops 'a terrible hunger for a destination'

(p. 113). Like the wild bush, in which a person can most easily lose their way, the new web of roads can also be wild and terrifying, leading to nowhere:

> All the roads multiplied, reproducing themselves, like snakes, tails in their mouths, twisting themselves into labyrinths. The road was the worst hallucination of them all, leading towards home and then away from it, without end, with too many signs, and no directions. The road became my torment, my aimless pilgrimage, and I found myself merely walking to discover where all the roads lead to, where they end.
>
> (pp. 114–15)

The recent colonial road has brought a crisis of identity and direction. But it gives way to a more universal and allegorical road – the road of life, subverting the image of the back-breaking colonial road gangs, into which Africans were hijacked, by one means or another, at the hands of the colonial authority. Much later in the novel Azaro observes strange beings frantically building a road which, Azaro learns from his spirit guide, they have been busy on for two thousand years and which they will never finish. The reason for this is that if they complete their road, they will perish because:

> they will have nothing to do, nothing to dream for, and no need for a future. They will perish of completeness, of boredom. The road is their soul, the soul of their history.
>
> (p. 329)

Azaro looks at the road 'with new eyes' and sees that 'it was short and marvellous. It was a work of art, a shrine almost, beautiful beyond description' (p. 330). He asks the spirit why it is so beautiful and he replies:

> because each new generation begins with nothing and with everything. They know all the earlier mistakes. They may not know that they know, but they do. They know the early plans, the original intentions, the earliest dreams. Each generation has to reconnect the origins for themselves. They tend to become a little wiser, but don't go very far. It is possible that they now travel slower, and will make bigger, better mistakes. That is how they are as a people. They have an infinity of hope and an eternity of struggles. Nothing can destroy them except themselves and they will never finish the road that is their soul and they do not know it.
>
> (p. 330)

While this universal road is a positive pathway, not populated by monsters, it is still portrayed within a mythical paradigm. The universal of greed is supplemented by the universal of goodness. Okri, moreover, contradicts this vision of hope by implication, given who is describing it. The storyteller in this case is not the familiar (although not necessarily trustworthy) Dad, but a decidedly suspect three-headed spirit who is attempting to beguile Azaro back to the spirit world and to his own death – the goodness may simply be a mirage. In other words, travelling this road is as hazardous for Azaro as taking the one inhabited by the greedy monster. Storyteller aside, however – and here is an example of the opaque narrative point of view – the depiction of the struggle to construct the challenges and dreams along our roads of life is by no means entirely false.

This road of life, along which we all struggle and strive, is reinforced in the book by means of a liberating image of the road towards wisdom and transformation. This road too begins in the realm of the past and of tradition, but it is a road that embraces change and embodies not warnings but their opposite – injunctions to explore and to grow. The king of the spirit world says to Azaro, just before he is born, 'You have to travel many roads before you find the river of your destiny' (p. 6). This king has himself journeyed many roads and embodies the image of the wisdom of the well-travelled:

> Our king was a wonderful personage who sometimes appeared in the form of a great cat. He had a red beard and eyes of greenish sapphire. He had been born uncountable times and was a legend in all worlds, known by a hundred different names. It never mattered into what circumstances he was born. He always lived the most extraordinary of lives. . . . Sometimes a man, sometimes a woman, he wrought incomparable achievements from every life. If there is anything common to all of his lives, the essence of his genius, it might well be the love of transformation, and the transformation of love into higher realities.
>
> (pp. 3–4)

Here, unlike elsewhere, transformation is unambiguously embraced. Azaro may encounter all kinds of hazards on his travels, he might well heed his father's warnings about wandering boys, but we are in little doubt that his exceptional growing understanding is linked to his itchy feet and his exposure through his restlessness to change, newness and strangeness – 'my feet started to itch again, and I resumed wandering the roads of the world' (pp. 143–4).

It is, in fact, this wonderful, curious restlessness that characterizes a central figure in the novel, a person who is the modern incarnation of the king – the photographer. He liberates himself by travelling the world. He is, at the same time, fleeing from persecution at the hands of the new politicians at home, to whom his skills as photographer pose a threat because he records the truth. He returns after an absence and tells Azaro that he has been hiding in his camera, 'travelling on the back of the silver light'. He has been 'visiting other continents. Flying round the universe. Seeing what men and women do' (p. 262). He is overtly constructed in opposition to the folklore of the ravenous road. He declares himself not afraid of the famished King of the Road and determined 'to travel all the roads of the world' (p. 262).

At the same time, Okri resolutely refuses to reinforce the most obvious polarities such as that between technological progress in opposition to the past. For example, the forest rebels against its violation by so-called progress. In a huge storm that signifies the end of the harmattan and the beginning of the rainy season 'the freshly laid tarmac had been swept away', and 'all those who were building the road intended to connect the highway had fled for cover and were nowhere to be seen' (p. 287). The white overseer and the workers who foolishly try to save him, are swept away in a stream of floodwaters ominously described as originating 'from the forest' (p. 288). The colonial road is reduced to 'what it used to be, a stream of primeval mud, a river' (p. 286). The storm, however, is figuratively linked to the new technology with the image of God as 'The Great Photographer' with lightening flash bulbs:

> Then the air darkened, the noise exploded again, and a bright light flashed over everything. The sky split open. And the path became a clearing.
> The world was still, as if it had momentarily become a picture, as if God were The Great Photographer.
>
> (p. 285)

This simile is suggestive. The elements, the bush, the trees, pre-colonial Africa, are linked to the avenging storm. But this storm, with its natural properties, is itself associated with the modern technology of photography; technology, moreover, that is desirable and a positive force in the novel, as we will see again later. The polarities are repeatedly contested even as they are established. The organic natural world of the pre-colonial past is not allowed to be pitted against the tech-nological scientific innovations of the white engineer and the society he represents.

To sum up, the road is many things. It is the danger of curiosity and adventur-ousness that can kill the restless traveller. It is colonial degradation, the African past, the universal human condition. It is simultaneously an opening up of the possibility of change and 'newness entering the world'. This possibility establishes some ironic distance from conservative warnings from the past, even when this ironic distance falters in the face of the writers' own trepidation and ambivalence.

What is clear, notwithstanding the labyrinth within which the road symbolism is constructed, is that Okri's society is the bizarre product of both new and old, tradi-tion and burgeoning change. It is one of the unevenly developed societies that spawns magical realism, discussed in Chapter 2. What is not clear, is whether Okri's road can be all things to all readers. The traveller, trapped in its labyrinth, has to choose a direction, a choice that will surely dictate the nature of the journey ahead.

Azaro observes the hybrid cacophony of African culture, of old and new, co-existing, typical of magical realist contexts:

> One road led to a thousand others, which in turn fed into paths, which fed into dirt tracks, which became streets, which ended in avenues and

cul-de-sacs. All around, a new world was being erected amidst the old. Skyscrapers stood high and inscrutable beside huts and zinc abodes. Bridges were being built; flyovers, half-finished, were like passageways into the air, or like future visions of a time when cars would be able to fly. Roads, half-constructed, were crowded with heavy machinery.

(p. 113)

Here, the mongrel culture is threatening and demonic, linked to the image of the labyrinth and the archetypal myth of the prison of the snake devouring its own tail. However, Okri also recognizes the reality of the mosaic, even if he does not unambiguously embrace it. Azaro saw:

women of the new African churches, who wore white smocks and rang bells, . . . I passed prophets emerging from the forest with dew and leaves in their hair, cobwebs meshing their beards, their eyes demented with visions. I passed sorcerers with machetes that crackled with flames in the morning light, making sacrifices at dawn of red cocks, who poured gnomic chants on the untrodden roads. I also passed workers who had woken early and with sleepy faces made their ways through the mists, pierced by the sun, to the garages and bus-stops.

My feet were fresh on the paths. Dew wet my ankles. Hunger dried my lips. News-vendors roused the dawn with their horns, announcing to the awakening world the scandals of the latest political violence. The industrious women of the city, who carried basins of peppered aromatic foods on their heads, tempted the appetite of the world with their sweet voices. The worms of the road ate into the soles of my feet.

(p. 114)

Edges blur between tradition and change, old and new, science and magic, forcing us to examine both the interactions between the human and the spirit world, and also relations between the three major sites of the novel – the road, which we have already touched upon, the bush, which is by now familiar, and the border interstices between them, Madame Koto's bar.

The spirits, reminiscent of Fagunwa's traditional forest of a thousand demons and ghommids, and of Tutuola's bush, are in the process of learning to cope with scientific changes and technological advances. They initially inhabit the dark forest with its concealing foliage:

I noticed that the forest swarmed with unearthly beings. It was like an overcrowded marketplace. Many of them had red lights in their eyes, wisps of saffron smoke came out of their ears, and gentle green fires burned on their heads.

(p. 12)

But the dense forest is being cleared and cut down to make way for the road:

> We were surrounded by a great forest. There were thick bushes and low
> trees between the houses. The bushes were resonant with the trilling of
> birds and crickets. . . .
> 'Do you see all this?' Dad said, waving his good arm to indicate the forest
> and the bushes.
> 'Yes,' I replied.
> 'It's bush now, isn't it?'
> 'Yes'.
> 'But sooner than you think there won't be one tree standing. There will be
> no forest left at all. And there will be wretched houses all over the place.
> This is where the poor people will live.'
>
> (p. 34)

And later again the changes are portrayed in this linear mode – the paths are
widening, workmen chanting, houses appear – 'it took longer to get far into the
forest' (p. 104). The connection is made between darkness, the forest and the
spirit world. As Azaro runs deeper into the forest, 'the spirits were all over the
place' (p. 138). On one of the many occasions that Azaro is about to die and
acquiesce in the call of his spirit companions, he describes the presence of the
spirits, the 'darkness' that rushes over him and 'a powerful wind from the forest'
(p. 229). It is clear that the spirits thrive in the safety of the darkness afforded by
the uncleared bush, and that the widening paths and the well lit clearings pose a
threat to the spirit world. A poetic microcosm of the exposure of the spirit world
by the relentlessness of modernization, of 'progress', is provided by photography,
to which we will keep having to return. The camera's flash of light blinds and
exposes the unwary ghosts. When the camera flashes, 'ghosts emerged from the
light and melted, stunned at his feet' (p. 5). This poetic metaphor is powerfully
and overtly extended when, much later, that lightening storm already mentioned,
opens up a bright path and:

> The clearing turned into a new world. Out of the flash came the sharp
> outlines of spirits rising into the air with weary heads. And then they fell
> down and bounced and floated over the stillness of the world. The spirits
> passed me, passed through me, their eyes like diamonds. And when the
> next explosion came, followed by another blinding flash, the spirits were
> obliterated.
>
> (p. 285)

However, there is no simple linear modernization as the road encroaches on the
bush. The spirits dwell as much in the past as the present, on the road as much as in
dreams or the spirit world itself, or even the bush. The spirits are, in fact, everywhere:

That was the first time I realised it wasn't just humans who came to the marketplaces of the world. Spirits and other beings come there too. They buy and sell, browse and investigate. They wander amongst the fruits of the earth and sea.

(p. 16)

Once they have recovered from the shock of the new technology, the spirits will adapt to it, even to the blinding photography. In fact, the photographer enters their world of magic:

After much prancing and mystery-making, as if he were a magician, the photographer lifted up his camera. He was surrounded by little ghosts and spirits. They had climbed on one another to take a closer look at the instrument. They were so fascinated by the camera that they climbed on him and hung on his arms and stood on his head. . . . When he had finished he couldn't be bothered to go all the way back to his studio so he hung the camera on a nail. The spirits and the children gathered round it, pointing and talking in amazed voices.

(p. 46)

They even become actively involved in the new party politics – 'Herbalists, sorcerers, wizards and witches took sides and as the trucks fought for votes in the streets they fought for supremacy in the world of spirits' (p. 495).

The spirits are everywhere, but they are extraordinarily present in Madame Koto's bar:

It seemed that I had walked into the wrong bar, had stepped into another reality on the edge of the forest. On the floor there were eaten bits of chicken and squashed jollof rice on paper plates. The walls were full of almanacs with severe faces, bearded faces, mildly squinted eyes, pictures which suggested terrible ritual societies and secret cabals. There were odd-looking calendars with goats in transformations into human beings, fishes with heads of birds, birds with the bodies of women.

(p. 271)

As we would now expect, the bar is another site of multiple meanings, the most obvious of which is the bar's own spatial positioning at the border between road and bush, at the gateway to the spirits, who enter from the bush, and haven to the new politicians, who enter from the road. As in Bhabha's border interstices, this is the zone of the mutant and the hybrid, women-birds and bird-fish, creatures, half human and part animal, and where Okri, master builder, constructs other, sometimes conflicting, meanings.

If the bar is sometimes the last stop before the bush, it is also the barometer for the nature of the modernizing, Westernizing changes. Here electric light will astound the people:

> The most extraordinary things were happening in Madame Koto's bar. The first unusual thing was that cables connected to her rooftop now brought electricity. Illiterate crowds gathered in front of the bar to see this new wonder. They saw the cables, the wires, the pylons in the distance, but they did not see the famed electricity. Those who went into the bar, out of curiosity, came out mystified. They couldn't understand how you could have a light brighter than lamps, sealed in glass. They couldn't understand how you couldn't light your cigarette on the glowing bulbs. And worse than all that, it was baffling for them to not be able to see the cause of the illumination.
>
> (p. 373)

The bar is where the gramophone will first, miraculously, blare – 'The next thing was that people heard very loud music blaring but saw no musicians performing' (p. 373). All of this is in the mode of the magical's ironic inversion of reality, where the spirits are a routine part of the mundane everyday, and electric light and sound constitute the awesome and the unbelievable.

In the last chapter, however, we saw the challenge to concepts of hybridity, as anthropologists like Drewal and Apter insisted on the dynamism of indigenous culture that incorporated transformations on its own terms. There are echoes of this in the novel where the spirits not only adapt and mutate, but also exact revenge and dictate the rate of progress on the building of the road. I have been suggesting – and in this modifying the anthropological view – that there is a fundamental distinction between everyday reality among ordinary people, and the ironic mode of the writer and intellectual, who have had a far more thoroughgoing Western experience and who look on the culture's uneven development with self-knowledge and some distance. They write magical realist novels, in which cultural hybridization is crucial to both their themes and narrative structures. Apter's depiction of the ritual sacrifice of the dog to Ogun, in order to protect the new Peugeot, is reminiscent of the ritual washing of Madame Koto's car. The following funny-tragic portrayal is a quintessential instance of the African intellectual's perception of the culture's patchworks:

> When the day arrived for Madame Koto to wash her new car, many people came to celebrate the ritual with her. Our landlord was present. People brought their bicycles and scooters. Many came on foot. There were old men whom we had never seen before. And there were a lot of powerful strange women with eyes that registered no emotion. We saw chiefs, thugs, and there were even herbalists, witch-doctors and their acolytes. They gathered in the bar and drank. They talked loudly. Eventually everyone was summoned for the washing. They formed a

circle round the vehicle. The great herbalist amongst them was a stern man with a face so battered and eyes so daunting that even mirrors would recoil and crack at his glance. He uttered profound incantations and prayed for the car.

(p. 380)

However, as the ritual degenerates into tragedy, ambiguity is created regarding the desirability of the changes. The great herbalist prophesies that the car will become a coffin, as indeed it does. Our faith in him is stretched when he drunkenly attempts to use his prophesy to grab a prostitute: ' "But if you give me one of these women", the herbalist said, lunging at one of the prostitutes, and missing, "then I will drive the coffin away from the car" ' (p. 381). But the ominousness of his prediction is powerful and when he focuses his bleary eyes, it is eerily on the forest and the wind howls and whistles 'along the electric cables'. The elements are at war with the new technology and the birds abandon the car top. Shortly thereafter, the driver loses control of the car, smashing into a beggar and the *abiku* boy, Ade, and horribly wounding himself. This leads to Azaro's mournful observation:

I think most of our real troubles began that night. They began not with the devastation of voices and chairs and the car, but with the blood mingling with rain and flowing right into the mouth of the road. I heard the slaking of the road's unquenchable thirst. And blood was a new kind of libation. The road was young but its hunger was old. And its hunger had been reopened.

(p. 424)

Nigeria's libations are in blood. Its road is an untravelled one, but the monster is ancient and sleeping and awakened by the blood, taking the society into a new era of terror – 'Our road was changing. Nothing was what it seemed any more' (p. 428). The whole incident is dominated by Okri's perceptions of strangeness and change, by his acceptance of the power of the old man, whose predictions are not contested.

Simultaneously, however, the car ritual in *The Famished Road* is pervaded by Okri's consciousness of the changing times and the futility of the libations in the face of the evil with which the society is about to be overtaken.

The bar is undoubtedly in one sense a border, a gateway, a moment of change, of welding between old and new, of mutation and transformation. This is not to lose sight of the fact that it is only so within an unstable location, given that it physically shifts around, problematizing our conception of linear development and contesting the evolutionary march of progress. The changes that come about, in other words, realign all the pieces and the players in complex ways, ensuring that the straight line between bush and road is obliterated – 'The bar had moved deep into the forest and all her customers were animals and birds' (pp. 59–60). Sometimes, as here, the bar is deep in the forest, sometimes it is there between

85

forest and clearing; sometimes it is in the clearing and Azaro has to walk far to get into the forest. He leaves the bar and finds that 'the paths had been widening', and that 'it took longer to get far into the forest' (p. 104). And again, as the customers mutate and exchange freakish and bizarre deformations with one another, the bar shifts once more:

> The mutant customers made the bar feel entirely different. They conferred on everything a dull yellow light. The bar itself gave the impression that it had been transported from its familiar environs of our area to somewhere under the road, under the sea, to a dimly remembered and unwanted landscape.
>
> (p. 133)

If Rushdie and Bhabha, Bakhtin and Marquez, celebrate borders, transformations and syncretisms, if Soyinka and Achebe seek solutions to the present within frameworks of the past, Okri continues to be elusive about the significance, desirability, or even the reality of change. These mutants that transport the bar to the murky and dangerous under-road landscape where the greedy monster of the road waits for prey, are described in the grotesque realism of carnival, with reverberations of the Tutuolan folklore tradition:

> There was an albino, but he was tall and had a head like a tuber of yam. The man who was bulbous in one eye was white and blank like a polished moonstone in the other. The two men who were sinister in dark glasses now had white hair and curious hip deformations. The youth who had no teeth was now a woman. I recognised them all beneath their transformed appearances.
>
> (p. 133)

Does the image of these creatures carry the transgressive function of carnival? If Azaro recognizes these creatures as those who were in the bar before, but who have now swapped features, then have they changed at all? Are these Bhabha's borders of a new postmodern, postcolonial era, or are they Tutuola's 'beautiful "complete" gentleman', ensnaring the wary and reckless traveller, part of the oral tradition of morality tales, desperate to conserve the fabric of ancient societies? Perhaps Madame Koto can provide some answers.

Madame Koto is medicine woman, pregnant hag, witch, ambiguous mother, businesswoman, brothel queen and supporter of the political party of the rich. She is chameleon, changing faces, images, roles and functions throughout the novel. 'She was often digging the earth, planting a secret, or taking one out' (pp. 75–6). She 'hung the fetish on a nail above the door. I noticed for the first time that she had a little beard' (pp. 85–6). She appears to be precisely that gigantic, obscene, unstable and hybrid creature, archetypal pregnant hag. She and the frequenters of her bar appear to have been drawn in the tradition of grotesque realism as defined by Bakhtin. For example, one such 'customer' devours a lizard in the bar and 'brought out his gigantic prick, and pissed in every direction. Madame Koto hit his prick with her broom. He pissed on her' (p. 85).

The overtones of Tutuola are also powerful. There are the spirits who exchange body parts and the sinister man in the impeccable white suit, already described, who is exposed as a horrid, hairy kind of human spider. The plenitude of Tutuola's fictional universe of tales that pour randomly forth with only the most tenuous structuring framework holding them together, is also reminiscent of the exuberance of Okri's images, interludes and poetry. However, we saw in Chapter 3 that Bakhtin and Tutuola represent very different politics. Does Madame Koto's raucous bar, sensual, rollicking and bursting with dwarfs, albinos, mutants, ghosts and spirits, contest the newly forming and corrupt Establishment, the fragile Law in the making, just prior to independence? We must look beneath the surface of the carnivalesque style and question whether Madame Koto and her bar are weapons of resistance against the obscenities of the times.

If Madame Koto's bar is an interstitial zone, a barometer of change, then increasingly she is depicted as having journeyed, through the bar, into the future of the new, corrupt politics. And so Azaro has the image/dream of spirits 'with blood pouring out of their eyes'. These spirits are 'sorrowful' and 'wise' and dying. When he wakes up and sees the customers in the bar, Azaro

> knew we were in the divide between past and future. A new cycle had begun, an old one was being brought to a pitch, prosperity and tragedy rang out from what I saw, and I knew that the bar would never be the same again.
>
> (p. 220)

The wealthy customers 'were elegantly dressed in bright kaftans and agbada and safari suits'. The thugs no longer looked like thugs – 'in spite of the . . . animal expression in their eyes, they looked like modern businessmen, contractors, exporters, politicians. Dressed in lace kaftans, with matching hats' (p. 220). Azaro is aware for the first time of the sinister new alliances that Madame Koto is forging – ' "My favourite customers, welcome!" Madame Koto said, in a voice of such extreme unctuousness that I turned to her, surprised' (p. 221). However, the portrait is still ambiguous, her bar gets smashed, 'she wept, quivering', but 'she too had crossed the divide between past and future. She must have known that a new cycle had begun' (p. 225). A bit later, 'the bar had changed again' and Madame Koto 'looked different'. Her image is even more strongly that of the Party of the Rich:

> She wore a new lace blouse, an expensive wrapper, coral beads round her neck, and copper bangles round her wrists. She wore eye-shadow, which darkened her eyes, and powder on her face, beneath which her sweat ran.
>
> (p. 239)

On the walls of the bar, 'there were two almanacs of the Rich Party'. However, the image is still fragile and situated along unstable boundaries. Along with the sinister new men 'with dark glasses' in the bar, there are also 'normal, decent-looking people' and the sweat running beneath Madame Koto's thick mask of make-up threatens to melt her face and her new role.

Gradually Madame Koto's instability, and the roots of the political corruption, tend towards the *abiku* image of circularity, universality and repetition, rather than on change, transgression and third time. Bakhtin's senile, pregnant hags are ambivalent life in death and death that gives birth. Madame Koto's grotesque body, by contrast, will only give birth to war, horror and violence, if it gives birth at all:

> And I saw that Madame Koto was pregnant with three strange children. Two of them sat upright and the third was upside down in her womb. One of them had a little beard, the second had fully formed teeth, and the third had wicked eyes. They were all mischievous, they kicked and tugged at their cords, they were the worst type of spirit-children, and they had no intention of being born.
>
> (p. 464)

It may be true that 'it began to seem as if there were many Madame Kotos in existence' (p. 375), but by the end of the novel, Madame Koto and her *abiku* children are strongly associated with the portrayal of the moment of Nigerian independence, which becomes a variant in the universal pattern of the insatiability of human greed. The following extract from the novel incorporates all the wild sensuality of the fair, all the grossness of the grotesque. But it also heralds a new version of power, rather than an orgy of rebellion against it. Living and dead, human and animal mingle, not in some sycretized hope for the future, but in the deformity of the present:

> Red lights flooded my brain and when my eyes cleared, the smells of a thousand perfumes, of wild sex on hot illicit nights, of vaginal fluids, of animal sweat, overpowered my senses. In the terrible heat of the dance I saw that, among the erotic dancers, the politicians and chiefs, the power merchants, the cultists, paid supporters, thugs and prostitutes, all moving to the beat of the new music, among them all, there were strangers to the world of the living. I saw that some of the prostitutes, who would be future brides of decadent power, had legs of goats. Some of the woman, who were chimeras and sirens and broken courtesans, had legs of spiders and birds. Some of the politicians and power merchants, the chiefs and innocent-looking men, who were satyrs and minotaurs and satanists, had the cloven hoofs of bulls. Their hoofs and bony legs were deftly covered with furry skin. Fully clothed, they danced as men and women when in fact they were the dead, spirits, and animals in disguise, part-time human

beings *dancing to the music of ascendant power.*

(pp. 459–60)[9]

Madame Koto may not be cut from the cloth of the mythical goddess Beatrice, but is herself a fearsome gender stereotype. Thus Azaro senses 'the emanations of an enormous feminine presence' and feels 'the intense gaze of an ancient mother':

> She sat in her cobwebbed niche, a mighty statue in mahogany, powerful with the aroma of fertility. Her large breasts exuded a shameless libidinous potency. A saffron-coloured cloth had been worn round her gentle pregnancy. Behind her dark glasses, she seemed to regard everything with equal serenity. She gave off an air of contradictory dreams. I was mesmerised by the musk of her half-divinity.

(p. 290)

This 'ancient mother', 'pregnant goddess', 'gave off the accumulated odours of libations, animal blood, kaoline, the irrepressible hopes of strangers, and a yellow impassivity' (p. 290). Both Tutuola's beautiful woman, who dared to try to follow her own sexual urges, and the powerful, grotesque woman, who is pregnant, ugly, old and disgustingly, unnaturally libidinous, are female sexuality portrayed as dangerous and deformed. Once again, female sexuality and fertility are either overpowering, or are metaphors for the sickness or health of the nation. Reality disintegrates beneath the weight of the mythology.

To sum up, not surprisingly for a chameleon, Madame Koto's meaning and function shifts as the novel progresses. What evolves and stabilizes (but only up to a point, as Okri always leaves a small escape hatch for her at the last moment of our passing final judgement on her) is Madame Koto as implicated in the corruption of modern Nigerian politics. She becomes the embodiment, the physical symbol of the new power itself, rather than its transgression, with her warring *abiku* triplets, ominously signalling the country's bloody civil war to come.

What is the nature of this modern Nigerian politics? This question brings us back to the elusiveness of the novel with regard to the possibility of change. Okri expresses unrelieved cynicism for the vices of the political parties. One ostensibly supports the poor and the other, the rich. There is, however, not much to choose between them – 'The three thugs of the Rich Party – or was it the Poor Party – lay writhing on the ground' (p. 194). There is the contaminated milk, distributed by the Rich Party to persuade people to vote for them, which ends up poisoning those who drink it. Then the Party of the Poor comes with loudhailers, leaflets and empty promises. And ultimately:

> It became quite confusing to hear both parties virtually promise the same things. The Party of the Rich talked of prosperity for all, good roads, electricity, and free education. They called the opposition thieves,

tribalists, and bandits. At their rally, they said, everyone would be fed, all questions would be answered.

That evening the van of the Party for the Poor also paraded our street. They too blared music and made identical claims. They distributed leaflets and made their promises in four languages. When the two vans, each packed with armed bodyguards, passed one another, they competed with the amount of noise they could generate. . . . The two vans clashed twice that evening. We kept expecting some sort of war to break out, but both parties seemed restrained by the healthy respect they had developed for one another.

(p. 390)

How does the novel explain this rash of greed, cruelty and corruption, disfiguring the new country which, like the *abiku* babies, is still in the womb, only about to be born? The image embodies the answer. When the spirits of old inhabit the politicians of new, and become indistinguishable from them, the political disintegrates under the burden of the grotesque, imprisoned within the cage of the universal human cycle of greed, the monster who endures under the road, the wicked *abiku*, who imprisons its mother in a cycle of despair.

Such a political milieu is not conceived structurally or historically, and the legacy of colonialism is only mentioned in passing. Okri has explained the reason for this, insisting that

> there's been too much attribution of power to the effect of colonialism on our consciousness. Too much has been given to it. We've looked too much in that direction and have forgotten about our own aesthetic frames. Even though that was there and took place and invaded the social structure, it's quite possible that it didn't invade our spiritual and aesthetic and mythic internal structures, the way in which we perceive the world. Because if one were going to be investigative, one would probably say that a true invasion takes place not when a society has been taken over by another society in terms of its infrastructure, but in terms of its mind and its dreams and its myths, and its perception of reality. If the perception of reality has not been fundamentally, internally altered, then the experience itself is just transitional. There are certain areas of the African consciousness which will remain inviolate. Because the world-view it is that makes a people survive.[10]

This is the language of Tutuola, of myth and conservation, of pure and inviolate African ways of seeing the world; it is diametrically opposed to the hybrid, to change and it is this which drives the area of the novel that is steeped in stories of universal greed and suffering, lifted out of historical context. The most that can be done is to warn a boy with wanderlust to beware the famished old monster that awaits him, just beneath the surface of the new road.

The novel's suspicion, moreover, that history and politics are governed by this universal and repetitive cycle of greed fuels the image of Nigeria itself as the *abiku*:

> Our country is an *abiku* country. Like the spirit-child, it keeps coming and going. One day it will decide to remain. It will become strong.
>
> (p. 478)

Nigeria is not only the wicked *abikus* in Madame Koto's belly, it is a combination of Azaro and his *alter ego*, Ade, the sweet ethereal spirit child who is determined to keep dying and returning to his spirit companions. Ade holds out some qualified hope:

> There will be changes. Coups. Soldiers everywhere. Ugliness. Blindness. And then when people least expect it a great transformation is going to take place in the world. Suffering people will know justice and beauty. A wonderful change is coming from far away and people will realise the great meaning of struggle and hope. There will be peace. Then people will forget. Then it will all start again, getting worse, getting better. Don't fear. You will always have something to struggle for, even if it is beauty or joy.
>
> (p. 478)

While there is tension between idealism and disillusionment, this vision is within the same paradigm of the impossibility of real change; the only hope is the creative human will.

This is not, however, the novel's only paradigm. The relentless cycle of the *abiku* is undercut by Azaro's decision to remain in the land of the living. This is not only the counterfoil to Ade and the more wicked *abikus* but to Madame Koto's decision to sell out to the forces of evil. Madame Koto's decision to cross over the border into evil territory and move her bar with her into the clearing for the new road was not part of the inevitable march of history. Okri presents her decision critically through the terrified dream of Azaro, an *abiku* boy, determined to stay and to break the universal cycle of repetition. Azaro sees that 'there were snails all over the ancient mother' and she speaks to him 'through the snails and objects in her chamber' causing him desperately to seek an escape route from the ancient, slimy circle:

> How could I find my way out of the maze of these dreaming objects which were all obstacles before me? How could I escape from the mystery of the head of a snake, its sloughed skin on a newspaper? How could I escape the stones blackened with the tar of new roads, or the single finger pointing at me in a jar of transparent liquid? . . .
>
> Sweat broke out all over me. I found myself caught in a strange immobility. Then to my greatest horror, she moved – as if she were about to

crush me into her pregnancy. I jumped down from her great body and fought my way through the tangle of cloth, screaming.

(p. 291)

He repeats the desperate question: 'How could I escape that labyrinth of objects?' (p. 292). The crushing weight of history's urge to repeat itself is couched again in the gendered image of the vulnerable male, crushed by the threatening female body and its powerful, sinister fecundity. However, Okri is also attempting to depict the necessity of breaking the *abiku* stranglehold. This necessity, and what a struggle it is to achieve, is reinforced throughout the narrative by the repeated attempts that are made on Azaro to abduct him back to his *abiku* dimension. As in a recurrent nightmare, Azaro encounters spirit and human oddities who are after him. Azaro is pursued by monstrous spirits – 'I shook off the men, but I went on running, for the world seemed populated with people intent on me for one obscure reason or another' (p. 114). The hope of the novel lies in Azaro successfully repudiating the *abiku* within himself and thereby, denying the inevitability of that mythical, Tutuolan road with its hungry, waiting monster:

I was a spirit-child rebelling against the spirits, wanting to live the earth's life and contradictions. . . . I wanted the liberty of limitations, *to have to find or create new roads from this one which is so hungry, this road of our refusal to be.*
(p. 487)[11]

Here Okri appears to contradict earlier reservations and to assert passionately the possibility of change, the condition for which is not solely, or even primarily, the mythical past. In this he is distanced from the more recent Soyinka or Achebe, and even the majority of African writers. This seems to be Okri's own perception:

The title of your new book, *The Famished Road*, raises memories in the reader's mind of Soyinka's *The Road*.
No, there's no connection. My road is quite different. My road is a way. It's a road that is meant to take you from one place to another, on a journey, towards a destination.[12]

In the battle of Azaro versus Madame Koto, Azaro's escapes her labyrinth and the coils of the past:

One night she appeared to me in my sleep and begged me to give her some of my youth.
'Why?' I asked.
And she replied:
'I am two hundred years old and unless I get your young blood I will die soon.'

Her enormous spirit lowered over me. Her spirit was about to swallow me up completely, when a great lion roared from above, quaking the house, and driving her spirit away. Then I realised that *new forces were being born* to match the demands of the age.

(p. 496)[13]

New forces to match the demands of the age. If Madame Koto exits from her bar only to emerge into the future as universal cycle of the past, then does Azaro break out of her bar into the future as newness entering the world? Put another way, what is the nature of the changes that Azaro's escape facilitates? Is it the possibility of social and political change, on behalf of the oppressed and poverty stricken people, and at odds with the meaningless and corrupt politics that Okri so devastatingly critiques?

Azaro's family is desperately poor, and their difficulties in surviving each day are graphically repeated throughout the novel. Mum endlessly tries to sell a few paltry provisions and more often than not, 'We didn't sell a single item' (p. 51). She is an exhausted victim, upright and moral and thus pushed out of her space in the market because she refuses to be bribed by the Party of the Rich for her vote (pp. 168–70). Dad, too, is persecuted by the politicians and is given ever heavier loads to carry in his back-breaking, poorly paid casual work. We see him drunk and violent, unemployed, suffering 'under the blistering heat-waves, looking for a job' and he 'had found none' (p. 52). He searches and searches and is frustrated, brooding and moody, always desperate to find work to feed his family and keep their rapacious landlord away. He is deeply humiliated when Azaro discovers him doing what he sees as the shameful work of carrying nightsoil as the only work he can ultimately get (p. 200). The grinding poverty drives him insane and feeds him with delusions of grandeur. Creditors endlessly plague the family, rats eat at whatever they can scavenge from the tiny room they all share. The demons he fights in his determination to become a boxer are as much the internal, restless fires as the demonic visitors from the other world – ' "Poverty is driving him mad", Mum said' (p. 352). We saw that the outcome of Dad's attempts to break out of his poverty and victim positioning is ambiguously portrayed in the novel.

The purpose of Azaro's heroic escape is not to be found in the awakening of the poor. They are depicted in the novel as misguided or downtrodden. Their passivity, amnesia, naïveté and delusions ensure that they are victims, victims moreover who conspire in their own oppression. When the Party of the Rich first reappeared, Azaro

thought there would be trouble in the area. I thought houses would burn and party vans be destroyed and thugs roasted. I thought people would remember how the very same party had poisoned them with bad milk and had unleashed their rage upon our nights. But people had forgotten, and those that hadn't merely shrugged and said that it was all such a long time ago, that things were too complicated for such memories, and besides the party had new leaders.

(p. 387)

Madame Koto is ultimately able to ensnare and torment them because ordinary people create her myth and expand whatever power she might have. It is 'the crowd' that 'was busily generating her myth' (p. 38):

> That evening was the beginning of her fame. Everyone talked about her in low voices. Her legend, which would sprout a thousand hallucinations, had been born in our midst – born of stories and rumours which, in time, would become some of the most extravagant realities of our lives.

(p. 37)

The virtuous, sad, tired Mum or the demented, raving Dad, will not bring forth much of a transformation. We have already experienced some difficulty in interpreting Dad's attempts to break out of his poverty into boxing. Look here at the caricatured portrait of his hopeless foray into politics, with his bizarre alliance with the beggars, who are themselves portrayed as not unlike the wicked and mischievous *abikus*:

> He tried to organise [the beggars] to clear up the rubbish, to sweep the road, to paint the stalls, to plant flowers near the gutters. Bristling with great enthusiasm, wearing his torn shirt, the plaster flapping on the side of his face, Dad went from house to house asking people to vote for him. He outlined his plans for a school, he suggested to people that they contribute to the beggars' upkeep, and everywhere he went people cursed him for bringing more trouble into their lives. The beggars cleared the rubbish from one end of the road and dumped it at the other. They crushed the flowers they tried to plant.

(p. 448)

What continues to be confusing about Dad is that some of Okri's heartfelt philosophies are mingled with the confusion. For example: ' "many people reside in us", Dad said, . . . "many past lives, many future lives. If you listen carefully the air is full of laughter. Human beings are a great mystery" ' (p. 499). This is central to the novel and explains the ever-changing Madame Koto but, attributed to Dad, seems to question whether such philosophy is appended, sometimes randomly and formlessly, beguiling us to interpret form and meaning.

Azaro does break out of the cycle, but through the good services of a dream-like lion, not dissimilar to Cheney-Coker's magical flying carpet, which we will encounter in the next chapter. Change is not achieved, by and large, by way of any structural challenge to Madame Koto on the part of the crowds who have invented her myth, not by way of any seizure of control of the Party of the Poor. Those 'who had no great powers on our side, and who didn't see the power of our own hunger, a power that would frighten even the gods, found that our dreams became locked out of the freedom of the air' (p. 496).

As always, this is slightly qualified, but the qualification returns us to the enigmatic figure of the photographer, who provides a pointer to the nature of Okri's solutions to his country's political demise. There is a moment in the novel when the people's resistance to the Party of the Rich is documented by the photographer and makes the newspaper headlines. Azaro explains that 'we were astonished that something we did with such absence of planning, something that we had done in such a small corner of the great globe, could gain such prominence':

> For the first time in our lives we as a people had appeared in the newspapers. We were heroes in our own drama, heroes of our own protest. There were pictures of us, men and women and children, standing helplessly round heaps of the politicians' milk. There were pictures of us raging, attacking the van, rioting against the cheap methods of politicians, humiliating the thugs of politics, burning their lies.
>
> (p. 156)

At this point the photographer is just one among the many heroes of the day, the messenger and not the saviour. This is not a position that Okri is able to sustain.

If anyone escapes the deadly circle with Azaro, it is 'the intrepid photographer'. When the Party of the Rich bring contaminated milk in the attempt to bribe the poor, and bring sickness and violence to their neighbourhood, it is he who ends up 'taking pictures of the thugs flexing their muscles' (pp. 125–6). Although he too has been poisoned by the milk, 'bravely, he took pictures of the milk-heaps and vomit outside the houses' and of 'men in contorted forms of agony, women in attitudes of hungry outrage' (p. 132). When the party thugs whipped people, 'the photographer frenziedly took pictures' (p. 154). For this he is arrested and tortured. His increasingly strong role is as mythical hero:

> Prison seemed to have changed him and he went around with a strange new air of myth about him, as if he had conceived heroic roles for himself during the short time he had been away. When he arrived the street gathered outside his room to give him a hero's welcome.
>
> (p. 155)

There is still a touch of irony in this, a degree of poking fun at the man who has turned himself into a heroic figure who 'could have selected quite a few wives from the admiring female faces of that evening if he had not already permanently entered new mythic perceptions of himself that excluded such rash decisions' (p. 156).

Ultimately, the photographer takes on the messianic function of saving the people from the evils of the day by way of the weapon of his photographs. He becomes in this role the saviour of the ordinary, poor people, who are too stricken by poverty to redeem themselves, beyond that one moment of resistance when they first oppose the Party of the Rich. There is strong evidence that Okri has self-consciously portrayed the photographer's function as constructing a new myth. Jeremiah, the photographer's name, was the seventh-century BC prophet who attempted to warn his fellow Jews against moral decay. Although his name is quickly forgotten and he is known only as 'the photographer', the association is established. The mythic persona of the photographer is further developed by his stature as political refugee, hiding from the wrath of the rich and corrupt new class, whose excesses he exposes. He goes into hiding, appears and disappears without warning and has all the aura of a larger than life Scarlet Pimpernel. He is also the Pied Piper, whose magical, special powers are invoked to rid Azaro's family of their rats. He has an heroic stature – 'his eyes were big and bright, full of fear and wisdom' (p. 189). He understands the sounds of the rats and can tell their size 'by listening to them' (p. 190). He tells Azaro that he knows a good poison for killing these rats that are plaguing the family, and he promises to bring some. In the morning he disappears, but he keeps his promise and returns with a magical 'little round, transparent bottle' with 'a yellow powder inside' which is 'the most powerful rat poison in the world' (p. 201). The photographer can kill the rats 'with his powerful medicine and my secret charms' (p. 233).

The Piper as political messiah to save the people from the vicious thugs and evil, corrupt politicians is furthermore made unambiguously overt. They must be killed because:

> 'They are like bad politicians and imperialists and rich people.'
> 'How?'
> 'They eat up property. They eat up everything in sight. And one day when they are very hungry they will eat us up.'
>
> (p. 233)

There are further overtones of Browning's poem in the description of the plague of rats that the photographer has killed:

> The room was a Calvary of rats, a battleground of them. They had died in every conceivable position. There were rats near my pillow, clinging on to the mat with their bared yellow teeth. There were rats all over my cover cloth. Some had died beside me, died beneath the cloth, perished on the centre table, their long tails hanging over the edge. Some had clawed their way up the window curtain and had died at the foot of the wall, leaving long rips on the cloth. They had died in Dad's boot, their tails mistakable for his shoe-lace. They had died with their yellow eyes open, gazing at us with a solemn vacant threat of vengeance.
>
> (p. 235)

In fact, 'lying in a thousand different positions – tails entwined, pale bellies

96

showing, teeth bared, snarling in their death-throes – was an unholy horde of rats' (p. 236).

But Okri's Pied Piper is also portrayed ironically, somewhat sardonically. Drawn as he is from a children's poem, he cuts a somewhat ridiculous figure, seen through the young, albeit exceptional eyes, of the child that is Azaro. He is clothed in the distinctive red and yellow – potential enchantment countered by blood and nausea – 'the strangest figure!':

> His queer long coat from heel to head
> Was half of yellow and half of red[14]

Okri's photographer has been beaten up by thugs, 'blood dripping down his forehead, past his eyes, and soaking his yellow shirt':

> His blood was on his hands. He wiped it on his shirt-front. The red on the yellow made me feel ill.
>
> (p. 189)

The harsh reality of the violence distances this piper from the quaint European fairytale version.

We can now appreciate better the significance of the simile linking the huge deluge with thunder and lightening to the photographer, whose mythic proportions are being developed as if the world 'had momentarily become a picture, as if God were The Great Photographer' (p. 285). But despite the fact that this vengeance on the colonial road derives from the pre-colonial world of the bush and the spirits who inhabit it, the photographer is not himself drawn from the past, from the wisdom of the ancients; he is not narrated at the grandmothers' knees around the eternal and universal fireside of the oral tradition. Steeped in the modern, he travels the paths of the world, seeking his own freedom and a global understanding. He returns from being 'Round the world and back' (p. 231) looking different:

> his face shone with health. His eyes were bright. His mood was buoyant as though he had discovered fields of hope somewhere in the night.
>
> (p. 230)

It was the photographer who contested Dad's ancient myth of the famished road in favour of fearless wanderlust and curiosity about the world:

> 'I am going to travel all the roads of the world.'
> 'And do what?'
> 'Take photographs of the interesting things I see.'
> 'Be careful of the King.'

'The king will die.'
'The King never dies.'
'How do you know?'
'Dad said so.'
'I am not afraid of the King.'

(p. 262)

All of this makes of the photographer a cosmopolitan even as he becomes a mythical messiah, a worthy member of the benevolent elite that writers often fall back on for their political solutions. An individual, or a small exceptional group of individuals, pits itself against the corrupt bloc of ruling interests. These are heroic figures, who are usually Western educated or artistic and specially gifted. They are Soyinka's strong breed of interpreters, Ayi Kwei Armah's healers or Chinua Achebe's Beatrice. Thus the messianic is a device that enables the resolution of the conflicts between the belief in the necessity for social change and the scepticism about its possibility. It is a resolution of the contradiction between a belief in the universality of the human condition of greed and repetitive evil, and in the uniqueness of the human ability to produce exceptionally talented and morally upstanding individuals. Archetypal and mythologized struggles are Manichean battles between good and evil, life and death.

Okri's photographer adds to this number, with one crucial difference. His messianic function is not sought and found by way of a reincarnation of the old gods, a re-birth which engages in a quite particular struggle for nationalist consolidation and healing. He revels in the experience of travelling the world and pits his cosmopolitanism against Dad's jealous monster of the road. However, Okri leads Azaro and his friend, the photographer, out of the labyrinth and into a political vacuum. The photographer's flash may light up a path, but there appears to be space only for the two of them to enjoy a kind of existential freedom.

Okri himself emphasizes this existential dimension, with reference to the struggle between life and death in *The Famished Road*:

> One of the central oppositions in the book is the choice between living and dying. . . . What seems like a constant attempt to pin down his identity is just that all of these different phenomena are different attempts to pull him one way or another: towards life or towards death. And it is part of his choice that he always has to move towards life.[15]

The photographer is on the margins – a complex and challenging figure. He is postmodernist in the overtones of ironic, multiple readings of reality. He shares with radical postcolonials the perception of oppression and a commitment to resisting it. He shares with the cosmopolitans a global framework that breaks out of narrow and blinkered straitjackets. In sharing, however, the messianic features of elite and individualized solutions, the photographer emerges from the maze, perhaps only to discover himself in a strange clearing that Okri has not signposted.

The Famished Road's critique of the decadence of Nigerian society is trenchant and brave. But the novel contradicts itself in its simultaneous representation of a journey as both a futile return in circles and also a road to a new destination. This contradiction manifests itself when universal mythological battles encounter political and historical struggles of the here and now. Okri's fiction is buffeted between existential issues: Life and Death, Good and Evil, individual uniqueness and the predictability of the human condition, the unjustness of the division between rich and the poor, and the creation of new social divisions in independent Nigeria. All of this seeks resolution in the benevolent, messianic figure of the photographer and the enlightened but unpredictable light of his camera's flash. There is, in addition, just one fleeting moment when Okri appears in the novel as himself, in the guise of the artist as gifted and wise carver of masks. This takes us into the narrative framework and the next section of this chapter.

The Famished Road carries an uncertainty at the heart of the narrative point of view. The boy is young, albeit exceptional, always with an immature voice, at an ironic distance from the author. The other storytellers weave a labyrinth as their tales contradict themselves and each other. The reality within the photographer's camera is too often obscured by the cacophony of the novel's language and imagery. Indeed, Okri himself has compared his novel to music, to a noise that resists being read as text:

> But it's difficult for me at this stage to say anything very coherent about
> this book, probably because it's not meant to be coherent. It's against the
> perception of the world as being coherent and therefore readable as a
> text. The world isn't really a text, . . . It's more than a text. It's more akin
> to music.[16]

The clue to the novel's significance may be closer to listening than to reading, but the imagery of its narrative framework is closer to seeing and watching than to hearing. Even when there is a moment of truth, it is depicted through the mediating and relative vision of the mask.

Azaro finds a mask that transforms reality.

> Not far from me, like a skull sliced in half and blacked with tar, was a
> mask that looked frightening from the side, but which was contorted in an
> ecstatic laughter at the front. It had eyes both daunting and mischievous.
> Its mouth was big. Its nose was small and delicate. It was the face of one
> of those paradoxical spirits that move amongst men and trees, *carved by an
> artist who has the gift to see such things and the wisdom to survive them.*
>
> (p. 244)[17]

Okri identifies with that artist, who has the vision to perceive life's multiple dimensions, especially as played out in his own society, with all its contradictions and intensities. This artist has the maturity to cope with the stress of these varied and co-existent realities. The mask is a hybrid face, which presents a different visor, depending on the angle from which it is viewed. It is big and small, intimidating and funny, threatening but also fun. Its creator can perceive the awesome riddles and paradoxes and capture them without being destroyed by the web of their infinitely changing patterns.

When Azaro looks at the world through the mask, what he sees is precisely the kaleidoscope of wild connections and syncretisms:

> I saw a tiger with silver wings and the teeth of a bull. I saw dogs with tails of snakes and bronze paws. I saw cats with the legs of women, midgets with bright red bumps on their heads. The trees were houses.
>
> (p. 245)

Azaro, however, lacks the maturity of vision that the carver enjoys and thus the view through the mask becomes tormenting and disorienting – 'I had begun to lose my sense of reality, confused by the mask' (p. 245) – and becomes menacing when a creature, 'incredibly ugly' 'devourer of humans' becomes visible. However, Azaro cannot easily take the mask off:

> I desperately wanted to take the mask off so I wouldn't have to see anything. I tore off the vegetable string, but the mask stayed on, stuck to my face. I tried to tear it off again, but it was like stripping the skin off my own face. And then the transformation of the wood into flesh became complete.
>
> (p. 247)

Again, ambivalence; the wise artist who carved the mask and captured the spirit of life's paradoxes had the maturity and wisdom to survive. He is fashioned by Okri in the mould of the traditional masquerade, where the ritual journey of discovery and spirituality is crucially linked to masking, where the spirits of the deities or of the natural world enter life and influence it through a masked specialist.[18] It is clear, however, that the youthful Azaro is not yet such a skilled specialist, and he is nearly destroyed by the vision of the mask and *his* maker – Okri, omniscient narrator – has to ensure that he tears it off:

> without caring, I ripped the mask off my face, obliterating its existence from my eyes. My face felt somewhat raw.
>
> (p. 247)

It has come close to entering his essence, but unlike the third eye which remains as a benevolent trace, a kiss of knowledge, the mask leaves his skin raw. The image is strikingly reminiscent of Salman Rushdie's nightmare of the syncretized, Anglicized Indian whose fusions are now terrifyingly permanent, that I described in an earlier chapter and which is so suggestive in this context of Okri's similar preoccupations:

> He had fallen into a torpid sleep, high above the desert sands of the Persian Gulf, and been visited in a dream by a bizarre stranger, a man with a glass skin, who rapped his knuckles mournfully against the thin, brittle membrane covering his entire body and begged Saladin to help him, to release him from the prison of his skin. Chamcha picked up a stone and began to batter at the glass. At once a latticework of blood oozed up through the cracked surface of the stranger's body, and when Chamcha tried to pick off the broken shards the other began to scream, because chunks of his flesh were coming away with the glass.[19]

It is Azaro's immaturity that distances us from his point of view, albeit that we perceive most of the novel through his eyes. It is his youth, and his *abiku* origins that make him so vulnerable to the guile of the stories of the three headed spirit:

> 'Are we travelling this road to the end?'
> 'Yes,' the spirit said, walking as if distance meant nothing.
> 'But you said the road has no end.'
> 'That's true,' said the spirit.
> 'How can it be true?'
> 'From a certain point of view the universe seems to be composed of paradoxes. But everything resolves. That is the function of contradiction.'
> 'I don't understand.'
> '*When you can see everything from every imaginable point of view you might begin to understand.*'
>
> (p. 327)[20]

Is Okri attempting to see everything from every possible point of view, or does he hide behind the screen of many voices because he is unwilling to present any point of view at all? We come back to the beguiling spirit with the forked tongue, who attempts with sweet words to entice Azaro back to the spirit world and his *abiku* existence. Part of his power hinges on the flaws in human nature:

> Then I found the three-headed spirit sitting beside me. He had never left. He had been waiting patiently. He could always count on the unintended callousness of human beings, their lovelessness, their forgetfulness of the basic things of existence.
>
> (p. 326)

We are, therefore, ironically distanced from anything this creature might have to say, although he expresses what are clearly many of the text's genuine and passionate beliefs. It was the three-headed spirit who pointed out the road to

Azaro, telling the inspiring story of how the road is being constructed by people themselves as part of life's challenge. However, the poetic language of this tale soon revealed its ironic underbelly when its narrator is exposed as the lure towards death.

The novel's purpose, moreover, remains elusive. The roadbuilders are actually 'strange beings' who have masks 'instead of faces'. These masks 'became more beautiful the longer you looked at them'. In fact, 'maybe their masks were their faces' (p. 328). Given the concealments and surprise exposures of the novel, the suggestion is that Azaro is deluded as part of his abduction and that aberrant ghosts and spirits might live beneath the masks. Again there are the unmistakable overtones with the folktale of the Perfect Gentleman. Here the boy is being warned, like Tutuola's drinkard's wife, that he may well be disillusioned on his ill-advised journey, given that all is not what it appears. Azaro's illusions must be shattered; he must not listen to the honeyed talk of the spirit, or else he will die:

> When we cross the river there is no turning back. Your companions and the whole of the spirit world and the goddess of the spirit-rivers will have a wonderful banquet awaiting you, because you are their prodigal friend.
>
> (p. 335)

The battle against the spirit and his stories and visions is a critical and resolute moment in an elusive narrative structure that has the floating aura of a dream. The fight for Azaro is at the level of perception and language, persuasion and vision, rather than, as in the epics of old, at the level of great physical battles and feats of strength. The river boundary into the otherworld is a vast mirror, whose reflected images dictate reality:

> It was only when I looked at the river properly that I realised it was a vast, undisturbed mirror. The canoe stood on a haze of light, without troubling the mirror's surface. The lights of that world, converging on its shimmering surface, made me utterly transparent, as if I had disappeared from reality, become a ghost. For a moment my eyes, suffused with light and silver, were blinded.
>
> (p. 336)

These reflections render Azaro insubstantial, like a ghost. The figure nearby the canoe, who Azaro wrongly takes to be the ferryman of the dead, turns out to be his champion, invoked, it is implied, by the herbalist priest. Her head is covered in a black cloak and, as we would expect, her unveiling is revealing. She is a hybrid woman, young and naked in body, 'with an old woman's face', and with 'the feet of a lioness', 'her eyes were those of a tiger' (p. 336). This woman and the three-headed spirit – Good and Evil – 'fought one another through all their reflections':

> Suddenly I saw both of them mirrored to eternity. They were everywhere and each reflection was real. And then, as if behind a glass window

illuminated at night, I slowly made out Dad's face. He watched me with
calm eyes, while the spirit fought the woman. They fought on the river of
glass, fought on the canoe, fought in the sky.

(p. 338)

The depiction is itself an extraordinary hybrid of ancient ritual and custom,
syncretized with the postmodern in its insistence on the crucial mediations of
perception and the deception of reality. In all the golden light of blinding reflection from the mirror, a shadow is cast by the herbalist priest, a shadow which
'expanded the spaces' and which filled the air 'with the aroma of wild village
shrines':

His dancing, fervent and insane, with red amulets and cowries cackling
round his neck, became the whirling torment of the twice-beheaded
spirit.

(p. 339)

Ultimately, the force of family and tradition triumph and illusions are
unmasked as the mirror is shattered and the beckoning demon of death is overcome:

The spirit fought vainly in the canoe as the chicken twitched. Its blood
dripped on my forehead. The herbalist fell silent. The spirit's head,
landing on silver, looked around, saw itself separated from its body, and
let out its final scream of horror, cracking the surface of the river. The
mirrors shattered. It became dark. Splinters and reflections caught in my
eyes.

(p. 339)

The pull towards death is shattered. However, splinters and reflections in the
eyes are deadly remnants of negative forces that will continue to colour the way
Azaro perceives reality; they are a reminder that nothing is absolute and the road is
indeed never finally complete in its construction.

Azaro is a first person narrator, whose perspective dominates the novel. He is
the receptacle for, and transmitter of, all the different stories, visions and possibilities. The novel buttresses Azaro's position as narrator with a grid of extended
metaphors and symbols of seeing, of eyes, masks and mirrors. Within Azaro's
stories, there are other storytellers and perspectives. We have already seen how
hard it is to pin the narrative down at quite crucial moments, such as the meaning
of Dad's wrestling matches against his destiny, or Mum's stories, or the nature of
Madame Koto and the meaning of her bar, or even of the central road imagery
itself. By continuing to map the mosaic of many stories and visions, what does
seem to emerge, as we shall see, is that the novel strives to see the world without
illusions. This it does within a sophisticated understanding that the truth hides

itself behind mirrors, masks and eye-glasses, and that reality is often not what it seems. There can be no simple unmasking, moreover, for what lies behind the mirror can simply be another illusion or nightmare:

> The goddess in wood spoke to me through all these things, but most of all she spoke to me with her eyes. I didn't understand her speech. Without thinking, like someone wandering around in a stranger's dream, I climbed the body of the goddess and took off her glasses. In the deep hollow of her sockets she had eyes of red stone, precious stones the exact colour of blood. My breathing seized. Her eyes fixed on me with such heat that I hurriedly put her glasses back on.
>
> (p. 291)

The ruby eyes, redolent of illicit, corrupt money, the colour of the blood spilt in the violence and greed of the time, are blind. They have exchanged sight for wealth and her sockets are hollow and empty. Not to be able to see, to perceive and understand, is the novel's nightmare. Hence the blind old man in the novel is a great force for evil. He, like Madame Koto, wants to see by the light of Azaro's youth. Azaro realizes that he has 'run right into the territory of the old man who had been blinded by a passing angel'. He turns his 'green and half-dissolved' eyes on the boy:

> 'Come here,' he said.
> 'Why?'
> 'I want to see with your eyes.'
>
> (p. 313)

Azaro ends up seeing a horrible world through the slimy green eyes of the blind man:

> Everything went dark. I tried to blink, but couldn't. As if I had woken into a nightmare, thick green substances passed over my eyes. They settled. Gradually, my eyes cleared. When I looked out at the world again, what I saw made me scream. Everything was upside-down. The world was small. Trees were like slow-moving giants. The rain was a perpetual nightfall, and night a perpetual rain. The earth was full of craters. It kept moving as if it were a monster fretting in sleep. The spaces between things were populated with the most horrifying spirits I have ever seen. They had wounds all over them which dripped pus. When they talked green spit poured from their mouths. I screamed. My eyes caught fire.
>
> (pp. 313–14)

Madame Koto's bar and the blind man's bungalow, therefore, both become threatening sites of attack. Seeing through the horror of the old man's blindness, Madame Koto emerges as a monster with the ruby eyes:

> out sprang a big yellow animal with blazing ruby eyes and long claws. It leapt into my eyes, and I fell back. (p. 314)

The old man, like Madame Koto's warring *abiku* triplets, is also Nigeria, unseeing creator of discordant music, reminiscent of the unnatural old man-child of Ayi Kwei Armah's first novel, completing the cycle from birth to old age at an accelerated speed, a country old and blind before it has even been born.[21]

Azaro frees himself from the old man and flees, but it is no coincidence that the man wrongly accuses him of breaking his window after this incident, resulting in a terrible beating by Dad. The shattering of glass, like the lifting of the eye-glasses, does not always lead to release and freedom. The emotional trauma of this beating makes Azaro vulnerable to the call of the three-headed spirit and the pull of death.

Azaro lives in many dimensions and tells his story through his life, his dreams, his entry into the dreams of others, even through the perspective of the duiker; he exists on the plane of his pre-life and perception of spirits and ghosts invisible to others. He is hijacked into seeing through the film of slime of the old man's decayed vision, and also through the mask of the master carver, whose vision of reality is as terrifying to the youthful Azaro as the blood and guile of the perspectives of Madame Koto and the three headed spirit.

Spectacles and unveilings, tearing off masks and white suits and revealing what lies beneath are part of the novel's cacophony. Madame Koto's spectacles may conceal her evil, bejewelled eyes, the colour of blood, but the blue spectacles of Mum's story told a different tale, one which syncretized the oral tradition with new technology. The different ways of seeing are inscribed in all the different spectacles, mirrors, masks and modern science, most especially, photography. And it is the eye of the photographer which comes closest to the vision of the wise carver, and which is ultimately able to expose the sweet talk and beguiling promises of the politicians:

> The only thing that was missing was the photographer to record the events of the night and make them real with his magic instrument.
>
> (p. 182)

Photographs are central in this novel of shifting reality and multiple guises, many of which hide spirits or animals under their human facades. The photographs capture and freeze a moment, but is this 'truth'? Initially, there is a question of the gulf between reality as lived and what the photograph projects:

> Hanging on crooked nails on the walls, there were framed, browning photographs of my parents. In one of the pictures Mum sat sideways on a chair. She had a lot of powder on her face, and she had the coy smile of a

village maiden. Dad stood next to her. He had on a baggy pair of trousers, a white shirt, and an askew tie. His coat was much too small for him. He had a powerful tigerish expression on his face. His strong eyes and his solid jaw dared the camera. He looked the way some boxers do before they become famous. There was another photograph in which I sat between them, small between two guardians. There were smiles of shy sweetness on our faces. As I stared at the photograph in that little room where the lamp produced more black smoke than illumination, I wondered where the sweetness had gone.

(p. 33)

In the first photograph both Mum and Dad are posing and are not as we come to know them – the over-powdered, coy Mum, like a village maiden, the Dad, squeezed into formal dress and daring the camera to contradict him. As for the second photograph, has the sweetness gone, or has it always been soured by poverty? Perhaps the greater reality is the lack of the photographic illumination, captured in the image of the black smoke produced by the lamp. In other words, at first the photograph captures only a very partial truth. In a novel that questions the nature of reality – that shares postmodern scepticism about privileged readings and employs devices of masks and mirrors – what better crucial image for Okri than that of photography?

Linda Hutcheon points out that photography is defined by its ambivalences – 'it is in no way innocent of cultural formation' and 'yet it is in a very real sense technically tied to the real, or at least, to the visual and the actual'. Postmodernists expose this contradictory relationship to the real, expose 'what may be the major photographic code, the one that pretends to look uncoded'.[22] In fact, 'the inherently paradoxical medium of photography' can act 'as the paradigm of the postmodern'.[23] Although we are reading text and not looking at photographs, the question of photography leads very obviously 'to the related issue of narrative representation – its powers and its limitations'.[24]

In a novel wracked by tensions and ambivalence, it is the photographer who comes closest to seeing authoritatively. This is not so right from the beginning. In the early stages of the novel, photographs enact the tension between capturing reality and photographic convention that codifies reality. If the old family pictures blur reality with their formality and sweetness, then so do the photographer's other early pictures, which are steeped in distorting extremes of poverty and joylessness:

When I looked closer at the pictures we all seemed strange. The pictures were grained, there were dots over our faces, smudges everywhere. Dad looked as if he had a patch over one eye, Mum was blurred in both eyes, the children were like squirrels, and I resembled a rabbit. We all looked like celebrating refugees. We were cramped, and hungry, and our smiles were fixed. The room appeared to be constructed out of garbage and together we seemed a people who had never known happiness. Those of us that smiled had our faces contorted into grimaces, like people who had been defeated but who smile when a camera is trained on them.

(p. 91)

Note, they smile specifically for the camera. The extreme misery, like the painted smiles, interrogates the photograph's veracity. What changes is that the photographer begins to capture not just portraits of families and groups, but the political scandals and corruptions of the new Nigeria about to emerge. What is the nature of the hope he represents? Because the degradation of society is almost total, events and people only exist if the camera creates and constructs them. But to destroy the photograph means there is no evidence, and no reality at all, as if the photographer had not been present. After the riots 'The only thing that was missing was the photographer to record the events of the night and make them real with his magic instrument':

We feared that the photographer had been murdered. His glass cabinet remained permanently shattered. It looked misbegotten. It became a small representation of what powerful forces in society can do if anyone speaks out against their corruptions. And because the photographer hadn't been there to record what had happened that night, nothing of the events appeared in the newspapers. It was as if the events were never real. They assumed the status of rumour.

(pp. 182–3)

This point is further illustrated by the vision Azaro has about the photographer. He sees thugs beat him up:

The camera fell from the photographer's hands. I heard people screaming inside the camera. The thugs jumped on the camera and stamped on it, trying to crush and destroy it. And the people who were inside the camera, *who were waiting to become real*, and who were trying to get out, began wailing and wouldn't stop.

(p. 173)[25]

Again the splintered glass is destructive. Eventually, Azaro imagines that the thugs catch himself and the photographer and

They shut us in a glass cabinet which would not break. Outside the cabinet chickens fluttered and turned into politicians. The politicians, wearing white robes, flew about the place, talking in strange languages. I stayed there, trapped behind glass, a photograph.

(p. 174)

In this sense, the photograph is terrifyingly powerful and even dangerous – the sequence is reversed as the camera constructs reality rather than reflecting it. Thus photography potentially violates boundaries, as freedom, truth and justice cannot exist outside its frames. This is the ultimate political critique of postmodernism running rampant and textuality dictating meaning. This being the case, people become trapped as much by the photographer as by the politicians, in that their only existence is within the frame of a snapshot. The people are at the mercy of the benevolence of the photographer.

A significant change in the depiction of photography occurs, however, as the photographer himself develops and becomes more and more socially aware and politically active, the polar opposite of the blind old man. His camera becomes his third eye and increasingly his pictures tell the truth, document history and capture social reality. There is less and less irony in the depiction. In a society of thuggery and corruption, of distortion of truth by unscrupulous politicians and businessmen, the only reality is that documented and pinned down by way of the physical proof of the photograph. Thus the ironic postmodern gaze with regard to photography is steadily lowered, as Okri sees the political possibilities.

This is not to say that there is a naïve conversion to the possibility of easily capturing reality. Firstly, the description acknowledges the distortions of reality brought about here by the effect of the newsprint on the photographs, so it is only just possible 'to recognise our squashed and poverty-ridden faces on the grainy newsprint' and 'the dreadful newsprint distorted her beauty into something wretched and weird' (p. 156). These are, however superficial distortions, by contrast with the enormous coup of having the evidence of what had actually happened to expose the lies. Unlike the immature vision of the young Azaro, the viewpoint of the more experienced photographer is authoritative as he has already travelled extensively and seen wondrous and terrible things in the world:

> There were pictures of a fishing festival, of people on the Day of Masquerades. The Egunguns were bizarre, fantastic, and big; some were very ugly; others were beautiful like those maidens of the sea who wear an eternal smile of riddles; in some of the pictures the men had whips and were lashing at one another. There were images of a great riot. Students and wild men and angry women were throwing stones at vans. There were others of market women running, of white people sitting on an expanse of luxurious beaches, under big umbrellas, with black men serving them drinks; pictures of a child on a crying mother's back; of a house burning; of a funeral; of a party, with people dancing, women's skirts lifted, baring lovely thighs. And then I came upon the strangest photograph of them all, which the photographer said he had got from another planet. It was of a man hanging by his neck from a tree.
>
> (p. 263)

The horror of the lynching is communicated by the photographer's description of it as taking place on another planet. But when he answers Azaro's questions he is aware that he should not frighten the child too much and, with a subtle touch avoids heavy political pontification. In response to Azaro's question as to why 'some white people' hanged the man, the photographer says that Azaro is 'too young to hear all this'. When pushed by the boy, he says it is 'because they don't like piano music', clearly communicating that 'he wanted to change the subject' (p. 264). This also serves to signal that the reader and the photographer have greater knowledge and maturity than Azaro. What is implied in the riddle of the piano music is the unity of the black and white keys, a metaphor of racial connectedness. This superior knowledge reinforces the authoritativeness of the photographer's voice. Echoes of the photographer pervade the whole novel – 'it was because of our fondness that I was sure that some day we would see him again' (p. 265).

Multiple narrative fragments form and regroup. There is masquerade in impersonation: Tutuola's Perfect Gentleman, the man in the white suit, the masked spirits. There is masquerade as masked performance: the journey of discovery linked centrally to the tradition of masking where spirits and deities are brought into the world and can speak. There is mask, in the sense of black skins and white masks – the colonial mimic in white suit and dark glasses, who, like Rushdie's Chamcha, finds his glass mask of acculturation has been grafted into his skin. There is mask as sunglasses, or photograph, or mirror, through which an apparently innocent and neutral reality seems to be reflected while being refracted, a postmodern image of the relativity of viewing, of the uncertainty of fixed positions. The shattering of the mask or of glass brings either further disaster inhibiting sight, or the liberation accompanying the destruction of illusions. There is also the photograph which delivers historical reality, but ultimately in the interests of the salvation of the photographer/artist/writer, who is himself existentially liberated, in the idealistic attempt to save the miserable masses in the process.

As Biodun Jeyifo concludes, again with reference to Okri's early fiction, but, for all its apparent newness, also relevant to *The Famished Road*:

> But what kind of redemption is envisioned by these novels? What Jeffia Okwe says in *Flowers and Shadows* could be fairly ascribed to Omovo's uneasy intimations at the end of *The Landscapes Within:* 'I was in no hurry. I had come to find peace with myself and my memories. I had long ago discovered there was no such thing as finding peace outside oneself in the heat of a life's journey or in the hustle for material acquisition. I had found it within me, in that calm centre where nothing could shake or disturb me like they used to. In finding it, I had found myself.' Ben Okri's fiction, to date, speaks eloquently and movingly for a *whole* generation. But like the very many models of the modernist novel of bourgeois individualism, African and Western, which are so influential on his novelistic art, the ultimate vision he proffers is reductively individ-

ualistic.[26]

> The road was the worst hallucination of them all, leading towards home and then away from it, without end, with too many signs, and no directions.
>
> (pp. 114–15)

I wish to conclude with a few words about *Songs of Enchantment*. I think that this sequel to *The Famished Road* highlights some of the tendencies in the earlier work that become more pronounced, with negative gender repercussions.

Michael Gorra reads both *The Famished Road* and *Songs of Enchantment* as one, and can do so because the second is a seamless continuation of the first. He says that Okri's narrative lacks logic 'and by "logic" I don't mean a European plausibility'. He explains that what he does mean is 'a sense of purposeful form and structure'.[27] However, in the new novel

> The 'political thugs' still terrorize the neighborhood in which Azaro lives with his parents. The sinister and otherworldly Mme Koto still runs her palm-wine bar in league with the Party of the Rich. The great pre-election rally that was in the offing for the last half of the previous book still hasn't happened by the end of *Songs of Enchantment*. So when after 600 pages spread between the two volumes Azaro sees 'the sight which was to bring terror into our lives,' I almost shut the book for good. Terror hadn't been there before? But maybe Azaro needed to remind us, for these characters are so perpetually on the verge of crisis that the reader stops believing in it. Or stops believing, rather, that the crisis will ever be in any way resolved.[28]

Songs of Enchantment offered the possibility of following Azaro after he has fought the demons of death and made the promised escape from the snake. But instead, the sequel not only falls short of this promise, but is also a work that is far more conservative and less brave. It has recourse to the myths of old at the service of the familiar nationalist project of cultural healing.

This is Ato Quayson's point when he refers to the fact that 'in *The Famished Road*, the whole of reality is sited on a continually shifting conceptual space'. He feels that what saves this novel from total escape from reality, is the distance it maintains from 'a total location in mythopoeia'. However, in *Songs of Enchantment*, 'the whole narrative takes a complete turn to mythopoeia':

> The object of the novel is to stage the elemental struggle between the forces of Good, represented by Azaro's Dad, and those of Evil, represented by Madam Koto and the Jackal-headed Masquerade.[29]

In this way, the novel is restricted to 'the closures of mythology in terms of the outcome of elemental struggles' and there is therefore 'a loss of the irony that often attended the relationships between Azaro and other characters in the earlier novel'. This results, according to Quayson in 'an implied moralism in the novel that derives directly from the socializing and morally affirmative tone of myth and folktale'.[30] This reinforces the crucial point made in Chapter 3 about the importance of ironic distancing from myth, if the stories of old are to be harnessed to a magical realist point of view.

What read as exuberant, busy and kinetic, even if to a fault, in *The Famished Road* becomes, when repeated in *Songs of Enchantment*, a paradoxical stillness, a fiction trapped in the labyrinth of its own formula, and in a far more reactionary politics. And sadly, the touchstone to the construction of this labyrinth of increased density is women as grotesque, powerful and threatening. While this was already clearly apparent in *The Famished Road*, in *Songs of Enchantment* the women, including the gentle and beautiful Mum, become strange and terrifying as part of this novel's organizing frame. The first change is in Mum, who gets fed up with Dad early on in *Songs of Enchantment* and goes off ominously 'in the direction of Madame Koto's fabulous bar', leaving behind her son and husband (p. 17).[31] When they go searching for her in the bar, it has once again metamorphosed, but significantly this time into an awesome stronghold of terrifying and powerful women. These women:

> were resplendent in their jewels and bangles and amulets. They were mostly mighty women with enormous breasts and eyes that were frightening in their invulnerable stare. They were busy around the barfront, milling about with tables and folding chairs. Their perfume was delicious to the nostrils and they bore themselves proudly, like a select people, or like members of a royal household.
>
> (p. 36)

Their mighty breasts, sensuous smells and frightening self-confident eyes make them formidable to the poor men who are searching for Mum among them. They laugh at Dad and emasculate him, reducing him to pleading for his wife. Azaro and Dad are overpowered and outnumbered – 'women swarmed everywhere' and someone who looks just like Mum (with the Okri loophole of doubt) acts just like a whore – not the Mum of old at all. She wears a gaudy 'gold-tricked wrapper'; she 'flashed smiles in all directions, red lipstick burning her face, her arms loaded with bangles'. So degenerate is this Mum that she cannot hear her child call above the music, and so menacing and unmotherly are the horrible throng of swarming women that they form a 'solid wall of women's bodies' preventing Azaro from reaching his mother (p. 37). The women tower over Azaro and chase and threaten him much like the spirits who wished to transport him into death did in the last novel:

> Having no choice, I ran into the bar, into the smells of sacrificial blood and ritual herbs, the juices and rich potencies of bark and earth.
>
> (p. 38)

The stench of powerful women, their juices bonded to bark and earth is extended to the description of Madame Koto herself. Azaro sees her asleep, completely naked, 'her mighty breasts heaving like gargantuan bellows':

> I followed her heaving form in the air, overwhelmed by her heated lust smells, by the deep essences of her enormous body stewing beneath the constraints of her convulsive flesh. Her craven volcanic desire made the air demonic. Around her lashed the fury of a lust that had been rising all her life, hurtling her deeper into the powers of her spirit, making her flesh blubbery with the over-ripeness of days without lust and release. It made her eyes sharper in their penetrating insight into the weaknesses of men. It made her centre riper, richer, voluptuous and soft. It made her face mask-like in the solidity of self-control and manipulation. It deepened her command of the psychic centres of men and women and invisible forms of power, drawing to her great body the magnetism of the earth's hunger for fertilisation.
>
> (p. 140)

Male terror of female power here is quite staggering, a power unleashed by the evil forces being born with the new nation's independence. This may reverse Achebe's idealized Beatrice as Priestess to the nation's recovery, but it is within the identical paradigm. Woman's body reflects the sickness, health or potential for recovery of the nation, and in the process loses its rightful autonomy. The nation's unnatural greed, grotesque desires and immanent volcanic eruption into civil war are symbolically represented by female attributes grown monstrous. Azaro has a vision that Madame Koto gives birth to the horrible three *abiku* babies who 'spent their lives divided, warring against each other, fighting for their mother's milk, savaging her breasts, and tearing her apart' (p. 142).

There is not only a strange new breed of women in the bar; the bush is rumoured to be populated with a secret sect of priestly females, who have great powers of transformation and have discovered 'the secrets of herbs and bark, of the earth and the night' (p. 79). They may be different from the whores and hags in the bar, but they share the association with the earth, and while these 'women of the forest' are opposed to Madame Koto's Amazonian bunch, they fulfil another familiar, stereotypical female function – this time as priestesses, as the custodians of traditional values and knowledge. There were those that:

maintained that the women, seduced by the spirit of the forest, were against Madame Koto and her ascendant cult. And Mum surprised me one night by telling me that the women were singing of the forgotten ways of our ancestors. They were warning us not to change too much, not to disregard the earth.

(p. 79)

After leaving Madame Koto's clutches, it is with these women that Mum becomes associated and she often slips away at night into the forest to participate in secret rituals from which the men are excluded. She becomes 'more beautiful, more aloof, like a seraphic priestess' (p. 80). She moves from whore to priestess, from sex queen to untouchable, and Dad, in his depleted, emasculated condition cannot even 'pluck up the courage to sleep with Mum on the bed' (p. 80).

Without the photographer to oppose the image, we are firmly situated in the realm of myth, of warnings about change, of conserving the ancient ways, where, among other things, women were good mothers and Madame Koto and her bar of giant breasted women did not exist. In other words, Okri's depiction of the women in his sequel to *The Famished Road* is as a barometer of the changes for the worse for the nation as a whole. This novel has clear overtones of Ayi Kwei Armah's *Two Thousand Seasons* and his African 'Way', the idealized purity of pre-colonial Africa.[32] And so Azaro sees in the great procession:

illustrious ancestors with caravans of wisdom, old souls who had been reborn many times in the magical depths of the continent, and who had lived the undiscovered secrets and mysteries of The African Way – The Way of compassion and fire and serenity . . .

These spirit-masters of the spirit universes brought The Way which had since been corrupted by succeeding generations, by greed and decadence, blindness and stupidity, by vulgar kings and dim-witted chiefs, corrupted and turned into sinister uses in the eternal battle of ascendencies. These invisible masters brought fragments of the Original Way in their silent procession, drawing back to its centre the valuable truths in our stolen heritage, our dispersed legacy, our myths coded with wonderful secrets of living, our splendid feats of memory and science and mysticism, art and learning, poetry and thriving in a universe of enigmas, our accomplishments denied by the dominant history of the short-sighted conquerors of the times.

I saw them with their celestial caravans of the forgotten and undiscovered African Way, and maybe I marvelled.

(pp. 159–61)

The photographer and his desire for change, for travel, for experiencing the world, for defying the famished monster of ancient warnings, even with his messianic mission, have all but disappeared. The grotesquely distorted women and their unspeakable bodies 'drenched with potent menstrual blood' (p. 141) have sent Okri back to mythical origins, beyond the border zone of magical realism, where newness has the potential to enter the world and to see it with the vision of a third eye.

This is not the note upon which to end the discussion of Ben Okri's fiction. *The Famished Road* is far more subtle, complex and nuanced than its sequel. It is flawed, however, by the ambivalence, contradictions and discordances of its music, and scarred by its refusal to move beyond individualized solutions for the nation state and to embrace change wholeheartedly.

In *The Famished Road* Azaro defies Madame Koto and finds a way out of the labyrinth. To what purpose is undeniably unclear. The disappointment is that she seems, with her squadron of formidable women, to have re-captured him. The abiding image, however, on which I want to end is not that of Madame Koto, but, with all the difficulties that attend his portrayal, with the potential inherent in the image of the African Pied Piper, the photographer in yellow, drenched with the red of blood, travelling the roads of the world:

> In the morning he was gone. I felt sad he wasn't there. He had taken pictures of everyone except himself. And after a while I forgot what he looked like. I remembered him only as a glass cabinet and a flashing camera. The only name I had for him was Photographer. He left a written message to Dad to say he was leaving and to thank us for our help. Dad was pleased with the letter and on some happy nights we sat up and talked about many things and many people, but we were fondest of the photographer. And it was because of our fondness that I was sure that some day we would see him again.
>
> (p. 265)

On his travels, the photographer appreciates the complex music of the piano of cross-cultural interaction. It is the same piano that the Ghanaian, Kojo Laing, to whose fiction we will turn later, celebrates in his poem, 'Nobody's song, nobody's colour':

> Today I can sing a long song for nobody's colour.
> He gives her new song back through a wild piano.[33]

'THE PLANTATION BLOOD IN HIS VEINS'

Syl Cheney-Coker and *The Last Harmattan of Alusine Dunbar*

The historical reach of *The Last Harmattan of Alusine Dunbar* is from slavery through colonialism to the post-independence period. Its geographical span is from Africa, through the middle passage to America and then the return to Africa. Beyond history and geography, the novel travels through time and space, from the real to the magical, from the living to the dead and back. Like Marquez's *One Hundred Years of Solitude*, which clearly influenced it, *The Last Harmattan* is also a gripping, epic tale of the generations. The long cycle of inhumanity and oppression is counter-balanced by strong, morally unwavering families – the founders of Malagueta, such as the Cromantines and the Martins, and later Thomas Bookerman, Phyllis Dundas and the Farmer brothers. Originally slaves, they return to Africa and become the aristocracy of the new African settlement; they are symbolic of the human urge to justness, righteousness and freedom.

These families are linked to the mysterious and god-like Sulaiman the Nubian, otherwise known as Alusine Dunbar, who has supernatural powers and who fore-sees all the unfolding events of the novel, and to his daughter Fatmatta, also endowed with unnatural powers. The Cromantines, original founders of the settlement, encounter Fatmatta as a very old woman on the boat returning to Africa from America. Fatmatta dies on the voyage, but not before she communi-cates her story to Jeanette Cromantine.

This story is complicated and begins with N'jai, a gold merchant who returns from one of his bouts of wandering with Sulaiman, who stays in his house. The lonely Mariamu, N'jai's wife, is desperate for a child, but seems to be infertile. She turns to Sulaiman whose unearthly powers she hopes can help her. He uses his very earthly powers and himself fathers Mariamu's child, a daughter called Fatmatta. Eventually Mariamu leaves N'jai and moves in with the loving and foreign Mulatto, who runs a local store. Fatmatta's life is not easy. Her unnaturalness includes an unearthly beauty, making her fatal to ordinary men. But one unnatural albino is destructive of her. He appears as a handsome suitor whom she marries, but who immediately disillusions her with the reality of his true self. Ultimately, Fatmatta is sold into the middle passage and slavery. She uses her powers to resist the sexual abuse of the white slavers and, in old age, finally sets sail for Africa, a home she never reaches.

The novel moves over time and space with great strides, carrying its reader breathlessly along and diverting into the life histories of its many and varied characters, only to return to its historical thread. It begins in present-day, postcolonial Africa, with a Prologue in which General Masimiara is imprisoned after his failed coup against a corrupt government in Malagueta. Throughout the rest of the novel, the flashback portrayal of the founding and growth of Malagueta is mediated by this irony that history has come full circle and Masimiara is imprisoned in the very island dungeon of the colonizers, and from which 'in centuries past' his countrymen and -women had been 'transported across the treacherous sea' into slavery (p. vii).[1]

Book one is set in America during slavery. Jeanette, the proud and free young African American, falls in love with Sebastian, a slave, and returns to Africa with him to found a dynasty, along with other proud returnees who include Gustavius Martins. The latter falls in love with a local woman, Isatu, against the terms of the agreement with the local African ruler, who distrusts the returnees. Eventually Gustavius and Isatu have a son called Garbage. Hostility and distrust between indigenous Africans and returnees leads to an attack on Malagueta when locals suspect that the foreigners are bringing them bad luck.

It takes another wave of returnees to re-establish Malagueta: 'Nine years later, Thomas Bookerman and his men, trying to find the spot where the first Malaguetans had established their settlement, were to pass through the region' (p. 94). The growth of the new town accompanies the growth of the narrative chain of new life stories, such as that of Phyllis Dundas, who will end up in a union with Thomas Bookerman. A new generation emerges, including Emmanuel Cromantine, son of Jeanette and Sebastian Cromantine. The returnees attempt to build a Utopia in the face of the prejudices of the locals and the shadow of colonialism, in the person of Captain Hammerstone, and which threatens a new enslavement. Bookerman and Phyllis are exiled to the Gold Coast as punishment for resisting colonial settlement.

Malagueta continues to grow and change, although colonialism is cruel and oppressive. But its victims – the 'grandchildren of the founders of Malagueta' – sow the seeds of anti-colonialism, forming the embryo of what will become a nationalist, educated elite. Arabs arrive and establish an evil coalition with the British, who now try to withdraw as the place is becoming 'ungovernable'. Masimiara becomes head of the army and the wicked Ali Baba and 'the forty African ministers took over the reins of Malagueta' (p. 381). They are corrupt and far more ruthless than the likes of the British Hammerstone. They are overthrown and the benevolent Masimiara becomes head of a military government with Colonel Lookdown Akongo as his second-in-command. Masimiara is, significantly, linked to the founding elite – his mistress is 'Miss Sadatu Agnes Cromantine-Doherty, great-granddaughter of Sebastian and Jeanette Cromantine, the founders of Malagueta' (p. 385). Sanka Maru is invited to head 'a new civilian government'. However, the tyranny continues until Sanka Maru comes to a spectacular end at the conclusion of the novel. When the 'old man', Sulaiman the Nubian, otherwise known as Alusine Dunbar, comes to get him, Sanka Maru has no premonitions about his imminent demise:

> President Sanka Maru walked to a window, pushed the curtains aside and saw a magic carpet flying in the air, not knowing that it had come a long way and that its arrival had been predicted by an albino afraid of light. Mesmerised by the occurrence, Sanka Maru thought he was seeing things when an old man lowered himself from the carpet, waved to him, and disappeared under a tree.
>
> (p. 395)

What role can magic carpets and predictions play in the political and historical drama of the assassination of a President? For the moment such questions will stand while we look more closely at Sierra Leone's unique history, and flowing from this history, at Cheney-Coker's own Creole identity, expressed in one of his poems (*Hydropathy*):

> I think of Sierra Leone
> and my madness torments me
> all my strange traditions
> the plantation blood in my veins
> my foul genealogy!
> I laugh at this Creole ancestry
> which gave me my negralized head
> all my polluted streams
> not one river shedding its pain.[2]

Cheney-Coker's background is very varied, as he explained in an interview with me in 1994:

> I was born in Sierra Leone, Freetown, almost fifty years ago. I went to secondary school in Sierra Leone. When I was twenty one I went to America to the University of Oregon on the northwestern side of the United States and later on did graduate work in Wisconsin. In addition to being a poet and novelist I've worked as a journalist and I've taught at universities on three continents – Asia, Africa and United States.[3]

He describes life in his part of the world – 'so utterly complex and exasperating' – and the importance of his 'exposure to various cultures, which are quite different from mine'. He himself identified the more narrow cultural ethnicity of much African fiction writing and, highly significantly for the argument that I am developing, he distanced himself from it:

117

> *The Last Harmattan of Alusine Dunbar* would not have been possible if I had narrowed myself to a kind of ethnic or cultural preoccupation that some people say you find in other African writers' work.[4]

If the substantive point is that it is their different histories that determine the fundamental divergences between postcolonial writers, then it should come as no surprise that it is a Sierra Leonian who defies ready classification as a 'decolonizer', as a cultural nationalist. Sierra Leonians are the syncretized result of cultural mingling between African, American, Caribbean and European cultures. The Creoles of Sierra Leone are descended from 'liberated slaves who were racially and, often, culturally akin to the indigenous inhabitants, but who had also been exposed to Western culture'.[5] This resulted in 'a syncretism of African and European practices' on the part of 'the majority of Creole society'. And in fact, says Leo Spitzer, 'there can be little doubt that in their everyday life most Creoles retained and mixed elements from traditional African culture with the ways of the West'.[6] This syncretism was not, as it never is, a smooth and seamless construction. As Cheney-Coker himself explains:

> If you have read my poetry, and of course my novel, it is clear that I am a Sierra Leonian with roots in the history of the middle passage. Initially I think I was trying to come to terms with defining what that history has meant for me and how in some ways it makes me slightly different, or so people feel, from other West African writers. It's clear that if you are dealing with other West African writers who write in English, their mind-sets, the traditional norms and forms that make themselves known in their poetry now and then, image clusters so to speak which they have inherited, have remained intact. But in my case its quite different because I'm having to contend with the admixture of an African life and the history of slavery – what those two have meant for us Sierra Leonian Creoles.[7]

It is this Creole identity crisis that leads Cheney-Coker in his poetry painfully to question:

> but from what plantation
> and from what people my rum
> in my country the Creoles drink only
> Black and White with long sorrows
> hanging from their colonial faces![8]

Cheney-Coker borrows from Fanon when he sneers at himself in his poetry, as in *Freetown*:

> and I think of my brothers with 'black skin and white masks'
> (I myself am one *heh heh heh*)
> my sisters who plaster their skins with the white cosmetics

to look whiter than the snows of Europe.[9]

This cultural crisis leads to what has been called 'defensive Africanization'. Desperate for a means whereby they can 'regain their self-respect and heal their battered race pride', the Creoles 'began to search back in history' seeking 'evidence of great deeds and past glories'. However, 'as a conglomerate community originating from the intermarriage of settler Africans from a number of different ethnic groups' they knew very little about 'the histories of their ancestors'.[10] A solution was to construct healing myths of origins – of heroic, homogeneous beginnings – to trace their history back 'to what they believed to be the general black African past – back to the glories of Roman Africa, ancient Egypt, and the greatness of the biblical Middle East'.[11]

This mythical recovery of the past is, of course, at the heart of the 'decolonizing impulse'. However, in the unavoidable hybridity of Sierra Leone it takes a distinctive turn, distinguishing Cheney-Coker from other African writers and attracting him to magical realism, however much he dislikes the term:

> It was also this feeling that the novel in Africa has been as it were cloistered within very prescribed forms. It was either you had a sociological view of the novel within the Achebean definition, or you were a political novelist within the Ngugian concept of it. There were all these perceived notions of what the African novel should be like. One hears so much about it – this novel should be written in this or that form because this is the way African literature is perceived. For me this was rather an intellectual humbug. I felt the need for new kinds of directions. . . .
>
> Inevitably the question arises, you know, is your novel magical realist? Were you inflamed by Marquez? The answer is yes and no. If we are discussing form, yes, but if we are discussing an idea then the answer is, no. . . .
>
> Whereas Latin American writers like Llosa and Carpentier and Marquez are enjoying themselves having a jolly good time writing, African writers have allowed the direction of the novel, so I felt, to be dictated by critics who limit the interpretation of writers' work within the mainstream of University teaching. In the process the very vital and energetic interpretation of life, I mean the great coalescence between life and death, between the past and the present, is lost.[12]

Cheney-Coker's poem *Freetown* is fascinating in its highly ambiguous recourse to a romanticized and essentialized mother Africa, in his search for a rooted cultural identity. I will quote the first and third verses:

> Africa I have long been away from you wandering like a Fulani cow
> but every night
> amidst the horrors of highway deaths
> and the menace of neon-eyed gods

I feel the warmth of your arms
centrifugal mother reaching out to your sons
we with our different designs innumerable facets
but all calling you mother womb of the earth
liking your image but hating our differences
because we have become the shame of your race
and now on this third anniversary of my flight
my heart becomes a citadel of disgust
and I am unable to write the poem of your life . . .

there are those who when they come to plead
say make us Black Englishmen decorated Afro-Saxons
Creole masters leading native races
but we wandering African urchins
who will return one day
say oh listen Africa
the tomtoms of the revolution
beat in our hearts at night[13]

Here is a cacophony of conflicting emotions, a poem about the inability to write a poem of Africa. It is about being an African, but an 'urchin', a wandering, lost child. It is a negritude praise poem to Africa which follows the conventions of contrast between the horrors of the Western city of neon lights and dangerous, killing highways and the safe, protective womb of Mother Africa and the heartbeat of the tomtom. There is the double distance from this mother with whom the relationship is ambiguous – the urchin is not merely an exile, struggling against the acculturation of the 'Black Englishman', but is also a Creole, struggling against the pressure of being the master of 'native' Africans, but a Creole who compares his wanderings to those of the 'Fulani cow'. Concealed like a pearl in the misery of the poem's uncertainties is the celebration of difference – the possibility that Africa is, in fact, a heterogeneous continent of many parts, given 'our different designs, innumerable facets'. But this complexity is reduced, romanticized and homogenized within the problematic image of us all being able to call Africa the 'mother womb of the earth'.

In *The Last Harmattan of Alusine Dunbar*, Cheney-Coker constructs the legend of the founding families of an imaginary Malagueta – obviously based on Freetown. This rooted identity is created through the heroic deeds of the ex-slaves:

By telling the history of what slavery produced in Sierra Leone, however fictional it was going to be, but along historical lines, I wanted to show how these remarkable people, in two hundred years (mind you its longer than two hundred years in my novel) did so much, not just for Sierra Leone but for West Africa. It was for me an act of celebration. I think in some ways I was trying to do what in a much larger context Derrick Walcott has done in his poetry.[14]

The search for such myths and heroes, seen through an ethnic prism, can result in a narrowing of concerns. Cheney-Coker is by no means lacking in vision, but his history will help to explain his ambivalence towards hybridity, the ambiguous politics of his novel and the crisis of moral authority at the heart of the narrative.

Syl Cheney-Coker is a postcolonial writer on the margins. He shares features in common with the magical realist cosmopolitans of the Latin American variety; he also has preoccupations in common with the cultural nationalism of some of the African decolonizers. His precise location, and its political and narrative implications, are revealed in the major themes of the novel, and its narrative points of view.

At the beginning of *The Last Harmattan of Alusine Dunbar* Sebastian Cromantine, still a slave, is haunted by a terrible dream and the voice of his father, 'a rootless man burdened by his inability to find a resting place' (p. 9). He will only be at peace once he is buried in Africa and it becomes Sebastian's sacred mission to return his father's bones to their origins. Already there is a tension between myth and reality. Sebastian is appropriately overwhelmed 'as he tried to imagine the untried chasm of supposition that he had to cross to understand the world of his father' (p. 14). He gains courage, however, as he evokes 'a lineage that was not defined by time, but by the spirit, by the force of all eternities and the running music of ancestral water that coursed through his blood' (p. 14). This spiritual lineage is a kind of blood knowledge, unmediated by experience or historical time. If his father's bones are his 'Magic Lantern', gaining him admission to his father's past, then his weapon to protect and arm him for the journey is not 'a gun' but 'his bloody history', and his hope is 'buoyed by the potency of the black man's sperm that had begun to explode and generate its force in the universal womb of woman' (pp. 14–15). The wish to return to Africa is depicted as a biological drive, an instinct lodged in the blood, racing in the sperm, lodging in the womb.

However, no sooner does Cheney-Coker espouse this ethnic essentialism, than he humorously distances himself from it with farce, with the image of returnees armed with bags of the bones of their dead 'which they were hiding under their bunks so that the crew would not find them. During the periodic storms at sea, the rattling of the bones in the bags helped to reassure their owners that they would make it to the shore' (p. 15).

On the boat back with the Cromantines is Fatmatta, the Bird Woman, who had a very similar vision to that of Emmanuel Cromantine, an urgent vision magnetically pulling her back to Africa, to where her afterbirth is buried:

> she saw a long ancestral bridge with a lot of people crossing from one end to the other, and suddenly everything was clear to her. Cut off from that coalescence of man and spirits, burdened by servitude, she had merely been fulfilling a destiny circumscribed by fate, by an old animated life rhythm that went round the universe like a great flame and then she knew that she would not die in the land of leeches but that she would return,

shed all signs of degradation and abuse. Because by the persistence of its look, by the grave and reverential distance it put between itself and other turkeys, the great bird had come to take her home to that land where her navel string was buried.

(p. 67)

This image of the return to the source is crucially entwined with the image of reproduction, of birth and the pull of umbilical cords, of ancient life rhythms. This linkage between woman and the land, her fertility as metaphor, is far from new. The symbolic link between Africa and nurturing mother is at the core of nationalistic yearnings, as we have already seen in previous chapters. However, once again the unpredictable Cheney-Coker does not allow Fatmatta the Bird Woman to return home. What is the symbolic significance of her dying on the boat, to return only in order to be buried, along with her birth cord, in Africa? Again, I think that the answer lies in the elusiveness of our author, who steps back ironically from the passionate avowals to which he has committed himself. Fatmatta's death on the boat is a warning that, notwithstanding magical looking glasses and flying carpets, the return to Africa is not going to be a fairytale.

Cheney-Coker's portrayal of the meeting between the locals and the returnees is wonderfully subtle. The newcomers are ignorant of local customs, as becomes clear in their negotiations with the king. Sebastian asks for land 'which they were prepared to farm, and pay him back from the harvest' (p. 69). This may be an American practice, but the king has to point out that this is not African custom: ' "Here, no one owns anything, not even the stones," the king replied' (p. 70). He grants them all the land that they need to use, but they are warned that this is conditional on their respecting 'our laws and the men keep off our women' (p. 70). The message that they are strangers is clear. At the same time, this sense of the difficulties of such returnees reveals the underbelly of essentialism and romanticization. Sebastian has a dream reminiscent of the one in which his father had appeared to him: 'he had been in that country before, and that he knew all its history so that nothing was hidden from him, and he could retell all that had happened before' (p. 70). In this vein, the returnees discover 'this dance which was part of a heritage that they had forgotten but was nevertheless in their blood' (p. 97). Then again, Cheney-Coker provides a wise portrait of the stresses of reintegration and even of the superstitions of local people. For example, when they succumb 'to the malaria scourge that would kill off many of them', they, 'contrary to reason' (p. 99), blame the foreign woman, Jeanette Cromantine, and her sweet potatoes:

But when their children succumbed to death soon after eating the sweet potatoes which the foreign woman had planted, they deduced with an age-old logic, contrary to reason, that the seed of the settlers' misfortune had been planted in their world, which not even the totemic power of their gods could halt.

(p. 101)

In terrible retaliation, the locals set fire to Malagueta and pillage it, destroying all that the new arrivals have worked so hard to set up. This is against the grain of the depiction of Fatmatta's ancestral bridge. And it is to Fatmatta that we must return in order to see how this tension between nationalistic myth and historical and cultural change is grounded in the portrayal of the woman's body.

Fatmatta, the Bird Woman, daughter of Mariamu and Sulaiman, is in reality offspring of no parents and mother to no child. She is mythologized into Goddess, Devil, Temptress, one of the breed of beautiful, supernatural women who torment men, and who are destroyed by the inexorable male desire for such women. She is an Africanized version of the mermaid of Western mythology. Sulaiman sees an image of his daughter – 'he saw the proverbial golden comb of a mermaid, which was not a comb but the tongue of a scorpion' (p. 35) – and poor Ahmed falls fatally in love with this scorpion mermaid, and is ultimately destroyed by her. The following passage is typical of this convention of woman as Other, as destructive Siren with a song deep in both Western and African traditions:

> Something greater than desire took hold of him, laundered his brain, and as he hastened his steps he heard the clear and hauntingly beautiful voice of a woman singing. Because it was dark and quiet, the voice filled the night with the deep riches of a praise singer's, melodic and divine. He walked on, more like a man propelled than like one possessed. His steps did not conform to any set pattern and he was not conscious of the fact that it was towards an area of the village forbidden to men at that time of the year that he was heading to, urged on by the swelling in his groin. . . .
>
> He went forward, freed of all trepidation, but his movements were fast and careless so that Fatmatta turned but she did not protect herself, and Ahmed saw the deep and treacherous valley of a temptress, straddled by shimmering breasts with their dark berry nipples. He had almost reached the woman when he saw in her eyes the scorpion, with the look which he did not know would produce a menacing rupture of the embryonic tissues of his youth. Suddenly, the hot and urgent fever pitch of his blood began to dry and he felt the solid evidence of his manhood turning into flabby flesh, drained of its liquid, like an udder. An immense pain gripped him, and he experienced the sharp needles of thorns growing in his heart, and he did not see the smile of a killjoy on Fatmatta's face as he collapsed, jettisoned by his quivering desire, into the slough of degradation.
>
> (pp. 43–4)

But Fatmatta, too, will be victim when she pays the price for her female power and is made to act out the part assigned to rebellious women in traditional folklore, as we saw in Chapter 3. Her story is the familiar one, the Tutuolan tale about the wayward, militant woman who refuses her father's choice of husband and seeks the perfect, beautiful gentleman, only to have him change into a skull. As Eldred Jones explains:

The folk motif of the girl who refuses all eligible suitors to marry a complete stranger who later turns into a devil is found in treatments as varied as Amos Tutuola's 'curious creature who turned into a skull' . . . to Syl Cheney-Coker's *The Last Harmattan of Alusine Dunbar*.[15]

In Cheney-Coker's version, Fatmatta's handsome new husband begins to shed the face he had borrowed, soon after their wedding. He is revealed to be a grotesque albino:

> Like all albinos he hated the sun, but when he had heard through the grapevine of the albinos about the beautiful woman who could talk to birds and had the power of a scorpion, he borrowed the body of the most handsome man to die of love, bought a bottle of lotion that the marabouts swore would restore his colour, and went off to marry her. He tried to move, to get to a small bag lying on the floor, for the lotion, but he had lost it in the schism of events for his wedding, and quickly, he began to disintegrate. He felt his skin turning yellow again and his soft hair becoming coarse. (p. 57)

This is the turning point in Fatmatta's life and her role and image radically changes. She has been brought into line and has learnt her lesson. She is still fatal to men but now only to the vicious and cruel white slavers, who buy her body and wish to possess it with all the violence and disrespect of human ownership. Now we rejoice in the moral rightness, the justness of the fate of such men. Female destructive power, however, may have been harnessed to a crucial cause, but it remains destructive all the same:

> Andrew McKinley pushed her down on the bed; but when he tried to take her he discovered that the power of the arousal that only that morning had been his manhood had been calmed by a prodigiously cold wind that seemed to be blowing in his own belly.
>
> (p. 66)

McKinley, not unlike Ahmed, sees the dreaded 'scorpion crawling in her eyes' and after a while 'the belief' spreads 'that she was a creature not of this world but of one where men would be tormented by the scorpion in her eyes and be tainted for ever by the curse of impotence once they had forced themselves upon her' (p. 66). McKinley lives to curse the day he had bought 'the woman he now regarded as the true sister of evil' (p. 66). Likewise, the colonizer David Hammerstone has a nightmare:

> Captain Hammerstone was dancing as he had never danced before; his partner was a tall, graceful woman who resisted coming into his arms. He tried to trick her, promising he would go to the bottom of any ocean to

retrieve sunken treasures if only she would stop avoiding him. When eventually she came into his arms she touched him at the back of his neck and Captain Hammerstone felt a lacerating, scorching heat run down his spine; he removed her hand and saw that it was spattered with his blood. He woke up violently, and, for the first time in his life, he saw the face of death.

(pp. 281–2)

The awesome and unnatural power of women may become an instrument against slavery and racism, but at the price of reinforcing, rather than breaking, the paradigm of female as fatal. Furthermore, the link between the body of the woman and political and national struggles is forged again. While women are also committed to these struggles, when their bodies are frozen into myths of the nation or of the continent as a whole, there is little room for flesh and blood women to take up other issues and articulate other needs and passions.

After death, this scorpion woman becomes the immortal, ancestral and spiritual protector of the pioneering families back in Africa, and particularly of the women of these families. But Fatmatta does not become a mother herself, and in this she is not the ideal woman-as-mother, as commonly portrayed:

She wore the glass beads which her father had immersed in crocodile fat as a protective charm against the brutality of men like Andrew McKinley and the voracity of other slave breeders. In that way she had aged and managed to avoid the circle of bringing mulatto children into the world, who themselves would be slaves.

(p. 67)

Fatmatta's deliberate avoidance of mothering children is a political act of defiance, highlighting the unnaturalness of slavery and the sexual brutality between white slavers and black slaves. This can only be fully understood within the context of the mother Africa motif, which places enormous pressure on women to mother children, if they are to be regarded as fully fledged adults and as contributing to the pride of the nation. This is a very difficult issue for African feminists, some of whom argue for there being alternative roles for women, while accepting and celebrating their possible function as mothers and nurturers. The mulatto child – that undesirable product of unions with white slavers – is avoided, but Cheney-Coker clearly grapples with the problem of how to depict Fatmatta as a mature and knowledgeable woman, albeit a childless one. He resolves the problem by having Fatmatta make the childbirth journey with Jeanette Cromantine, 'transmitting her strength to the woman who was losing hers'. This journey is mythically retained as the true road to womanhood, a road that allows Fatmatta her dignity and respect as a woman, but which freezes women in their traditional roles:

Then, as she began the long road to knowing how the real side of womanhood began, she saw, as if in a dream, a woman of exceptional beauty coming to lie beside her. The pains that had begun to tear at her insides stopped, and Jeanette Cromantine saw the celestial face of Fatmatta the Bird-Woman.

(p. 109)

Fatmatta comes to Jeanette again when her son is killed, and also at her death. On this last occasion the connection between women's organic role as nurturer, symbolically tied to the land by the umbilical cord of her essential fertility, is made unambiguously. Fatmatta reminds Jeanette of

> the glass beads that both had worn, at one time or the other; about how it had helped them to understand that in the beginning, God had made women to give life and joy to men; to bear children, raise them, and, hopefully, derive some pleasure from this life, which was eternal, and that once they understood its endlessness, its transcendence over such imperti- nent humbugs like a slavebreeder named Andrew McKinley and the pirate David Hammerstone, they could go on living for ever, supporting each other with that fearlessness that God had given them, to bear testi- mony to the birth and growth of Malagueta: their child.

(p. 354)

In sum, Cheney-Coker manages to juggle a number of different roles for Fatmatta, none of which quite manage to break out of female stereotypes. She is *femme fatale* and nurturing mother; she is rebellious slave, but whose rebellion takes the form of destructive female power; she is revered ancestor, but one whose female body is cast into the mould of the struggle against slavery, against colo- nialism, but never against patriarchy.

However, this is not to underestimate the ways in which *The Last Harmattan of Alusine Dunbar* simultaneously battles to re-write the script of gender stereotype. Cheney-Coker's stance is often respectful and admiring of women as equal part- ners – sexual, economic and political. For example, the depiction of Isatu carrying Gustavius' dead body is particularly poignant and enlightened:

> With a great strength belying her now unbearable grief, she lifted the limp form of her husband and came into the hallway. The hills dwarfing the garrison were alive with the voices of the creatures of the night, but Isatu Martins was not afraid. She walked slowly, carrying the man, as she had carried him in other times, though when in the past they had reached the bottom, it was not clear who had carried whom.

(p. 251)

There are other relationships of respect and love, of sensuality and equality between partners – Jeanette and Sebastian (with Jeanette probably the stronger and certainly more responsible for their economic survival), Phyllis and

Bookerman and Louisa and Emmanual. Played out here is the proud tradition of men and women standing together against the oppression of slavery and colonialism. In these depictions, Cheney-Coker picks up a point of difference between Western and African feminists. African feminism often expresses a tension between, on the one hand, a political and emotional identification with men who have also been oppressed and, on the other hand, an opposition to the oppression of women by men in the home. This imposes an additional burden on African feminism – a pressure on women not to take up so-called 'divisive' issues of domestic oppression, but to stand 'shoulder to shoulder' with men in battles against racism and imperialism. Such solidarity between men and women accounts for the change in the role played by Fatmatta, who is cast in the role of *femme fatale* until she is herself a victim of slavery and becomes the ally of black women, but also of black men, as they struggle against slavery and colonialism.

This sense of the political role of women flies in the face of the more questionable portrayals. There is, for example, the wonderful description of the prostitutes in the yellow house, who refuse Hammerstone and his men, and who have a brave sense of political rights, and their own allegiances. And there is the women's magnificent storming of the garrison, liberating their men who have been imprisoned by Hammerstone:

> Forgetting that they were facing men who had only recently killed in battle, Isatu Martins, the mothers, wives and sweethearts forced the gates open and entered the garrison. Paralysed by the incredible bravery of the women, the soldiers watched them as they quickly began an assault on the place. Just where most of their men were being held was unknown to them, but that did not seem to deter them from their objective. When the first sound of the wreckage began, it was already too late for the surprised guards to realise what was happening.
>
> 'Let's burn dis place down and get de men out of here', Isatu Martins said. Minutes later the flames of torches had engulfed the building; most of the soldiers who had been reposing in another part of the courtyard came too late to be able to stop the fire spreading. The wind that was blowing from the hill fuelled the flames, and the angry, whistling voices of fire rose in the rooms as the blaze began to spread.
>
> (p. 248)

Nevertheless, it is in their conventional roles as the mothers, wives and sweethearts that the women force the gates open. While the garrison is stormed, the position of women in the home seems impregnable. The archetypal power of the mythical African Mothers is both threatening and messianic. Cheney-Coker expressed this very clearly in interview:

> Then again, if you look at the history of West Africa I am sure you are aware that some of the strongest forces in West African politics are the

market women. If you go to Accra market, if you go to Lagos market, all those women who are not necessarily educated in a Western sense of the word but, by golly, they are powerful women! They can make or break you. They don't want to wear anybody's pants but they are strong. They deliver the goods. There are many men in West Africa aged 40 and above who would not be anybody but for their Mothers.[16]

The women have the power to make or break their men; as mothers, they make their sons. These powerful matriarchs stand for Malagueta, for the nation, and for Africa itself.

The novel is not immune, moreover, from stereotypes that relate to the gendering of the men. If women veer from goddess to whore, from angelic wife to waspish temptress, men are consistently depicted as driven by inexorable sexual needs. Males are repeatedly typecast as hugely virile; if women are harnessed to nature by their reproductive cycles, then men are so harnessed by their involuntary sexual instincts and animal drives.

Two positive and powerful male characters in the novel are Masimiara and Garbage. Masimiara is unambiguously heroic. He resists the corrupt regime and dies for his political courage and principles. His relationship with his mistress, Sadatu Cromantine-Doherty, is given unquestionable approval in the novel. As the descendent of the founders of Malagueta, she is a vital link in the narrative chain:

> He fell under her spell: the lure of her charm and the legend of her name. He bought books about her famous grandparents which he tried to read, but gave up the effort because he was not a great reader. Before meeting her, general Tamba Masimiara had been happily married to his wife for fifteen years and, except for the soldier's indiscretion in the loneliness of Burma, no woman had troubled his soul that much.
>
> . . .
>
> She introduced him to the joys of folk and classical music, the pleasure of driving to the countryside and the refinement of good wine. . . . She never gave him her soul, for that was reserved for the task that Sadatu Doherty had chosen as her life's work: the writing of a full-length biography of her legendary grandfather, Emmanuel Cromantine.
>
> (pp. 385–6)

Even within this benevolent depiction, the woman carries unnatural power – he is under her spell, responding to her lure; she troubles his soul rather than his conscience. His wife of fifteen years made him happy and is described as 'good-natured and exuberant' (p. xvii). They are so in tune that a dream of hers convinces the General that the time for the coup was ripe. Yet Akongo, in better days 'lied to his wife for him' (p. xvi), which information shows us how close Akongo and Masimiara were, and the magnitude of Akongo's betrayal, rather than being a commentary on Masimiara's secret affair; there is no hint that it is wrong for men to deceive their wives. Quite the opposite. The women who made him happy were 'his wife who had given him sons, and his bookish mistress who had introduced him to the fantastic poetry of Garbage' (p. 394). In a novel where the narrative point of view is often unstable, the perfectness of the arrangement of wife and home and sons, and mistress and poetry, is given as ideal. Could Jeanette Cromantine have had an affair? Her husband was often unstable and unaffectionate, and she was as virtuous a woman as Masimiara is an upright man. What is appropriate for them is quite different; double standards are written into the script.

It is in this light that the extraordinary approval given to Garbage's way of life needs to be understood. Isatu despairs of her son finding himself a woman because 'she knew that her son was stamped with the sign of a free spirit' (p. 333). Being a free spirit means Arabella being 'prepared to share him with Malagueta, with the world, and even with other women' (p. 352). She 'happily' waits for when he decides to come and then they would 'spend a night in the aura of her love', thereafter 'she would release him into the whirlpools of other loves' (p. 352). He and Arabella have a son. Then 'he had another child', this time by a woman who relentlessly chases after the poor man, following him from poetry reading to poetry reading and promising 'never to bother him if only she could have his child'. Of course he obliges. Then 'he had more children' – twins by a 'girl' who did not understand the poetry but is nonetheless 'captivated by the magic of his readings'. Then 'he had another child', this time 'by the granddaughter of the Chinese' and finally 'he had one last child' by 'a Scottish lass' (p. 352).

The authorial approval for all of this has three aspects. There is the free spirit of the poet – 'he never married any of the women because, as Arabella Garrison had known, he was married to the world' (p. 352). Then there is the virility of man – 'to those who complained to her that her famous, but very virile, son had "ruined" their daughters', Isatu Martins would deliver 'the arrows of her reply': ' "He must have what it takes as a man", she said, "for de girls to flock to him like dat" ' (p. 353). And, incredibly, there is class politics – given the background of 'the girls' Isatu 'derived a wicked pleasure' at the misery of their mothers, given that some of them 'had hoped to marry them off to some aristocrats' (p. 353). If we are in any doubt at all about authorial approval for this situation, look at the utopian reinforcement for this state of affairs, beyond the fires of youth, into the mellowed wisdom of middle age, with images of tea, ducks and cake – 'Garbage was grateful to Arabella that although they had never married, she had made her house a home for him where he could come to be happy, relax and drink the teacups of her refreshing love' (p. 370):

'I always knew that if I freed you to love me in your own way, you would always come back to me, and we would grow old together', she told him one evening when they had settled down to cakes and tea, the ducks in the pond that he had built for her swimming leisurely in the soft light of November.

(p. 371)

How is one to deal with such male typecasting without adopting the stance of the killjoy Virgins of the novel, who entirely lack joyful or sensual parts? All I can do is to interrogate Garbage's so-called free spirit, Masimiara's right to deceive his wife, and Sulaiman's fiery loins. While we will see in a moment that in the case of Garbage and Sulaiman there is some authorial distancing, the gender stereotype of implacable male sexuality is not seriously contested.

The tensions inherent in a symbiotic relationship between gender and national myths of reconstruction are nowhere more apparent than in the events leading up to the birth of Garbage.

Going against the injunction of the king, and in the face of prejudice and superstition, the returnee Gustavius marries the local woman Isatu and they are deservedly happy. Isatu's knowledge of the terrain – how to get food, shelter, water and protection from wild animals – means that 'she had virtually assured the survival of the exiles'. Gustavius was proud that he had a wife 'who respected the supernatural extremes of her world and had bridged theirs together' (p. 188). This is a very different bridge from Fatmatta's ethnic, ancestral connection. However, Cheney-Coker proceeds to romanticize that supernatural world, as the coalescence between mortals and spirits and as the spiritual life-blood of humanity. It is given as a superiority of being, which is lost when Africa is left behind and which can only be restored on returning to Africa and by the ritual cleansing of the impurities contracted in exile. Thus Isatu brings to the marriage 'the resources of a heritage to which he had lost all claim to knowledge' (p. 188). The loss is the key to why the marriage is, highly symbolically, not blessed with a child.

Why should the marriage between ex-slave and local African not be so blessed? Isatu had neglected her family who had opposed her marriage to a foreigner, and when she suddenly and instinctively felt the need to go 'home', her father had died. It becomes clear that she must go back to her roots before she can conceive a child, that she must be cleansed of all the impurities with which she has been contaminated by a foreigner. When they arrive back at her father's village, Sawida Dambolla informs them that 'we will have to wash you and your husband' (p. 198). She then (with authorial approval, given the evidence of Isatu's barrenness), goes on a tirade against the culture from which Gustavius comes, in the true tradition of negritude:

> They have a dubious notion of freedom so that man is perceived as living in a world where he is independent of nature. Space is a thing they have not learnt how to deal with, because they are pulling down everything: trees, groves, shrines; insulting the souls of the dead. Rites that help us into adulthood mean nothing to them, the spiritual is suspect, and very little thought is given to the relationship between what we bring into this world and what we take with us to our graves. Or for that matter to the little things that are much more important than the big ones in our lives.
>
> (p. 198)

The link between this sacrilegious culture that Gustavius, as foreigner, involuntarily brings and Isatu's miscarriages is made explicit. Before he died, Isatu's father, Santigue Dambolla, consulted a medicine man and this diviner, according to Sawida:

> saw you in a grove where your child was imprisoned among other children with hairs that had become entangled in the roots of the trees. No woman, diviner said, could hope to bring forth a child from that confusion of limbs.
>
> (p. 198)

Isatu had had four miscarriages, and what is evoked by this is the *abiku* myth of the wilful spirit children who torment their parents by coming briefly to the living, only to return to the spirits. The image of the confusion of the limbs of foetuses is directly linked to the union with a foreigner and Santigue felt he had sacrificed his daughter to 'what he called the Oporto, the white/black people' (p. 199). This also has overtones, of course, with the adventurous woman, who marries the beautiful foreign gentleman, against village custom and the wishes of her father, and is punished. The dead father walks about the house and only Gustavius Martins does not see him because 'years of being in the wasteland of America had stripped him of the power to make contact with the dead' (p. 202). Yet again, woman's fertility is linked to the African soil and traditional customs, and the process of spiritual cleansing and regeneration is begun with the 'couple from Malagueta' becoming farmers and bringing Dambolla's farm back to life:

> Then it was that the couple from Malagueta became farmers in the translucent world, surrounded by the ghosts of some of the founders of that town, who had achieved a permanence among the trees and the fields, and who made the burden of the transformation easy for the Martinses.
>
> Six months later, when the dry clouds had sucked up the rain, they looked at the field and were content with their labours. They had restored the trees to good health, planted three varieties of rice, got the cows milking again, and had the potatoes, yams and corn ready for the harvest.
>
> (p. 203)

This return to the land is the first major stage of the ritual they must undergo. The return is redolent with essentialist connotations of the biological and natural cycle of things with which they had to be in harmony before being able to participate in the human natural cycle of reproduction. The next stage involves the visiting dwarfs and appears to be written in the mode of the carnivalesque:

> One day, without warning, two small dwarfs, one of them also a hunchback, appeared in the town. They were colourful little creatures with large

heads and noses that were too small between glassy eyes. Although they insisted that one was male and the other female, it was hard for people to tell, because they wore the same type of wild, brightly patterned clothes, sported moustaches, laughed and swore and wrestled together until they both became exhausted. Gifted with acrobatic skills and wiles unknown in the town, they soon attracted a lot of attention, on the hot afternoons of summer, after they had set up camp under a large baobab tree.

(p. 204)

'Referring to each other as brother-sister so as not to give away which one was a man or a woman', they are hybrids between male and female, human and animal. They dance wildly and acrobatically, throwing 'the crowd into a state of hysteria' (p. 204). They appear to contest bad, ancient customs and promise that they can 'bring back the twins who had been driven away from the land as possessors of evil' (p. 204).

However, the dwarfs' hybridity is somewhat deceptive. They invoke the *abiku* myth within the framework of the quest for successful fertility through cleansing, through recovery of a pure, unsullied African spirituality. They

related the story of how they were the last members of a race of dwarf children who had been trapped in a grove by an evil spirit, which had once been a beautiful woman who had consorted with the devil.

(p. 205)

The dwarfs concur with Santigue Dambolla and the medicine man's verdict regarding cultural impurity in that one of them declares that 'we are suspicious of those who have lost the power to understand the origins of man . . . ' and 'Gustavius Martins knew right away that he was referring to him'. The dwarf clarifies that he and Isatu are pure of spirit and mind but are 'tainted by the garbage of your union' – the garbage clearly being the fact that Isatu married a 'foreigner'. They have to be cleansed by being 'washed with the sap of the leaves of the grove where the foetuses of your wife have been trapped for years'.

It is important to look at this ritual cleansing in some detail:

A week later, Gustavius and Isatu Martins stood naked in front of a boiling cauldron, inhaling the pungency of leaves and roots which the dwarfs had gone to the forest to find. Spirals of smoke rose from the pot, and the senses of the man and the woman were filled with a vapour that made them innocent and childlike in the baptism of their second coming. When they were beginning to feel their feet moving into the territory of their regeneration, the dwarfs touched them with the tails of horses soaked in the cauldron. The voices of the dwarfs spoke as if in a dream, and the woman felt the encrustation of the dirt and garbage that years of marriage to a man without the roots of the forest had imposed on her, while the man felt the garbage of the world across the sea of blood rubbing off his body, so that they were one again, cleansed of all impurities, and could touch each other with their feathery hands which had been anointed, and with their bodies which had been repossessed by new seeds, so that the fecundity of the woman could respond to the male-power of the husband.

(p. 206)

What we have here is the quest for a mythical kind of cultural purification, stripped of the history of slavery, of change and of the fertile mixture of multiple experiences; Gustavius can only be at one again with his wife, can only unite with her and bear the fruit of their love, when the rubbish, the debris, of his life experiences of the middle passage and of foreign places, are washed away. Cleansed to the bone and at one with the African soil, the two people are their essential, animal cores – male power and female fertility.

The dwarfs, who were instrumental in creating conditions conducive to the birth of Garbage, leave clear instructions that, if a child is born, 'when it came, must be thrown at the foot of the plants, near the garbage, where Santigue Dambolla was found dead' (p. 206). It must be immersed, in other words, in the land, the roots. Thereby the *abiku* cycle is broken – the scream of Isatu's birth pain frightens away 'the other children in the grove' (p. 207). According to instructions, the child is thrown near the garbage, from which he is rescued by his dead grandfather and cleansed. The purified child, wrapped in 'ornate silk' is named after the rubbish from which his parents have been purified.

However, in the tug-of-war between belief and irony, magical realism does not relinquish them to nation building without a struggle. Farce, parody and ironic distancing qualify this myth-making in the very moment of its construction. The dwarfs, who belong in the fairground where they perform spectacular tricks, and who have effected this cultural cleansing, are hardly the solemn, larger-than-life heroes that are more usually depicted as legendary nation builders. The baby that indeed is conceived through all this purification carries with him the impurities of his father's history and is called 'Garbage'. We will see later that, while the circumstances of his birth lend him tremendous authorial weight as a character, his strange name simultaneously effects ironic distancing from this authoritativeness.

At the same time, the nature of the birth of Garbage is a further example, like the portrayal of Fatmatta's resistance to slavery, of where gender is put to the service of race. The woman's body is the barometer of the spiritual health or sickness of the race. Another example, one in which the woman's body unambiguously signifies the sickness of her race, is that of Hediza Farouka, who is part of a race of wandering Arabs. If the stern dwarfs reverse the contaminations of slavery, then nothing can be done about the grotesquely fecund Arabs, who exemplify the impurities brought by colonialism.

Early on in the novel, Sulaiman reveals through his 'trembling looking-glass' how the 'scourge of the wandering Arabs would come' and bring 'their smell of garlic, their belch of onions, their parasitic breeding and pugnacious competitiveness' (p. 30). While this perspective is here refracted through Sulaiman's eyes, there is corroborating evidence for authorial approval of this attitude. At first the Malaguetans are enchanted by the Arabs, who 'turned the streets . . . into a boisterous carnival with the men beating their drums, while the nymphs danced over flaming gourds and swallowed gold coins which the enthralled Malaguetans threw at them' (p. 375). Garbage sees through the antics of the first wave of Arabs and petitions for their expulsion, but they are allowed to stay and are depicted as spreading and multiplying in the most alarming and terrifying way. The carnivalesque is again pulled towards an essentialist view of racial characteristics. If the dwarfs almost transform into stern nation builders, then Hediza, the 'breeding cow' and archetypal Arab woman, becomes the pregnant hag. Hediza herself makes the familiar transformation, that ends up being merely more of the same, from fatal temptress to unnatural mother:

> Her name was Hediza Farouka, a breeding cow who was once the most beautiful female in Damascus, but who had also driven men to their death because she would appear in public without a veil, causing the men to tear their eyes out over her. Instead of stoning her to death, the guardians of morality had offered her mother the other choice of selling her to a caravan chieftain famed for his vagabondage, and who promised to take her to a place where she would no longer torment men.
>
> (p. 374)

The guardians of morality punish the wayward woman once again. When the famed chieftain

> tried to sleep with her, he discovered that she had grown to the size of an elephant, driving him out of the tent, but she reverted to her original size the next morning.
>
> (p. 374)

Later, however, she permanently retains her gross size and produces ten little girls, who multiply in a menacing and terrifying orgy of fertility:

> Spread they did, on the day when after eating a giant pumpkin, the ten girls all grew to the size of full women and went on to produce one hundred women who themselves in a short time produced one thousand women, so that the rumour of the prowess and parasitic breeding of the Arabs, their pugnacious competitiveness and the smell of their garlic breath reached an alarming proportion in a few years.
>
> (p. 376)

There is little ironic distancing in the authorial voice, which is here omniscient, authoritative and backed up by Garbage's fears and misgivings, which prove to be utterly founded. Hediza Farouka with the ten tiny little endlessly multiplying girls hidden under her skirt, represents the threat of total submergence of the Self by the foreign Other.

The Arabs first of all peddle cheap jewellery which they pretend is magical, reminiscent of the slavers of old. They prosper, and ominously open 'little shops' and become the allies of the colonial regime. Although the account of the Arabs as trading from 'the bazaars of Damascus and the factories of Istanbul', 'helped by the colonial regime which, because of its antagonism to the rebellious Malaguetans, offered favourable concessions to the Arabs so that they could spread their influence' (p. 376), has a historical integrity, it is cast in images of uncontrollable breeding habits and innate greed. The novel bemoans how 'Malagueta was slowly being bought up by the Arabs' with 'their Byzantine cunning for buying up ruined relics' (p. 377). The omniscient narrator tells us that

> Garbage was not the only one who wondered at the turn of events in Malagueta brought about by the rising influence of the Arabs, who, once they had started buying up the old properties facing the sea, wrote home to their peasant mothers who sent them brides dressed like mummies because they could not stand the glare of the sun.
>
> (p. 377)

Ali Baba, who along with his forty thieving African ministers, takes over the reigns of government after independence, is evil, corrupt and wicked because his African blood has been contaminated by the Arab. He is referred to as 'the half-caste' – the degraded product of liaison between European and African. Hediza Farouka and Ali Baba stand with the fearsome Albino and exemplify the horrors of transgressing boundaries.

But why is there such an enormous discrepancy between the depictions of Ali Baba and of Captain Hammerstone, white colonizer? Both represent exploitative, invading powers. In many ways, Hammerstone is quintessential colonizer:

> He foresaw the day when he would be dealing with the great trading houses in Manchester and Liverpool, and in time the flames of pride would leap in his heart for opening this backwater to the great cities of commerce and civilisation. For he was clever with schemes and played with the naivety of others to make him rich. He knew without being told that because of its proximity to the equator, it must have the same riches as Ceylon – vast jungles to be explored and untold riches to be exploited. Besides being a soldier, Captain Hammerstone was a businessman.
>
> (p. 243)

But the novel also goes to great lengths to describe his hopes and dreams, sadness at lack of family life, love affairs, disappointments, and even his courage, pride and individualism. He was a man who felt that 'life was like a journey through an underground tunnel in search of happiness' and his world 'had been shaped by his vision of beauty and fulfillment' (pp. 153–4). He gives away most of his inheritance from his uncle to charity and in this way 'hoped to atone for the pain in his heart for not having loved his parents too much' (p. 156). On hearing that Hammerstone was returning for a renewed attack on Malagueta Bookerman's comment is 'So he had balls after all, dat captain. Now we gon show him how not to mess with our lives' (p. 218). As a man, he has guts; as a colonizer, he must be destroyed.

In my interview with Syl Cheney-Coker, I asked him about his portrayal of Captain Hammerstone:

B.C.: I was also interested in your portrayal of the white character, Captain Hammerstone, who structurally, historically, plays the role of a villain who should be despised and hated.

S.C.-C.: I hope not

B.C.: Precisely. You take a lot of care to give a rounded picture of his complex life too and in a funny way one respects him as a worthy adversary. Is that what you were intending?

S.C.-C.: That's exactly what I intended. Captain Hammerstone is a worthy adversary because he did bring something. However misplaced his values were, some of the developments that one encountered in Malagueta would not have been possible but for the fact that he had come. Also the role that he personifies is not the usual naked colonial role of just wanting to conquer and grab everything. He was himself in search of something. The universal thing about understanding the world as I see it is there are a good many lonely people walking around in *Alusine Dunbar* whether as conquerors or as conquered.[17]

What is unambiguous, in a novel riddled with ambiguities, is that Hammerstone was a complex man, like many of the other characters, in search of achievement in the world and fulfillment in his emotional life, both of which are hard to find and elusive to keep. But why does the writer not give the same degree of complexity to the nature of his other foreign conquerors, the Arabs?

Perhaps it is because, being far more unambiguously Other, whites can be excluded from the boundaries of cultural identity, from which safe distance they can be scrutinized with more perspective. The Arabic influence, by contrast, was much earlier than the European and it syncretized far more deeply with African culture. It perhaps poses, for this reason, far more of a threat to an African nationalist identity, an identity which Cheney-Coker appears to be adopting in this particular aspect of his novel.

Cheney-Coker is also aware of the nature of alliances, based on interests and material needs, that cut across the identity of race. Such alliances, political and immediate, clash with the view of history as moving in cycles of repetition that is also expressed in the novel. Hammerstone is able to recruit strong black men on his side, men who 'liked neither the old Malaguetans nor the white men who had hired them, but who, pushed by the voracity of hunger, came to the fortification' (p. 166). This class perspective undercuts and mutes issues of race. At the same time, and beyond race and magic, carnival or slavery, everything is tainted by the fact that, when Malagueta has self-rule, after slavery and after colonialism, Africans exploit Africans with the same ruthlessness and cruelty as the slavers or the colonizers exploited them. This cyclical view undercuts the portrayal of struggle as a means of social change even while making complex social analyses.

Political corruption is clearly a major preoccupation of Cheney-Coker's. In the interview he says:

> We have just changed the government in Sierra Leone where there have been some of the most corrupt politicians imaginable (there, of course, are corrupt politicians everywhere from New York to Istanbul). These are the chaps I went to school with, who had the finest education, who went to Cambridge, Oxford and took PhDs. They have no business being corrupt. I have come to the decision that the last people you want to put in government in Sierra Leone are people who have been educated. They make the worst criminals. So there you are.[18]

In the novel, the new ruling class is as vicious as the old slavers. The treacherous Lookdown Akongo, who betrays Masimiara in the coup, is motivated by the fact that 'he wanted so much to swim in the reserved swimming pool of a princely grammar school' (p. 386). However, this penetrating social critique is qualified by recourse to a universal condition of human barbarity – the savage irony that the grim dungeon into which Masimiara is thrown is the very same one 'where, in centuries past, the blood of his countrymen and -women had mixed with their own excreta and vomit, before they were transported across the treacherous sea to die in the swampy bleakness of another world' (p. vii).

In the Prologue, General Masimiara 'shook with rage' recalling 'the infamous headline':

> 'US company to dump nuclear waste off African coast'. It was his country, all right, there was no doubt about it. He read how for the sum of twenty-five million dollars the president had agreed to have the toxic waste dumped in the waters of his country, and kill off all the children.
>
> (p. xi)

People are still being sold and dying long after slavery has been abolished. How do these cycles of violence and oppression intersect with, and mediate, the harsh historical realities that Cheney-Coker does not flinch from confronting? As we move through great cycles of repeated cruelty – slavery, colonialism, post-independence corruption – as we move across those 'great landscapes of time', through the generations – we have to question whether we are in the mythical time of universal repetition or whether we are in the potential 'third time' of the magical realist.

When I interviewed him, Cheney-Coker was adamant that his novel was not cyclical and in this he distinguished it from *One Hundred Years of Solitude*:

B.C.: You were very categorical regarding the difference in ideological content, in the way of seeing the world, between your novel and Marquez's *One Hundred Years of Solitude*, while acknowledging that you were influenced by his fictional method. Can you enlarge on that?

S.C.-C.: I think its the case that the Latin American situation with its repeated revolutions they had, with the rise and fall of dictators, is very different. Look at the way he treats the major character in *One Hundred Years of Solitude*, Colonel Aureliano Buendia, the revolutionary who starts and loses 17 wars. At the end there's an almost nihilistic acceptance of the hopelessness of life. I don't see it that way. For me in spite of all the sadness and suffering, and Jeanette Cromantine does suffer a lot in my novel, at the end there is hope. The political side of the novel is a very small section which I leave until towards the end. I hope it is clear to the reader that what I am dealing with is our version of the cyclical nature of life. After 350 years when Alusine Dunbar comes back, his reason for coming back is to see if what he had divined initially will not be destroyed by very ordinary people. He had perceived and prophesied that Malagueta was going to be created. It was going to be messed up, but at the end something, however infinitely small, was going to be preserved. This is why he stands there and watches the last political character, Sanka Maru, being destroyed. When the other two people who were party to the destruction of the general whose treason starts the novel, when these two are themselves carried away, I hope it is clear to the reader we are going to start all over again. It's not that I am going to start to a new novel. Malagueta as a place is going to continue its existence.[19]

There is a tension here between repetitive cycles and the hope of change and of new beginnings. While the novel certainly contests the distinction between linear and circular time, with its powerful sense of both history and of repetition, *Alusine Dunbar* tends to be contradictorily cyclical, rather than forging a new time dimension. For example, struggle, intervention and transformation are blocked by the suggestion that:

Everything was mirrored in the looking-glass: the octoroon woman who would bring the potato plague, the albino who would marry the most beautiful woman in the world, the man who would be afraid of snakes and would use the skull of his father as a guiding light, and the one-eyed man who would lead a great mission in the atmospheric darkness of the forest tracing the first strangers who would be wiped out because of the potato plague. So the coming of the woman was not unexpected; he had known at what time she would come.

(p. 25)

Within this cyclical view the growth of class difference, which emerges early in the history of Malagueta, has its roots in universal human greed, rather than emerging out of historical forces. Isatu is aware that they will start fighting each other one day 'because they were already beginning to talk of the poor and the "aristocrats" among them and develop serious notions of class' (p. 191). Thomas Bookerman is contemptuous about 'the rise of an oligarchy':

> men who only yesterday were shopkeepers with bad teeth and could barely read now ordered evening jackets in black Venetians and hopsacks; women who only yesterday were content to wear hand-me-downs and keep clean houses had taken to buying gold and parading in silk and brocade at church services.

(p. 213)

A colonial mentality develops, from which some Malaguetans listen 'with awe and respect' to stories of England, stories of

> the rich who could afford butlers and chambermaids, of the latest types of furniture, the invention of the steamship, the advantages that could be had by going there for a while to give their skins the right colour, away from this mosquito town. How it was not such a bad idea if some of them sent their children there so they could learn how to speak 'the king's English' and dress like English men and women.

(pp. 213–14)

This growth of class consciousness is a central factor enabling Hammerstone to use to his own advantage an internal vulnerability that will enable him to establish British colonial rule – 'some of the rich men in the town were all for declaring a truce [with Hammerstone] so that they could go on making money' (p. 228). In fact, class consciousness begins to dominate the social fabric of Malagueta:

> The children of the noveau riche mixed with the few sons of the colonial administration in the grammar schools. Their expensive jackets and ties marked them out as belonging to a special breed; they stood out like precious bulls: proud, stubborn and opinionated. They had a brazenness and arrogance which came from a claim to the world that was the

preserve of those who wielded power and meted out justice. If life had been an enigma for the children of the old families, the new ones regarded it as a large dinner to be eaten at one go.

(p. 325)

However, in making a critique of the new oligarchies and despots, Cheney-Coker contrasts them with a benevolent elite, the founders of Malagueta. In other words, humanity is salvaged by a blood elite of innately better, messianic healers and matriarchs who fulfil ancient obligations to establish roots deep in the soil of Africa by reproducing themselves through the cycle of birth. Look how privileged the founding aristocracy has itself become. Louisa is overwhelmed by the possessions adorning the house of Jeanette Cromantine. She

> saw the finely wrought wood of the parquet floor, the expensive sofas stuffed with ostrich feathers and draped with flowery damask, the solid Jacobean chairs, the rococo mirror on the wall that told her how beautiful she was, the golden samovar that the first Russian to come to her shop had given Jeanette, the grandfather clock with a bird-shaped pendulum, and, going into the dining room, the Chippendale cabinet where she kept her expensive Wedgwood wares. The bedrooms were large and airy, and covered with the same wallpaper that had a sea motif. But it was the chiffonier in Jeanette Cromantine's room, the solid mahogany bed, and commode and fine Moroccan rug on the floor that took Louisa's breath away.
>
> (p. 243)

When Gustavius Martins dies, Sebastian Cromantine painfully remembers the hopes they had shared for their sons – privileged hopes of the upper classes:

> When he thought of the dead man, he was reminded of all the things they had planned to do together; how they were going to send their children away so that they would come back one day and check the spread of the disease brought about by the behaviour of the small aristocratic class.
> If anything hurt Sebastian more than the loss of his friend, of the feeling that he might never see his son again, it was the way the new class of aristocrats were beginning to influence the social life of Malagueta.
>
> (p. 263)

There is no hint of irony here in Sebastian Cromantine's grief. These two men are Malaguetan founders and eventually revered ancestors; Martins dies the heroic death of a committed activist. Yet the dividing line is thin between their sending off their sons for a privileged education in England and the colonial mentality described earlier. What are the guarantees that these blessed sons will return anything other than members of that 'small aristocratic class', except for it being in their blood to be brave, good and without the greed that characterizes their class? In fact, 'no sooner had the news leaked out that Emmanuel Cromantine was considering going to England to study to be a doctor than the sons and daughters of other merchants began to pester their parents to send them away' (p. 214). The implications and consequences of this are not fictionally explored. An inviolate line seems to divide the nature of the founding families from the common, decadent wealthy classes. Class analysis clashes headlong into the myth of the superiority of the founding families, the myth fuelled by the urge to construct roots.

In the brief spell that the original founders have of running Malagueta them-selves, before colonial rule is finally triumphant, there is no hint of democratic government. Thomas Bookerman seems to have the right to bestow the details of the running of the town onto 'the Farmer brothers and a committee of ten men'. However, 'he did not entirely turn his back on the running of the town. Recognized as the sole arbiter in all matters, he saw to it that no one was subjected to any law that was unjust' (p. 209). There is no better example of benign autoc-racy. No-one must be subjected to unjust laws, but Bookerman remains sole arbiter of what which these are.

The difficulty inherent in establishing and maintaining this distinction between the elite of founding families and other upper class elements that are growing within Malagueta, is revealed in the character to whom we keep having to return – Garbage. Garbage refuses to organize a new revolt against the English because 'poetry was a much more dangerous weapon than a whole army' (p. 351). Nonetheless, somehow through his poetry, Garbage becomes a leader of the workers and the students, despite the fact that his credentials are those of a paci-fistic poet and 'the son of one of the original founders of the town' (p. 351). This is a romantic and a flamboyant kind of populism. Disorganized, it is no surprise that the workers are simply mown down by police bullets when they rebel, resulting in a massacre reminiscent of that of the Banana Company workers in *One Hundred Years of Solitude*. The colonialists withdraw and the wicked Ali Baba and his forty African ministerial bandits take charge of government. They allow the country to fall into ruin. Garbage then has a vision that his many children out there in the world will return because 'they belonged to a race that had Malagueta in its blood'. Being superior beings they 'would never be eaten up by the voracious passions of greed and the narrow visions of race' (p. 383). Ali Baba and his mandarins are over-thrown and Sanka Maru becomes President, ultimately to be destroyed by way of the magical, by the device of the flying carpet and the wizard, Sulaiman.

Cheney-Coker describes quite precisely how this dramatic carpet came about:

> Marquez describes how he had gone out one day and seen a woman hanging her laundry and the wind came and a piece of laundry was being blown out and this is how he decided he was going to send one of his characters to heaven, Remedios the Beauty, she was going to fly. I remember someone saying to me that on the night that a major character

in my novel, Tamba Masimiara, the general, died (you know he was modelled on someone who really lived in Sierra Leone) the night that the real soldier died, there was such a strong wind. It was just incomprehensible. There hadn't been a wind like that in a long time. So I woke up one morning thinking about it and I said: well, why don't you have Alusine Dunbar flying on a magic carpet and let this wind with its enormous power. . . .

Things would come to me like that. I am really at a loss to understand how people can mistake all this as just a mere example of magical realism. It is a book to celebrate and to understand so much complexity in a world that, on one hand, is a very simple one to deal with, but yet at the same time contains possibilities for creative imaginative writing.[20]

This is exactly what magical realism is all about – a genuine outrage against modern politicians motivates the novel which employs devices that are supernatural to make the point boldly and memorably. What, however, are the political implications of the revenge on Sanka Maru? Is the carpet an allegory for the collective memory? Is it a device which defeats its political purpose by collapsing social and economic struggles into magical explanations? And who is Sanka Maru himself? He is both a critical satire of the Sierra Leonian President, Siaka Stevens, and he also carries overtones of the demonic Soumaoro, the enemy of the heroic Sundiata, taken from the epic oral tale of old Mali. Soumaoro had defeated nine kings 'whose heads served him as fetishes in his macabre chamber. Their skins served as seats and he cut his footwear from human skin'. He was 'an evil demon and his reign had produced nothing but bloodshed'.[21] The epic *Sundiata*, reverberates with the same fatalistic refrain of *The Last Harmattan*; 'everything had been foreseen'.[22]

Sanka Maru, as both Stevens and Soumaoro, stands as a symbolic shorthand for the novel's tensions between historical and mythical time. By identifying his work with a famous, traditional African epic, Cheney-Coker, the Creole, is attempting to ground his writing and his identity in African indigenous traditions. The question is whether, by so doing, he mutes his mixed origins and cultural kaleidoscope with yearnings for nationalistic purities.

These tensions in the novel, between historical and mythical time are replicated in space through the diverse fictional sites in which it is situated. The space in which the plot is played out is multi-dimensional. The jungle and garden, the living and the dead, interact and cross over. Sebastian Cromantine goes off into the woods, 'beyond the last house of the town', and is unnerved 'as the neat gardens with their smell of jasmine and gardenia gave way to the unruly growth of the wilderness and the cries of the creatures of the evening' (p. 75). His dead father also makes journeys to him 'beyond the border of the living' (p. 88). Sulaiman happily journeys across the globe, across the spaces of life and death, across time. He decides to return to Malagueta when from 'the high plateau of the dead he saw how the living were messing up their lives' (p. 288). He comes 'through the idyllic gardens of the savannah and saw the pageant of the migratory birds going back to Europe' and strays for a while in the desert 'to see what changes the discovery of the compass had made since the days of the camel'. This modern technology leads him to rest 'on the stones in the rock garden of antiquity' and eventually he is led to Malagueta by 'the clouds of the locusts which have no respect for the borders between wet and dry regions' (pp. 288, 289). Garbage, who will receive Sulaiman's wisdom and continue the narrative line, is a kindred spirit because 'the boy was free to wander, as he himself had crossed the meridian of life and death, to be present at the turning of the wheel which was about to begin in Malagueta' (pp. 295–6).

What is the meaning of the free travel between and across these borders and dimensions? Is this the African cycle of the living, dead and unborn celebrated in the oral tradition, or the border traffic of opposite parts in embrace, propagated by Bhabha? Or is it, contrary to Cheney-Coker's protestations, the cycles of Marquez, repeated for all the magical journeys and transformations celebrated by the fiction?

The ambiguity surrounding time and space is concretized in the novel in the portrayal of three houses that are both domestic spaces and also decaying wildernesses, that are home and sanctuary and also prison and hell. Space, time and narrative structure entwine most powerfully in the image of these three houses, which both do and do not survive over the spans time and are the sites of the enactment of vital narrative moments. Firstly there is the house of Mariamu and 'the Mulatto', re-discovered by Bookerman. Secondly, there is that nightmare hovel where 'the albino' took Fatmatta, his bride, for a fleeting night and finally that of N'jai, the gold merchant, the house where Sulaiman and Mariamu conceive Fatmatta. The last two are re-discovered by Garbage and it is in the last that he portentiously encounters Sulaiman and receives his heritage of history and wisdom.

Behind Antonio the Mulatto's shop 'was an old stone house of red laterite, thatched with palm fronds and protected by a fence of liana and guava stalks' (p. 44). It is 'a strange house' (p. 48) but a wonderful one, a space that escapes the cruelties and crises of life. Mariamu and 'the mulatto' are both misfits and they find love and a sanctuary. Antonio is a cultural hybrid, neither local nor foreign. Here the Creole, Mulatto identity is celebrated. This house, albeit decayed with time when Bookerman and his friends find it, syncretizes the savage and the civilized:

> When they walked in, they saw evidence of a life that had been full of luxury: they saw the two fine chairs where the couple had sat, the golden pelicans that the bugs had begun to devour, and the flute with the silver mouthpiece which, according to the people who lived by the sea, the man used to play to attract the dugongs to the shore. They saw the brass four-poster where they had made love, the china plates with the pictures of the dowager queen, the silver candelabrum which had lighted the living room.
>
> (pp. 210–11)

It was haven, escape, and narrative anchor. It contains not only Mariamu's diary, which will be found by Bookerman and add to his story, but the link to a central character who spans the human and the godly – Fatmatta, the woman/goddess, who is both daughter and not daughter to Mariamu. Bookerman finds 'the bronze figure of a woman holding a bird in her hand with a snake round her body' (p. 211). Human and godly, survival and decay, civilized luxury and barbaric destruction, all co-exist in this fertile and hospitable fictional site.

Not so the second house, which seems to have been degenerate for all time. Here the benevolent Creole as kind Mulatto is terrifyingly transformed into Creole as unnatural, sick Albino. In this archetypal fairytale location of horror, the infringement of borders destroys rather than enriches. Here a terrible price is exacted for crossing the line between human and animal, normal and abnormal, white and black, male and female. The Albino's house is the site of a culture's nightmare of rape and deception and stands as the turning point for Fatmatta, victim for once at the hands of a handsome black husband, most horribly transformed:

> there in the middle of that wilderness of a forgotten age was a small house overgrown with the century of iridescent plants that had flourished in that humid region. It was a yellow dusty house and as evidence of its decrepit state were its windows that were coming off their hinges, and the musical birds that flew in and out of the rooms, and the feeling that no one had lived there since the time of the flood, because at any time its roof of a lush garden of moss and lichen could collapse.
>
> Fatmatta went up the steps leaning on the arms of her husband. She did not see the diaphanous skulls on the veranda which were used as plant pots, ossified by neglect, but felt a cold shiver run through her as if she were entering the deserted house of the lemures.
>
> (pp. 55–6)

Bonded with this traditional tale is the conservative warning against foreigners, against syncretism and against women who rebel against the patriarchy; it is in polar opposition to the image of the kind and healing mulatto with whom Fatmatta's mother finds sanctuary. Eldred Jones comments, with reference to the inclusion of the traditional tale in works such as Cheney-Coker's, that in reaction to the corruption and misery all around them, some of the writers 'take a backward glance at the cohesion which characterized the small ethnic societies'.[23] However, this story and this house also enter Malagueta's arsenal of legend and become a part of Garbage's search for his African roots as he explores the town:

> He located the house, much talked about, with the overgrown garden, with the large banyan tree in the back, where hundreds of dipsomaniacal blood-sucking bats made their home. No one had lived in that house in living memory because many years before the first war between Thomas

Bookerman and the captain, someone had seen a horse-faced albino dragging a beautiful young woman there, from where she never came back.

(p. 283)

The first house signifies escape and the second the horrific inability to escape.
The third house seems to be situated between the two possibilities. It is itself a
boundary embodying many of the novel's crucial narrative events and crossovers –
between savagery and civilization, magic and science, universal cycles and history.
It is the house to which N'jai, the gold merchant, brings Sulaiman, resulting in the
liaison with Mariamu and the birth of Fatmatta. Early on it is destroyed by a 'great
herd of baboons' who 'demolished it in no time, going through the rooms, pissing
on the expensive Moroccan rug where Mariamu had conceived Fatmatta' (p. 37).
Significantly, the site of the house becomes the shop of Theophilus the apothecary,
but by the time Garbage finds it, it is already derelict and long abandoned. Sorcery
and medicine combine with the smells of decay and abandonment. It is both
'fairyland' and 'sorcerer's den', Mulatto haven as well as albino horror:

> Then, as if he were returning to some fairyland where he had played
> before, he pushed the door open and came into the shop with its smell of
> combustible peat and the musk of dead animals. He saw, as if someone
> had arranged them on a table, the jars filled with acaudal lizards, whose
> skins had dried up in the harmattan. He saw the alembic lamp that
> Theophilus had used for distilling and heating his potions, the Florence
> flask in which he had fermented the entrails of lizards, the dried bark of
> the quassia tree and the urine of goats which he had prescribed to dispel
> the intestinal worms of death.
>
> If he was afraid of being in that sorcerer's den, Garbage did not let it
> show.
>
> (p. 286)

He did not let it show because entry into this house of time and timelessness
involves crossing temporal borders – from being a boy of ten, he 'had passed, in
one swift moment, into the crypt of manhood' (p. 286). It is in this house that his
search for the past, through wandering about in Malagueta, crosses over into an
exposure 'into the future where Malagueta was a wounded doe and the voracious
birds of prey, the treacherous hyenas in the town and the incendiary bombs of the
new foreigners would bring her down' (p. 295).

Time battles against circularity; space is multi-dimensional and time and space
intersect in the houses, in which the narrative is perpetuated, amidst possibilities
and polarities that remain ambiguous. Mariamu took a chance, coming to the
Mulatto, who she hardly knew. She found peace. Her strange daughter took a
similar gamble and lost out. Time veers between the magical potential for third
time, a time dimension in which history and the supernatural syncretize, and

mythical time, in which universal cycles of human cruelty relentlessly repeat themselves.

Garbage comes to his house of destiny to meet with Sulaiman. What he receives is neither heaven nor hell, but the poet's escape from the action into narrative, as he becomes the next in a line of storytellers. And it is to the storytellers that we must now turn in the attempt to unpack the complex and elusive narrative points of view of the novel. As the thematic tensions we have been identifying seek resolution in the negotiations between irony and passion, farce and political commitment, we witness the way in which narrative structure enacts the political crisis of Cheney-Coker's Creole identity.

Like Bakhtin's Rabelais or Dostoevsky, Cheney-Coker's novel teems with life, exuberance, carnival and multiple speaking voices. Cheney-Coker saw his novel as a celebration and used farce, humour and the boundless imagination to fuel the return voyage from slavery, from colonialism and even from the betrayals of his own, contemporary Africa. However, the many voices also conceal an ambivalence and uncertainty regarding the particular history Cheney-Coker wishes to recover, the particular fight he wishes to commit himself to. At the same time, what does appear to emerge out of all the Creole conflict is the myth of the voice of the founders of Malagueta, who become a strong blood-line to establish an African Creole nation within Sierra Leone, to try to lay to rest Cheney-Coker's own crisis of identity, so poignantly motivating his fiction and also his poetry.

The writer's uncertainties are inscribed in the novel's narrative structure, where many storytellers clamour for a voice and are heard with varying degrees of clarity. What does ultimately become established, however, is a strong narrative chain, forged by the founding families of Malagueta. This is the content deeply embedded within the narrative structure of *The Last Harmattan of Alusine Dunbar*.

The Last Harmattan, like much magical realism, is a meta-narrative in the sense that it overtly ponders the nature of the telling and the writing of stories, of which it itself is an example. There are many storytellers who are engaged in the task of writing the history of Malagueta. The major voices are those of Alusine Dunbar, Thomas Bookerman and Syl Cheney-Coker himself, in both his persona as poet, manifested in the character of Garbage, and in his persona as omniscient narrator of his own novel. Ultimately the narrative is eternal as its thread is taken up by successive descendants of the founding elite.

Sulaiman the Nubian, or Alusine Dunbar, appears to be an all-powerful narrator with god-like powers to look into mirrors, to be immortal and to not only tell, but predict and then ensure that his prophesies materialize by acting on his predictions. In true magical realist style, however, the narrative confirms his powers and simultaneously, ironically, distances itself from him.

The novel begins its first book on the first page with: 'She had been prophesied in the looking-glass of the Nubian, Sulaiman of Khartoum, a hundred years before' (p. 1). This opening both establishes and detracts from Sulaiman's narrative authority. His magical powers of prophesy are mediated by the passive voice signifying an even more omniscient narrator, who is telling the story of Sulaiman as well as of the women, Jeanette Cromantine, who, in the tradition of Snow White's evil stepmother, Sulaiman foresees in his magical looking-glass. The simultaneous confirmation and cancellation of the authoritativeness of Sulaiman's narrative voice is illustrated when Mariamu appears before him in search of a remedy for her barrenness. We saw earlier that in the language of prediction of the novel, he knew she was coming to him because 'everything was mirrored in the looking-glass' (p. 25). However, Sulaiman's more mortal interests emerge when his solution to the beautiful Mariamu's problem is that he, Sulaiman himself, would impregnate her. This solution has occurred to him many times before:

> He had never married but his memory was alive with the images of women in veils, perfumed with the spices of Arabia, who had offered their bodies in appreciation for some changes he had brought into their lives: curing their sons of stammer, of polio; getting their husbands back from mistresses who had paid practitioners of the occult to turn them against their wives; or for bringing back the potency to their husbands. In those dimly lit rooms of the desert, in those tents smelling of couscous and goatmilk, protected by all those women who had flocked to him, Sulaiman the Nubian was certain that his seeds had sprung up and become sons and daughters who had been given to unsuspecting husbands happy that their wives had produced 'the spit of my father'.
>
> (p. 27)

When in ancient old age and at the height of his power and his wisdom, when all the accumulated weight of his knowledge and magic is situated in his illuminated testicles, we must remember with a degree of cynicism the return that he had received throughout his life for the gifts that he bestowed on women. The link is made unambiguously – Mariamu discovers that Sulaiman's 'esotericism was dissolved in the hot molten fires of his loins' (p. 27). More than cynicism, the comic and the grotesque, in league with the magical, mediate the serious force of the image. In his first encounter with the aged Sulaiman, the boy, Garbage, is terrified to see

> two small rays flickering on the floor, beaming from the old man's crotch. There, almost touching the floor, like a bloated udder, Garbage saw the herniated testicles of the old man, the cylindrical notches in the drooping pants.
>
> (p. 291)

It may well be that it is 'the glowing light of his knowledge flickering between his legs' (p. 294) and 'the power of his illuminating testicles' might well be 'awesome' (p. 295), but its awesomeness is compromised by the herniated image. The nature and extent of the compromise, however, remain ambiguous. The testicles have real magical properties and have taken over from the looking-glass as the vanities and sensualities of youth have been replaced by the force and wisdom of age:

> When the rays of the light of the illuminating testicles rose in the dark room, Alusine Dunbar saw in the distant edges of the surrounding forest a large one-eyed man, flanked by a beautiful woman and a young man with the lean face of a poet, leading a large group of well-armed men, and he saw in the harmattan of another time the dust raised by those people as they had begun the journey to Malagueta.
>
> (p. 305)

The tone is passionate, poetic and auspicious. More importantly, unlike the mirror that merely predicts, the testicles have real power to intervene, to protect the just and assassinate the wicked. Again however, Cheney-Coker muffles Sulaiman's narrative authoritativeness when he guides the column of good men on their way to fight the just war for Malagueta by describing how Sulaiman 'trained his balls so that the men would be guarded by their light' (p. 305). Not testicles here, but 'balls' and the reader has to smile at the image of not a gun, but of these spectacular balls trained on their target.

Sulaiman is a reincarnation of Marquez's Melquiades. He too roams, returns, enchants and foretells in the exotic language of crystal balls, magical mirrors, flying carpets and spectacle:

> Using a small hoe, Sulaiman dug several holes at random in front of some huts, and while the crowd watched he unearthed parrots' feathers, monkey heads and medieval bracelets which the first pirates had traded for gold and salt.
>
> (p. 23)

He is both very mortal man and godly magician – the grotesquely real. He entertains us, works for change and retribution of evil, within the contradictory framework of fate and prediction.

The 'large one-eyed man' illuminated by Sulaiman's magical balls is none other than Thomas Bookerman. It is he whose version of history will assist us in the pursuit of the nature of the significance of Sulaiman. Bookerman had been 'inspired by the fantastic tales of the incredible Malaguetans who had founded a town' (p. 101) and therefore he and his team had resolved to cross the ocean and find these pioneers. Moreover, not only is he a man of action, a founder and defender of towns, but he is also both inspired by stories, and determined to write the history of Malagueta.

Book three of the novel begins with Thomas Bookerman working on his *History of the Founding of Malagueta* (p. 209). He searches for written evidence 'to enlighten him further' and finds the house in which important bits of the narrative structure live, where Mariamu wrote her diary 'over a hundred years before his arrival on the scene'. This makes the narrative link not only with the past and future of this novel, but with that other fiction, *One Hundred Years of Solitude*, which, as we have seen, greatly influenced Cheney-Coker's own story and mode of telling it.

Bookerman cuts an heroic figure, ensuring that Malagueta is re-founded and bravely defended against great odds. Cheney-Coker, who despises the writer whose work is only fit for university study, portrays in Bookerman precisely the kind writer-activist that he himself aspires to be. Bookerman as narrator therefore carries great authority. He discovers in the auspicious house, the name of Sulaiman the Nubian and

> he deduced from the fragmentary evidence that Sulaiman the Nubian had been a mystic with a remarkable power of premonition who had seen the destruction of the area that was now part of Malagueta because the town was in the direction of a cyclical wind that blew once every fifty years, unleashed by the imponderable hand of a remarkable king.
>
> (p. 212)

As activist-writer, Bookerman presents one of the novel's solutions to the polarity between historical, linear time and the cyclical knot of fatalistic time, between radical politics resting on class analysis and god-like magicians who predict the outcomes of the actions of larger-than-life heroes. This he does by way of his view of history as farce and of the heroic as the funny and even eccentric, like Sulaiman himself. He insists

> that he and other men were engaged in a task that was a farce, because life was circumscribed by pathos. He saw that all he and others had laboured to build would one day be destroyed not only because of greed but because it had been laid down that although Divine Providence had blessed Malagueta, it had also given it some of the most unfortunate people on earth whose children would make the bones of their ancestors tremble in their graves because of their greed and servitude in the face of tyranny. The real heroes and heroines, he concluded, were those not arrogant enough to see themselves as conquerors or builders, but who had been engaged in only one pursuit in life: making others happy.
>
> (p. 212)

Farce is the operative word. In the carnivalesque tradition, where laughter, sensuality and irreverence cover the border zones between reality and magic, the people that Bookerman honours 'when he sat down to write the first chapter of the *Founding of Malagueta*' are 'those who had made them laugh during the lugubrious afternoons in the new region'. It is those like Fatmatta who sang 'bittersweet ballads'; it is 'Simon the Blind who had lost his right hand because he preferred playing his banjo to working on the field' (p. 212). It would undoubtedly include Sulaiman, 'chanting in an alien language' and revealing 'to the startled crowd an armadillo which in that part of the world had disappeared' (p. 24).

How transgressive is this laughter? Sulaiman might wreak his vengeance, but magic might simply replace struggle. Sulaiman, flying on his magic carpet, and in the face of historical forces and necessities, overthrows the evil Sanka Maru, who is both historical leader and epic myth. The tension between mythical and historical explanations is released and seeks alleviation by way of Bookerman's recourse to laughter and farce. Bookerman's political heroism is impeachable; his perspective is wise and authoritative, but he sees not with a third eye, but with only one eye. In other words, Bookerman's own positioning is as another narrator, who is both trustworthy and also simultaneously unreliable.

Here history has itself split into different orders. At the level of the big events and actors, fate and magic and predictions and heroes are lumped together in a farcical and eternal dance of power mongering and futility. At another level, ordinary people make a different impact, one which is both meaningful and unpredictable. This political stance is fragile, shying away as it is from either total cynicism or political commitment on a structural level.

Another proffered solution to the potential rift between historical and epic time is that of the language of poetry. The poet-narrator is a pivotal character and teller. He is the one with the ironic name of Garbage. ' "So you are the poet", Emmanuel Cromantine said to him. "Let's hope you write about this when it is all over" ' (p. 317). We saw that Garbage as the son of Gustavius and Isatu Martins is, significantly and symbolically, the offspring, the fruit, of the union between American and indigenous African. A Creole and a poet, like his creator, he is on the margins of society. As one of his classmates comments: 'That Garbage boy is not like us'. He tells his mother that he is getting an 'instruction' from 'a voice at night' (p. 258). From this marginal place, he becomes heir to the magic and wisdom of Sulaiman and inherits the mantle of teller of the story of Malagueta. Garbage can only recover the history and turn it into a continuation of the narrative after exploring the landscape in the tradition of his ancestors who established and defended Malagueta in the first place. He exhibits a 'passion for seeking out what had gone on before his time' (p. 283). He turns his mother into storyteller and forces her to fill in 'the details of the history of the town' (pp. 283–4). Sulaiman has found his disciple onto whom he can pass all his accumulated experience of life and death. The old man 'knew he had struck a chord in the mind of the ten-year-old boy who had the intelligence of a twenty-year-old' (pp. 287–8). Cheney-Coker proceeds to mould the narrative chain, whose strongest mortal link is that of his own persona as poet, ironically cast, not in gold, but in garbage.

What is the extent of the irony attached to the name? At first contact between them, Sulaiman makes reference to Garbage's name, which whatever significance we will see that it has for the politics of the novel, it also has the effect of distancing us ironically from the narrative voice of the poet.

I know, for instance, that you were given a name which in other times, to other people, would have been an embarrassment; but to you, it was an act of love, when your parents looked at you.

(p. 288)

We have seen that Garbage's name has a hugely positive meaning derived from the particular idiosyncratic mythology around the African soil that Cheney-Coker constructs. Garbage's role as authoritative narrator, moreover, is fully and seriously established by his genealogy, his formal encounters with Sulaiman and the omniscient narrator's obvious identification with his character, politics and actions. However, Syl Cheney-Coker's own uncertainties regarding the role of poetry in his society, and the ambiguous position of the poet himself, is inscribed in the distance between what Garbage says and the more conventional meaning of what he is called – not just Rubbish, but its American version of the term. This is particularly meaningful, given the writer's depiction of the American father's contamination by foreignness.

The poet, notwithstanding his undeniable authority and power in the fiction, is brought down to size. It is funny when the mayor and publisher of the town describes to his daughter the receipt of the poetry 'by that young man with the incredible name of dustbin' (p. 329). In addition, right at the beginning of the novel, Cheney-Coker himself uses the word conventionally, albeit in a quite different context, but with obvious implications for our interpretation of the ironic use of the poet's name:

Everywhere you looked, you could see the dogshit and dead dogs where once there had been beds of violets and fountains in gardens with clear alabaster statues. The general felt something had to be done. Garbage has a way of producing more garbage.

(pp. x–xi)

The irony, however, is weaker than the sacred role that Garbage inherits, only after personal growth and at the right moment of historical development. In other words, if Garbage could only encounter Sulaiman once he had explored the landscapes of historical place and story, then he could only begin the job of narrator-poet once the old era, signified by slavery and the return to Africa, had ended. He is the poet of colonialism:

[Garbage] had woken up from the daze that Alusine Dunbar had thrown over him, and started to run in the direction of the house with the lycopods. When he got there, all traces of it had been wiped out, as if a great hurricane had blown it off the face of the earth, carted it away into the depths of the sea, like a fabled ship full of the wonders of that magician, beyond the vertigoes of rediscovery.

(p. 318)

The destruction of the house coincides with, and is linked to, the death of Emmanuel Cromantine. On the night of his death, Bookerman and Phyllis were exiled to the Gold Coast, this being described as 'one last thread of the old Malagueta was being severed' (p. 319). The narrative thread, however, is not and its magical wonders are not shipwrecked 'beyond the vertigoes of rediscovery'. Garbage 'began to sail with a flourish of words':

> He searched for Malagueta in the tempestuous seas of former times where the conches of its birth stones had been trapped by the planktons of oblivion since the time of the first war. He brought back from the unfathomable bottom of the sea the coelacanth that had guided Sebastian and Jeanette Cromantine, clumsily navigating the route to the promised land. When he had put their trembling feet on that land, and welcomed them with garlands of sea lilies, he made them drink from a gourd of aged wine, so that their parched lips would be healed for ever. He wrote more poems; poems about his mother in the vista of his own childhood, when the two of them had been drawn together by the blues of his dead father's soul; poems for even the Virgins, because, in the drabness of their gowns and the rigidity of their comportment, they had meant well for Malagueta.
>
> (p. 329)

The house in which he met with Sulaiman may have been destroyed but the stories live on. He receives the 'gift of knowledge' from Sulaiman in the form of 'a large carton of books without any postal stamp or note, delivered anonymously to his house' (p. 371). He is sure that 'the elusive saint' will re-appear in Malagueta. We are not surprised then when he indeed returns quite spectacularly, on his magic carpet, to exact his vengeance, as once again this dispersed narrative delivers up its scattered links and threads.

If Garbage is Cheney-Coker in poet persona, then an omniscient narrator ultimately knows and tells it all – Cheney-Coker, the novelist. Throughout the narrative, a voice speaks that is even more clairvoyant than Sulaiman's, one that has the power to comment on the magician himself:

> A blazing light, like a giant constellation, shot out from the testicles of revelation, and Garbage saw the celestial face of a beautiful woman appear, borne by the wings of an angel. Swooping down like a bird, she caught Emmanuel Cromantine before he hit the ground, kissed him on the forehead, leaving everyone confused, except for Alusine Dunbar, who knew through what crypt a great scorpion had passed to light up the eyes of the woman so that she could come through the looking-glass of all eternity, with the golden amulets round her arms, to stop Emmanuel Cromantine falling into the slough of degradation.
>
> (p. 318)

Bookerman perceives through the one-eyed lens of farce; Garbage, named after rubbish, sees with the aid of the light of revelation of Alusine Dunbar's testicles; Dunbar sees through the looking-glass of all eternity, but only the omniscient storyteller can know that Alusine Dunbar alone was not confused. Throughout the novel, this narrator provides us with bits of information that assist in pulling the pieces of the narrative together. These are clearly not given in the auspicious, ponderous and biblical voice of Sulaiman, who would have the magical powers of prediction.

For example, the author of the novel is commenting on Sebastian Cromantine's 'terrible dream' by informing us that 'he did not realise then that the meaning of his dream had more to do with what a magical looking-glass had predicted a long time ago in a place far removed from where he was living' (p. 9). We are told that in the future Malagueta 'would cease to be a small town' (p. 231) and when Bookerman would be exiled from Malagueta. Malagueta is growing and changing and among the new workers 'was a man named Sheku Masimiara, whose grandson was to stage an unsuccessful coup against a corrupt president seventy-five years later' (p. 326). The chronological precision is the author's and contrasts with Sulaiman's supernatural future-telling use of the figurative language of poetry in preference to the historical language of exact dating.

The author's voice may be omniscient, but it, like the other voices, is also muffled by uncertainty. The following, judgemental comment on the Creole nature is given somewhat obliquely through the looking glass of Sulaiman, but its heartfelt bitterness is unmistakable:

> despite the sanctimonious public display of piety by the black people who would come from America before the Arabs, despite the regulated formula of their baptism in the name of the father, the son and the Holy Ghost, as God was his witness, despite the farcical re-enactment of the beating of Judas Iscariot on Good Friday, those bastards would hate one another in their parsimonious hearts; what would you expect of the children of those men who would never never lose their tricks of a monkey with black hands, and would be prepared to sell all they had built because they were used to selling and being sold for a hundred pieces of silver, for a yard of cloth, for gunpowder, for gold and – worse – for liquor? People who would spit on their God, if you would pardon his language, so much so that it was enough to make a holy man like himself puke.
>
> (p. 30)

Cheney-Coker is such a Creole descended from slaves. His monkey is not the reified signifying, defiant, symbol of resistance; is not Henry Gates' artefact of cultural pride and nationalism.[24] It is the rolling eyed Uncle Tom, the surviving alienation and trauma bestowed on Creoles by history. The novel is shot through with a scarring self-hatred which fragments the authority of the author's voice and accounts for the desperate search for a healing myth. The myth is vested, as we saw, in the nature of the founding families, who returned to Africa from slavery, and it is they who have the final narrative word, beyond even the writer's omni-science. The narrative chain is eternal and the novel ends with Sadatu Cromantine-Doherty, who is the descendent of the founders of Malagueta. She has taken up the sacred pen of narration of their story. Her soul, we saw,

> was reserved for the task that Sadatu Doherty had chosen as her life's work: the writing of a full-length biography of her legendary grandfather, Emmanuel Cromantine.
>
> (pp. 385–6)

The Last Harmattan of Alusine Dunbar is a magnificent fiction crafted by a master at the art of storytelling. But the structure of the narrative is fragmented and dispersed. Its narrative voices are many and complex. I think that the reason for this is that the politics at the core of the content of the form is itself uneasy and contradictory. The questions remain to the very end. We have seen that Cheney-Coker struggles with questions of identity, his own social and political insertion in Africa, and with the politics that he both wishes to express passionately and to triv-ialize through farce. The distinctive history of Sierra Leone has determined the writer's stance with both riches and with angst. It accounts for the excavation, finally, of a nationalistic myth of a return, of an elite of purified and strengthened returnees, who are able to grow their roots in Africa.

This is not to simplify the fact that the fiction is barricaded with masks and protective devices which distort the clarity of our reception. Sulaiman's bizarre glowing balls, Bookerman's one eye, the nation builders as androgynous dwarfs and, most importantly, a central figure in the founding dynasty, whose name means 'rubbish', delightfully undercut the novel's politically conservative urge towards the myth of pure origins – the base of national reconstruction.

Appropriately, then, I will end this discussion of Syl Cheney-Coker with the ultimately irreducible magic and poetry of his writing, with the unsolvable mystery of the ring for a prince. We never discover who the prince is and why he deserves the beautiful golden ring that Sulaiman is sculpting for him. The ring is the golden pleasure that remains after the critique and analysis have been completed:

> Sitting Buddha-like, he was working the bellows that regulated the flame of the fire, which sprang from the live charcoals burning in a forge. Garbage had never seen anything like that before and stood speechless.
>
> 'You have come just in time to see me making a ring for a prince who is coming here as soon as this rain stops falling', said Alusine Dunbar.
>
> Enthralled by the magic of the dancing flames, Garbage forgot about the rain falling outside; he stood riveted in one spot while the gold ingot

came alive in hues of yellow and red, and the dancing snakes of the smoke rose above the head of the magician who worked the goatskin bellows.

(pp. 303–4)

6

INTERMEDIATE MAGIC AND THE FICTION OF B. KOJO LAING

'I don't understand a magic that can put a ring round an aeroplane yet fail to bring it down', de Babo hissed to himself, hoping Kofi Senya would hear. He did, and replied with a growing grin: 'Intermediate magic always finds its own way later!'.

(Kojo Laing, *Woman of the Aeroplanes*, p. 44)

Intermediate magic has limited power. It is a progressive kind of magic that furnishes a kick start, the critical spark, that will culminate in movement only if there is a keen and competent driver in the seat, a motivated and trustworthy protagonist at the helm of the narrative. Perhaps the driver is a pilot controlling an aeroplane, perhaps a scientist, inventor of a magical contraption, like the crucial stupidity machine of Laing's second novel, *Woman of the Aeroplanes*. Perhaps she is a good witch with weakening powers, as in Laing's first novel, *Search Sweet Country*. Perhaps he is a paradoxically pacifistic soldier, Major Gentl, of the third novel, who has rented 'two rooms on the moon' from which 'he would use magic to see far into other countries'.[1]

In his fiction Laing depicts a desirable modernity, which has placed limits on magic. His novels search for a humanity, a mortality capable of spirituality in the modern world where the supernatural is on the wane. Laing embraces change, but if change and newness are unambiguously advocated in his fiction, strategies for accomplishing these changes, solutions to the enormous problems in the Ghana of postcolonialism, are not as forthcoming. The magic might enable Major Gentl to see far into other countries, but there is little comfort in what he sees, and great problems in what the novel suggests he should attempt to do about it.

Laing was born in Kumasi, Ghana, in 1946. He attended school in Ghana and then, unusually by comparison with the life histories of other African writers, in Scotland, where he afterwards took a degree at Glasgow University. If Okri's para-doxes are shaped by his long, voluntary residence in London, if Cheney-Coker's uniqueness is the product of his Creole past, then Scotland is one of the sources of Laing's often exciting, cosmopolitan regard for international syncretisms. This may be so not least of all perhaps because Scotland is itself in many ways culturally and economically peripheralized.

In answering a question about the ways in which his sojourn in Scotland has influenced his portrayal of European culture in his fiction, Laing has commented:

> I fell in love with the hills and isolated streams, pines, mist etc. My acquaintance with Europeans was already extensive in Ghana before I left for Scotland. I view people without colour except for specific purposes, artistic or otherwise. I married a Scotswoman but have been living in different continents since 1981. I made no emotional difference between European literature/art and the African equivalent.[2]

Laing's cosmopolitan positioning, however, is increasingly at war in his fiction with the more familiar quest for healing myths sought within an idealized African, pre-colonial past. I will be able to substantiate this claim by reference to Laing's second novel, set in fictional twin towns within Ghana and Scotland, later on in this chapter. In the meanwhile, we must search, with Laing, in his first novel, for his 'sweet country'. At the end of the chapter I will touch very briefly on the third novel, *Major Gentl and the Achimoto Wars* by way of a conclusion. We will see that while the three novels, and particularly the first two, share themes and preoccupations in common, they also develop away from each other.

'Change everything except the roots that do the changing!'

(p. 189)[3]

The quest for how to bring about genuine change without losing the basic supporting framework from the past is the search that dominates Laing's poetry and fiction as a whole, for all the differences that exist within them. In answer to Adewale Maja-Pearce's question in an interview, about what 'could be salvaged from the past', Laing had this to say:

> When I deal with the traditionalists in the book I criticize them not neces-sarily in relation to anything external, but in relation to the fact that stagnation is there, and I push this view beyond what the average Ghanaian would consider sensible. Take, for instance, the pouring of libation on the blackstools, the stools of dead chiefs that have been covered with ash and certain other things. To suggest that there should be a change in the way that libation is poured is something which the average Ghanaian would be shocked at. But the point is being made that change must come even there, just at that point where the Ghanaian feels that no change is possible. That is precisely the point where the change must come. And as a corollary of this, I'm not saying that there should be sweeping change across the board, some sort of mindless change.[4]

Search Sweet Country offers different options for achieving this quest through the choices and ways of life of its characters. It is structured, in other words, around the characters, and their interactions provide differing perspectives on the question of controlled change. We will see, however, that these perspectives are mediated through, and moderated by, the author's distance, for one reason or another, from all of these characters. Ultimately, his point of view comes through most powerfully and unambiguously by way of the poetic language of the novel itself. We shall see, in other words, that language attempts, along with the characters, to demonstrate how to effect the desired syncretism between transformation and conservation – the medium becomes the message.

The novel is set in Ghana, Accra, in the 1970s. The symbolic function of the characters is introduced immediately – 'Beni Baidoo was Accra' (p. 1). He links together Accra's many different parts and the novel's many characters:

> Thus, shrewd and shrivelled, he went around Accra with his one obsession: to found a village. And if some of his friends were making serious and half-serious searches in their lives, he felt it his duty to balance this with his own type of search. The search of a fool touches other lives . . ..
> Beni Baidoo usually had as much laughter with his food as possible, and finding himself in 1975, had broken up the year into different grades of laughter, sharing the teeth and noise among his friends Kofi Loww, Kojo Okay Pol, 1/2-Allotey, Professor Sackey, Dr Boadi and others. He brought to friendship a fine quality: nuisance value; and then flowed with his one obsession in and out of the lives he met.
>
> (pp. 1–2)

Beni Baidoo is the plot thread that weaves the different characters together – his friend Kofi Loww, who leads us to Boadi, Okay Pol and his woman, the good witch, Adwoa, who in turn will bring us to her friend, the English witch, Sally Soon, who becomes entangled with the 'good' academic, Professor Sackey, as opposed to the 'bad' one, Dr Boadi. Sackey, in turn, is entwined in an intriguing relationship with 1/2-Allotey. Beni is able to do this – is able to be the spirit of Accra, of the old culture undergoing metamorphosis in the city – because he is fashioned in the mould and tradition of the trickster. Pietro Deandrea asks:

> why does this character take to the extreme all the characteristics of Laing's language? The figure of an African trickster or of a mythical Ananse come soon to the reader's mind, because of their wicked humour, their penchant for tricks and taboo-breaking which Baidoo certainly shares.[5]

He appears and then disappears without warning; he goads and taunts and challenges the other characters, is beggar, rascal and wise elder, all in one – 'Baidoo was involved with driblets of divination; he was the explainer whose buffoonery ranged over the city . . . fools got reputations fast in Accra' (p. 26). He has knowledge of the living and the dead:

> Awura, I know something of the dead: the dead are full of tricks: a few hours before dawn, they send their eyes up to an inch above the earth, and the graveyards shine with the light of dead eyes, for those who have eyes to see such things. Brown eyes above brown earth, that's also my life!
>
> (p. 130)

Beni's trickster persona may go deep into the culture of the past, but he is reduced here to old age and begging. His own laughter is interrupted by his awareness of the fact that he does not have the resources and respect that traditionally would have been his, at his stage in life:

> But what really worries me at times is that my shabbiness breaks a few cultural taboos: as an old man, with so much experience, so much wandering on the very soils of Ghana, I cannot maintain the neatness that is supposed to stretch to the spirit. I can't afford the expense of keeping a neat and modest spirit.
>
> (pp. 130–1)

There is a precarious balance between the surviving witty wisdom of the fool and the social malaise that no longer values its clever trickster:

> Beni Baidoo vanished and left the saliva at the corners of his mouth dangerously close. His laugh was fresh but his donkey was feverish.
>
> (p. 131)

Baidoo appears and then vanishes, like a mischievous spirit. The spittle that remains after he has gone is a mixed image of both his laughter that entertains and the disgust that he, in his decrepit and shabby circumstances, provokes. Why is the saliva dangerously close? A spit is an insult one that is horrible for the recipient if it hits its mark. Ghanaians must beware of denigrating their trickster. Beni is entertaining, insulting, warning, and in a society that is undergoing shaky transformations, he is split, like so many other of Laing's characters; he is human and donkey, comedian and sick old man.

By the end of the novel, he will have died and his role been supplanted within a changing Accra. In the meantime, who are his friends, and what vision do they represent? Kofi Loww is a central figure. He has the aura of the author's own persona, in his search for the meaning of his life and of that of the city, with all its diverse and disparate elements. Loww wanders around Accra seeking answers – 'the sun broke into his face and bisected it. Kofi Loww, now thirty and living on the wandering side of doubt, walked along the High Street of Accra' (p. 6). His quest is the familiar magical realist one, to discover the nature of the splitting and joining of the weird cultural dislocations, contradictions and dualities in his society and, by extension, in himself, 'bisecting' his face. This discovery, therefore, will lead to finding himself as well:

> The cries of goats steadied the concrete in a bank building, and pushed Kofi Loww in no particular direction but certainly towards his own sense of being.
>
> (p. 113)

We have to unravel the images through very close reading, as if the novel were written in verse, poetry moreover abounding in riddles and paradoxes. The modern bank is, paradoxically, strengthened, steadied in its structure by the goats, animals of the past and the rural present, which impinge on the city. However, by contrast, the fancy, new glass office block attempts to distance itself from the sordidness of the poverty of the masses in the street; it 'was trying desperately to throw off its reflection of the horror of gutters' (p. 113).

Loww's own image is equally described by way of clues, poetic symbols and images. His reflected image is itself split, as he is, in the reflection of twin buildings, which creates 'two completely different images of Loww' but briefly 'these two crushed images . . . defined him completely' (p. 113). He is both sleepy snail, snug and unmoving, and also restless wanderer, head full of goals. In splitting, he encompasses the city's oppositions and 'as he walked he seemed to be binding parts of the city together with his clumsy broad feet' (p. 113). Syncretizing these splits and dualities will create something new. If Okri's goal is to see with a third eye, then Loww's wish is to walk with a third leg, to be 'the first two-legged man with one middle leg in Accra' (p. 113); there is always the middle as a third space.

In finding himself, Loww will find an answer for the city in his binding of its disparate parts together, like the goat which reinforces the bank's foundations. The sexual overtones of the third leg will become overt when Loww ultimately finds what he is searching for in his relationship with Adwoa Adde. But he has not succeeded yet. His two years at the university as a diploma student 'had increased his need to graze in the quieter savannas of the mind'. However, 'he cut up his life into little pieces, and did not quite know which piece to pick up first' – if he did not return to university 'the sun would only shine through opaque glass and through his father's tears and worry'. Equally, there were problems 'if he continued to drift through the streets finding aimless hours so healing' (p. 114). A side of him is obsessed with the gutter filth and excrement that follow and enrage him on his journeyings:

> But now, Kofi Loww walked on, past all the uncovered food for sale, past the jolly kaklo, the gari, the fish, the tomatoes, the cooked rice and stew, past all the flies that few sellers covered anything from. He stopped, thinking: the flies, the gutters, and the latrines had become a symbol far more powerful than all the excuses, including poverty, made from them.
>
> (p. 115)

Here, he is frustrated by Accra's population that refuses to take responsibility for improving the quality of its own life and uses urban decay and degradation as an excuse for its own lack of motivation. As he walks past 'the open stews and sewers', he reflects how:

> he could never understand a people who bathed so often, yet were so actively indifferent to dust and flies on their market food, so careless about spit and latrines. But of course you did not have your European plagues here! At comparable stages, Ghanaians had been far more fastidious than most people, he thought, with their villages constantly swept with fast brooms but slow history. He shouted suddenly without thinking, 'Why don't you all bath your streets and buildings as often as you bath your bodies!'.
>
> (p. 115)

The images of urban decay are a part of a symbolic shorthand within African fiction. They are found in Soyinka's *The Interpreters* and most significantly, in Laing's countryman, Ayi Kwei Armah, where such images of excrement form the narrative structure of *The Beautyful Ones Are Not Yet Born*. This is not the flamboyant carnivalesque grotesque signifying transgression and healthy, bodily rebellion. It is the sick despair many writers express in relation to the politics and culture of the postcolonial countries they inhabit. And these magical realist writers are no exception to this disillusionment, that is crucially linked to the nationalist project, in its preoccupation with the sickness of the state. We saw this in Cheney-Coker, and even more strongly, in Okri's fiction. The urge towards national solutions tends to call on unities, which fall back on tradition, rather than on diversity that links to change. There is, in other words, the pull towards the ethnic balm of the celebration of colour, the embrace of race that collapses difference:

> The sun was the brightest sister! The sun was a baker: heads, laws, fish, backs, beauty, chiefs, and history all browned under it; and the deepest assessment of the two-sided coin of life, the life of fufu, the life of pito, ended up with the same brown. And it was exactly this brown that Kofi Loww saw in the faces that laughed, frowned, mocked, and loved.
>
> (p. 7)

This romanticization can become a celebration of a mythical, idealized and unified Ghanaian mosaic:

> The old fisherman mending his net had hair the same colour as the passing clouds; and this same colour was thrown down in different shades onto so many buildings, buildings sharing among themselves the poverty and richness of different decades, different centuries.
>
> (p. 7)

Bright sister, mother Africa – splitting and difference unified under a national banner of race identity. However, Laing illustrates this racial identity paradoxically, by way of a warm and happy 'mixed' marriage between a Scotsman and a Ghanaian woman, which weakens the point even as he makes it. In negritude-style, happiness stems from the 'brown' that EsiMay has brought into Andy Pinn's life through his children's colour:

> Their children brought brown into their lives; after them, all colours changed, Loww could see. From the inside came the bursts and rhythms of talk and laughter.
>
> (p. 20)

Pinn was 'a careful man born in the heather whose wife broadened his roads' (p. 20). This broadening is associated with the warm sun of Africa that browns everything so wonderfully, given that the heather grows in 'the frost and smog of Glasgow' (p. 21). EsiMay's family 'wondered what its energetic daughter was doing picking up such a loose, pale pebble from such a deserted beach, the beach of life . . . and then marrying it' (p. 20). Laing's ambiguity is wonderfully captured in this brief comment. The deserted beach with its pale, loose pebble has to be Scotland, but he immediately backs off from this by calling it the beach of life and by explaining that EsiMay's family change their views 'over the years' because their son-in-law is a good man. Nonetheless the negritude polarity between sun, colour, rhythm of noise and happiness, contrasting with the cold, pale isolation of Britain, remains intact, as a stereotype.

This is not to underestimate Laing's ambiguity; he is as split as Loww, his protagonist, riveted with doubt and seeking direction in his own fictional wanderings. The unnatural homogeneity of race cannot cover up the passionate doubt that dogs Loww's three legs and the quests and searches of the other characters. Moreover, Loww qualifies his gloom and realizes that 'even in this city there were quiet men – sometimes even noisy ones – who did not make money or status an obsession' (p. 114). Like Armah's nameless man, Kofi Loww is incorruptible. He resists the attempts of the dishonest and repulsive Dr Boadi to buy him off. Boadi is terrified that Loww is going to subvert some of his illegal dealings that Loww observed at the airport, where Boadi was smuggling in some valuable racehorses. We see Kofi Loww's absolute integrity in relation to the bullying and bribing tactics of Boadi. This has a good influence on Boadi's assistant, Okay Pol, who is himself capable of changing and becoming a central figure for us by the end of the novel.

Linked however, to the mild cultural nationalism of the homogenizing 'brown', is Loww's problem with the university and the reason that he does not wish to go back to it. His fear is of taking in 'other people's ideas' which amounts to 'imported philosophy' from Europe. While he is attempting to 'find what he could do with both old and new', he does not want 'imported philosophy'. Crucially, then, the synthesis for which he is searching is not between European and African culture –

'neither marxism in palm-wine nor existentialism in pito' (p. 24). At this stage, however, he cannot even say what the different, opposing forces in play are – 'He ate shitoh, kenkey, and doubt: but what was old, what was new, after all?' (pp. 24–5). Interestingly, here he bumps into the 'omnipresent' Beni Baidoo who awaits the time that Adwoa, who is in touch with the spirits, witches, ghosts and ancestors, will settle Loww down, hinting at the answer Loww seeks – how to incorporate the old spiritual life into the modern and the mortal?

Already on his wanderings, Loww himself crosses the borders between the living and the dead and observes the ancestors. They are to be found in the cross-roads of the marketplace. Of immediate note is the idealized description of 'perfect African time' that enables him to have this insight:

> He stood still caught in perfect African time – time that existed in any
> dimension – and blocking the paths of other sellers with this same time
> that brought ancestors to the market, that touched the eyes of sellers and
> buyers now, that moved beyond those yet to be born.
>
> (p. 117)

He is able to see 'all sorts of dead faces moving among the living' such as 'she that seller of shea-butter, who finally died of grief because she could not have children' among others (p. 117). Somewhere within this vision is what Loww is seeking. He will find it only in and through Adwoa Adde.

If Beni Baidoo is the thread that binds a whole range of typical Ghanaians together by day, then Adwoa Adde, the good witch, connects with the supernatural forces of the city, as she flies over it by night:

> Adwoa could not believe it as she saw the sky lightening with the descent
> of hundreds of witches, most of them speaking silently of blood and
> bone, as snakes slithered into bodies again, and as pots, rings, beads,
> padlocks, knives, disembodied hearts, and black powder lay charmed.
>
> (p. 34)

Adwoa Adde has been 'pulled into magic and witchery' (p. 26) by being bequeathed her powers from her grandmother and from early on in the novel we see her flying over Accra, communing with the dead, as well as with the spirits of the living – 'Adwoa saw the dead as more adventurous, as more prepared to experiment', and Kofi Loww's spirit is 'as confused as he was' (p. 33). Again, as in the writing of Ben Okri, Cheney-Coker and Amos Tutuola, the boundary between the world of the dead and of the living is erased. Given the central issue of change in his novel, what is Laing saying through his portrayal of Adwoa Adde?

Ato Quayson sees Adwoa as 'defined in terms of indigenous spiritual beliefs'; 'the notion that witches are bequeathed their craft by others and that they can fly is widespread not only among the Akan but also among several African peoples'.[6] Significantly, Adwoa is ambiguous about her inheritance and her powers because, by becoming a witch, she is pulled into evil as well as goodness, an evil which threatens to destroy her. She begins to feel the venom of other witches in her bones:

> The witches were tying their knots and throwing their black powder. They pressurised Adwoa's blood, they wanted to pump her blood out high in the secret blue sky; and make a meal with her pretty bones.
>
> (p. 131)

She is also split and yearns for wholeness – 'she could make only half her darkness a force for good' (pp. 26–7). And 'Accra was cut up into varying intensities of light and dark, of good and bad' and she cannot distinguish what was good and what was bad, for she was forced into relationship with everything, and her pulse was the movements of thousands in sleep' (p. 29). While her portrayal may derive from traditional beliefs, she flies around with white witches and the overtones of European witches on broomsticks intermingles with the traditions that are being described.

Adwoa's dilemmas as a witch become acute in the face of her mortal desires – for the love of a man, of Kofi Loww, for mothering babies, for achieving her full humanity – which are blocked by her superhuman flights and supernatural powers. This theme will become the central one in the next novel. Mortality is won at the cost of the loss of supernatural power. Modernity for Africa is achieved at the expense of the old beliefs. The paradox is that the loss is an immense gain, as long as the transformation retains the spiritual source, the good side, of the old powers. How can it do this? In Laing's words:

> My hope in change is eternal, is located in seasonal changes, personal situational change and in the desire to see more of it everywhere – provided there's an authentic base.[7]

Adwoa's power may be traditional but for Laing the ancestors and the ancient customs are not inviolate. Adwoa's powers are, in fact, waning because she does not wish to be a witch, to have to incorporate the evils of supernatural power along with the good. Laing is expressing an interesting ambiguity of his own here about the consequences of having and using such power in his society. Communing with the spirits of the living and the dead means that 'Adwoa was completely exhausted' (p. 134) and 'did not do much with her grandmother's gift passed on so lovingly to her: she became a benevolent witch flying over Accra like an aerial sister of mercy' (p. 124). In fact, Quayson concludes that 'Laing is not so much interested in reflecting indigenous beliefs as in getting a surrogate for spiritual beliefs in general, be they indigenous or Christian'.[8] This is borne out by Adwoa's declaration that 'my grandmother has made me a witch, a witch for Christ, a witch for Ghana' (p. 155).

The question of indigenous beliefs, in other words, is bypassed as Adwoa becomes representative of spirituality in general and across cultures, as

Christianity merges imperceptibly with traditional spirituality. In this instance, Laing refuses to buy into the more dominant and respectful position with regard to the traditional gifts handed down by the grandmothers. Again, it is language that appears to flow over and engulf the plot, wresting it from more predictable thematic outcomes. This is what Quayson means when he points out that:

> From the point of view of the narrative's discourse, the significant thing is that Adwoa's characterisation hints at the potential sources of indigenous beliefs upon which the experiments with form may be grounded as a way of problematising narrative representation. But, because this potential is shown to be peripheral in terms of the course of the action, the force of the non-realist experiment resides largely within the play of the highly aestheticised language of the novel.[9]

If language – aestheticized, tricksterized and paradoxical – increasingly appears to provide clues to where the new, sweet country may be found, on a macro scale, Laing has not lost faith in the healing nature of loving relationships in the more micro picture. Ultimately, Kofi Loww and Adwoa Adde will find their solutions in each other, and will turn away from the enormous problems and crises of the country. Kofi, still riddled with doubts, eventually goes to the house of Adwoa Adde:

> Poor Adwoa, it was not that he had no love, but that the only way to make sure of it was to make sure of himself. After all what was wrong with a crisis of identity, for himself and for his country, even under the bright-ness of the sunflower?
>
> (p. 153)

The manner in which he expresses his crisis here, and that of the country, is also interesting. Again, with faint negritude overtones, African culture is stereotyped as bright, yellow and sensuous – sunflower or mango. Laing, however, almost imme-diately retreats from a cultural celebration of superior sensuality by insisting that it is a brightness that also blinds and damages:

> It was precisely the yellow pull of sunflowers and mangoes, dances and wisdom, that hid so many problems and crises underneath. This quiet man thus wanted to kill beauty and energy, so easily available; or at least to postpone them until the way was clearer.
>
> (p. 153)

As always when approaching Laing's writing, however, we must also read between and on the lines themselves. The language of paradox and riddle, linked to searched solutions, provide the key to what is being sought. This quiet man wanted the opposite of killing beauty and energy, but is seeking alternative ways of nurturing them than the conventional ones associated with an, albeit stereotyped,

Africa of killing intensity, heat, rhythm and brightness. The subtlety of the image, the nuance of the paradox, provide a path forward in the search for the new, based upon the old.

They make love, which is when Adwoa tells Kofi about being a witch. She is afraid that this information will alienate him – instead it provides the possibility of 'a big, new mystery which would finally stop his own searching: that big space of questions he had would be filled with something concrete at last, something so strange in someone he loved so much' (p. 155). Later, when 'Adwoa's people of the night world' come 'crowding the compound', Kofi will assist and support her. She cries out to him – 'Kofi, they have come to me when I have no powers left at all! How can I help them?' (p. 157). She panics and begs Kofi Loww for help as she has no power to cope. We see this as his moment of resolution as he 'took a chair and stood on it, shouting out "Bring your lives, bring your lives here! We are all suffering together!" ' Adwoa prays – 'When Adwoa came out again, there was a new determination in her eye. "I've prayed," was all she said' (p. 160).

Kofi, then, finds what he is looking for in caring for Adwoa and the people who come to her:

> Over in the eastern compound, Adwoa Adde rubbed her hands together, as if she were rubbing the world down or away. 'So you've borne all this yourself, all these months,' Kofi Loww said, the intensity gone from his eyes, his face full of pity and admiration for Adwoa. She said quietly, 'We are supposed to be together as a people, we go to each other's funerals, we laugh at a lot of things together. But we don't really care for each other at all. This made me so sad when I was flying, it makes me so sad now.'
>
> (p. 162)

Again the negritude stereotype that all Africans care for each other is exploded at the same time as being retained. This tension seeks resolution by way of this peculiarly personal solution to an enormous metaphysical and political set of problems. They have a 'happy household' where they:

> had decided to pursue or even run after their studies. Loww had a new brightness about him, he no longer looked grey under the tropical sun, for Adwoa was carrying half his weight.
>
> (p. 244)

Instead of being split, his burdens are lightened by being joined and united with Adwoa. However, the search for larger solutions to the country, to Ghana which is undergoing its shaky transformations, is not abandoned. Kofi and Adwoa have run their distance. The search is a relay. Who takes it on now? Surprisingly, given Laing's reservations about imported ideology at the university, but at the same time predictably, given the fusion between Christianity and traditional religion in the portrayal of Adwoa Adde, the search continues in the spaces provided by a kind of African Christianity.

The central questers in Laing's fiction work in pairs – Kofi Loww and Adwoa Adde and, as we will see later, Professor Sackey and 1/2-Allotey, among others. This is integral to Laing's focus on splitting, twinning, pulling away and the simultaneous urge towards uniting. The Church partners are the Bishop Budu and the priest, Osofo. They have different qualities and have to find a way of sharing the best of both of them. The kind and conciliating Budu clashes with the passionate Osofo, whose obsessive goal is the Laing ideal – to modernize the church by grounding it in the old ways:

> Osofo hounded and pounded the consciousness of his bishop: he insisted that certain practices of fetish priests had to be introduced into the church; he thought the church should know healing trees and sacred trees, powders and herbs. Sometimes Budu reacted to these pressures of the new with wild charges of heresy. But when he calmed down, he watched his own pot cooling as Osofo filled it with food for thought. And after the calm, he obliterated the one road that made the crossroads a crisis: he remembered his own one-way break from the Anglican church.
>
> (p. 50)

The pastiche of traditional healing, fetish priests and an African Christianity of a special kind, that has broken away from Anglicanism, sets up anxieties in Budu, who warns Osofo not to forget that

> we must have ritual and continuity before we can attract new members . . . and I see a little contradiction in your passion – you booklong people may call it paradox! For someone who wants so much change, why do you want to introduce so much more tradition? Why not try to invent a new Ghanaian culture fresh from the mud oven? You want to make the new out of the old old things and ways!
>
> (pp. 54–5)

The novel repeatedly emphasizes the contrast between the zealous Osofo, uncompromising, intense, too much energy, and who alienates people, and Bishop Budu who 'calmed and cajoled the sick' while Osofo 'overwhelmed them' (p. 135). The first real evidence of the fact that Osofo's vision and his church are a major source of spiritual newness, indeed able to retain the roots of old, emerges with the description of Osofo curing the boy in a magical, Africanized Christian ritual, which also brings him closer to Bishop Budu in a bond of opposites. He cures the boy through Jesus in the mode of traditional healer:

> Osofo went behind three crosses, and called God; Osofo went behind four crosses and called Jesus. Then he rushed back from the fifth cross,

lifted the boy gently, and asked him, 'Which side of Jesus is hot, which side of Jesus is cold?'.

(p. 138)

He prays 'in a mixture of Twi and English', enacting the unities and connections for which he stands, and gives blessing with 'new incense mixed with herbs' (p. 139). He uses traditional herbs 'shown to him by his own father' (p. 140). The boy is healed and Bishop Budu acknowledges Osofo's powers and

> Osofo saw, also without words, that the only way to make his little innovations possible was to have this easy almost totally worldly man anchored there beside him, yes even ahead of him, giving him, Osofo, a weight to pull against, a light against which he tested his dark and inexplicable moods.
>
> (p. 140)

All of this is preparatory to the developments between Adwoa and Kofi. In a dramatic moment, Osofo sees a crowd coming between the trees – Adwoa Adde and Kofi Loww and their whole band of spirits and mortals, including Beni Baidoo. They plead with Osofo, Christ-like, to save them, to take over the spiritual burden of Adwoa, which prevents her from taking her rightful mortal place as Kofi Loww's wife. Beni Baidoo, Accra itself, speaks on behalf of Adwoa, adding to her plea. He explains to Osofo that she 'is an angel' who has saved them, but 'we are now getting in her way, leading her into areas of experience that may even pull her away from him [Kofi]. You, see, if you save us, then you save them!' (p. 217).

Budu tells Adwoa to go away and make her life: 'We will see to your children, your spiritual children. You go and start your earthly children' (p. 219). In the meanwhile, Osofo seems aware that he has inherited the quest, feels that God has shown him the way at last:

> They must see us in procession through the streets of Accra. It has to be a procession of truth! Praise God!
>
> (p. 219)

This triumphal procession of the Church, built as it is on the union of Kofi and Adwoa, has all the overtones of the marriage between the spiritual and the modern that Laing seeks. The march grows 'all around the electric passion of one man: Osofo Ocran, whose huge hands tied the crowd' (p. 221). But then the plot becomes opaque. Policemen appear and buy the crowd off with food. Osofo's flock 'ate itself out of his life'. There was 'even the old catechist himself, taking his badly-fitting false teeth out of his cassock . . . and attacking the food like the rest' (p. 226). Like Jesus, Osofo is betrayed and has to start again. He thinks bitterly about the fickleness and superficiality of Ghanaians:

'C'mon, you can't sneak a look at the heavens like this! You are a Ghanaian . . . all you have to do is to throw a symbol, play a drum, burn the incense . . . then you can touch the infinite!'

(p. 226)

All that will happen is that 'they will always betray you . . . !' (p. 226).

What can this mean in the light of the complex deliberations about the Church and its syncretisms, the suggestion that the solution to Accra's modernization is in this new Africanized Church? Laing himself remains uneasy about this pessimism – the procession might have betrayed him but by the end we are optimistically informed that 'Osofo's new church was growing and growing as he mellowed' (p. 248). Is it growing only to be betrayed again by an untrustworthy populace? The impression is left that ultimately what has been gained is the personal growth of Osofo, as we see the process of his warming and softening.

What is clear is that the lovers – or the new Church – are only partial and ambiguous destinations in the searches of this fragmented narrative. Another solution, perhaps equally ambiguous, is the relationship between the races. This brings us to the witch from London, Sally Soon.

In constructing Adwoa Adde's 'flying crew of back and white sisters' (p. 124), Laing has gone against the tide. His inclusion of the white sisters, and especially of Adwoa's 'friend Sally Soon', is a significant departure from the more predictable and negative depictions of whites:

> She was an English witch sent over on a secret assignment against Ghana, but she had now fallen in love with Ghanaians, and had thus almost neutralized her own powers: the weaker she became the more she became Sally Sooner, the weakest she became the most she became Sally Soonest. She usually travelled the degrees of her surname. But she was now huddling behind the moon, crying over her own contradictions.

(p. 124)

This is in parallel with the liberating loss of supernatural power experienced by Adwoa Adde. Both of them have to lose these powers in order to become fully mortal, in order to achieve full humanity. Adwoa can only experience the joys of love and mothering if she throws off her traditional, inherited powers; Sally can only become a decent person, as opposed to a spy and a racist, if she throws off her colonizing ways, which, in turn, neutralizes her own witchy capacity.

Laing has drawn a complex picture of Sally Soon, Sooner, Soonest, recognizing that it is possible to throw off your background, but that this is not easily done. Sally is lonely and sad and misses her own culture, represented as steak and kidney pudding. She experiences what it is to become invisible because of skin colour:

169

Adwoa saw Sally Soon crying into the aeroplanes; there were hailstones in her handkerchief. She couldn't be seen in the sky for her blondness. Sally ate long-distance steak and kidney pudding. There was colonial history in the stars where she sat. But Adwoa went on, a little impatient to do her work, to brush the trees with her belly.

(p. 130)

The colonial history written in the stars cannot be obliterated by the hailstones she weeps and Adwoa, while being her friend, has different tasks from Sally. But ambiguity begins to surface as Sally becomes a lone figure, distinct from the other white sisters in the crew of witches. Sally has to find her own voice, her own place in the elements, in the sky and the sea. But she is lost in the infinity of the waves whose cyclical movement with the tides she cannot change:

Sally Soon was conducting an entirely technological choir in the heavens, she was losing herself in the minor scales of a fish without a key to the sea. She was the sole singer above the waves she could not turn.

(p. 131)

Reminiscent of the discoveries of Adwoa, Kofi and Osofo, the humanity that Sally finds in Accra seems to amount to a personal discovery, rather than an historical intervention. And again the achievement rests most fully within the personal relationship between the black and white good witches, a relationship which is warm, supportive and humorous, but obviously limited as a solution for the country:

They both laughed the laughter of tipper trucks: it carried all the worry behind them and dumped it in some bola far away. The planets were the dancing hearts of vulnerable witches. Accra could harm the hearts of beings hundreds of feet up in the sky. Accra be sweet-ooooo; only, avoid the history, avoid the gutters.

(p. 134)

Again by using playful language to say the opposite of what he means, Laing is underlining the limits to this friendship that thrives literally in the clouds, far from the filth of poverty and the reality of history. This avoidance, is, of course, another version of the ambiguousness of Laing's attitude to Sally Soon and to the issue of race.

Sally becomes less homesick and more Ghanaian, as kenkey replaces her home-sick yearnings for steak and kidney pudding. This symbolic device suggests her acceptance of a superior culture, in the tradition of negritude. Food imagery is found elsewhere in the novel. Sackey 'was thinking that food spoke through the language of oil in Ghana, oil the okyeame!' Sally, staying for supper, finds the food 'delicious' and when questioned – 'Does this beat British cooking?' – answers 'Of course!' (p. 232). The friendship between Sally and Adwoa is genuine, but, like the other questers that have gone before them, it becomes an end in itself, rather than structurally symbolic of the possibility of alliances across races and continents. It is at the expense of Sally giving up her own background and life almost entirely in the process of changing her political attitudes. She could have confronted her imperialistic history and retained the dignity of her own cultural pleasure in steak and kidney pudding. She tells Professor Sackey:

> 'I intend to settle in Ghana for years, if Adwoa would agree. You see, we flew together . . . O!' 'You what?' asked Sackey with interest. 'We studied together,' Soon corrected herself, blushing, 'Adwoa is my closest friend in this or any other country. I trust so much in her that I would let her choose a whole life for me without prior consultation!'
>
> (p. 233)

While the passionate declaration of friendship is positive, it is also an abdication from Sally's sense of self. Witch turned academic, she has come 'to book a date for an interview on aspects of the Ghanaian intelligentsia'. She is studying for a doctorate on 'Development and the Informed Ghanaian Psyche' (p. 230).

This leads to another area of tension in Laing that we have already touched upon – his attitude to the University and to academic pursuits. Sally turns from being witch to being intellectual and what is given jokingly, but critically, is the academic's urge to self-aggrandizement:

> Adwoa, can you transfer the copyright of your aerial history of Ghana to me? I would love, just *love* to be famous through the people of Ghana!
>
> (p. 134, original emphasis)

This joke hides Laing's mixed feelings and leads us directly to the character who most expresses Laing's ambiguous attitude to scholarly work, Professor Sackey:

> But at the door stood the very blond Sally Soon. England was all finished in her blue eyes . . . the Channel did not toss or cross there . . . for she had been eating enough kenkey. She had lost her powers of witchery, at the same time as Adwoa Adde had lost hers. She felt so vulnerable without Adwoa, but she had to continue her interviews, now that she was normal again.
>
> (p. 230)

While Sackey mocks her for her Britishness and academic naïveté, the portrayal is sympathetic and affectionate and atypical of how white women are represented in African fiction:

> But Sackey had already laughed, and was asking Sally, 'You have, I presume, decided that the Ghanaian psyche exists? As for the 'Informed' I wouldn't bet on it! 'Out of form' more like it, 'out-formed!' Now, young

woman, I must warn you now that I don't give interviews! Certainly not to fresh, young London rabbits.

(p. 230)

While the joking relationship embodies optimism around cross-racial interactions, it does not seriously address the possibility of generating new intellectual knowledge as part of the solution to the quest for rooted change.

If authorial distance from Kofi Loww is achieved by his indecision and his gutter gloom, from Osofo by his harshness, from Sally Soon by her background, then from Sackey it is accomplished by his irascibility, intensity and obsessiveness. His terrible moody anger and bad temper is destroying his marriage – 'Sackey, Professor of Sociology, could not manage the society of his house' (p. 57). We very quickly get to the root of his mission and his fears – he is a restless, powerful and violent man, who is afraid that his brains have deprived him of 'the rural peace of my grandfather' (p. 58). He will seek this rural peace through his opposite, his *alter ego*. Like Loww, who has to find Adwoa, and Osofo, who has to bond with Bishop Budu, so Sackey seeks an embrace with the life of 1/2-Allotey.

Although Sackey is a man of the mind and 1/2-Allotey is a man of the land, close to the earth, they are not simply polarized opposites. Allotey has already been searching for a syncretized relationship between old and new. The portrayal of his character is original in that he is as much at war with parts of himself as the other questers. He is as split as Baidoo, Loww or Sackey, hence his name – '1/2'. In other words, he is no rural stereotype of village yokel in harmony with nature, with the seasons, with the ancient rhythms of land and climate. Quite the opposite. He loves the land and works it, but is also at war with it and hates its conservative hold on his village, which is steeped in archaic customs. He has 'a quarrel with the earth', is having a 'fight with the mother of mud, the earth' (p. 71). Again what is called for is change that transforms the plant but does not destroy the roots of tradition – 'for him there was too much substance, too much continuity in his village' and what he wants to do is to stretch that village existence such that

> after the stretch he hoped there would be balance: a new commitment, together with the roots below the green, the roots still deep there holding the stems.

(p. 71)

Bonded as he is to the land, he resists 'the bulk of ancient barks', the preordained pattern of the seasons, and as a result 'the ancestors shared bits of him with that playfulness that often hovered at the edges of horror and destruction' (p. 72). He has no support at all in the village, least of all from his brother. He 'shocked the elders of Kuse by actually suggesting changes' even in relation to 'the pouring of libation'. His brother's angry stare is described as 'reincarnated' and Allotey feels 'the weight of centuries staring at him' (p. 73). His disgusted brother says:

'So of all the things you can change, with Accra so near, why change what
would turn the ancestors into mad wandering screaming Ghosts? . . . We
don't need your mad changes! We will go at our own speed, you hear!'
The crowd that had gathered was on the verge of dragging Allotey down
and beating him.

(p. 73)

So he decides to leave 'his forest and his clearing to his elder brother' and to
forsake the conservative place. He gets himself another small farm, on 'land of
fewer roots' (p. 73). He goes to the university at Legon because he needed a
market for his fish and his beans, but 'when he realised that some of the
lecturers wanted to study him, he stayed away again' (p. 75). However, he needs
the money so he goes back to the university where he makes the connection
with Professor Sackey, that leads to a tempestuous relationship and a great bond
of affinity, as they attempt to assist each other in their quest for meaning.

Laing, to begin with, has no rural romanticism about what is being sought, a fact
that is initially emphasized:

It brought a smile to 1/2-Allotey's face again to think that at Legon they
thought he was leading an interesting life, a life of 'traditional' searching.
Trees enjoyed him, made fun of him then protected him, but to say that
his life was interesting would have to mean something far easier and far
more answerable than he could see.

(p. 142)

In fact, the lives of neither Sackey nor Allotey are stereotyped or romanticized.
Sackey's life of thought and research torments him, but is his path to understanding. Allotey's body is in his land, quite literally as we will now see, but this
terrorizes and haunts him.

Allotey enlists Sackey's help in understanding a problem he has with his *okro*
farm. The magic in the following description is powerful and highly significant.
The *okro* farm at his village 'was taking over my body'. He

watched the okros grow, and the first one that matured – a fine thing with
a slight bend to it – was the exact copy of my . . . of my thing! The same
thing is happening now above my blue earth.

(p. 78)

So now in the hills of his new land, the exact same farm has magically reappeared 'and it seems to have planted itself alone!' Allotey explains how

it vanishes on certain days, and reappears on others, and brings with it a
blue earth. Yes a blue soil. Professor, don't look at me as if I'm mad! It is

an automatic blue farm in the hills.

(p. 78)

This is modern magic, but written in the paradoxical language typical of riddling. The man, who is attempting to break away from the great, ancient trees, sheltering generations of ancestors that strangle him, finds that his body is being horrifically taken over by the plants. And his struggle is characterized as an inversion of the basic realities of his society. The soil changes places with the sky and turns blue. The *okro*, as replica of his penis, enacts the depth of the land in his being, a fact that makes him dreadfully vulnerable, as evidenced by the use his wife makes of all of this to torment and humiliate him. His escape from the village is not absolute, given that this ghastly blue field of penis-shaped okro has followed him to his new land, although it is not clear what it will do to him there – 'I don't know what it plans to do this year' (p. 78).

The authorial tone is utterly dead-pan and classically magical realist; the author respects the point of view of Allotey and the events he describes have to be accepted by the reader as part of the modified worldview he brings with him into his future – a kind of new supernatural. At the same time, the surreal ludicrousness of the landscape distances the author from the point of view of the character, despite the fact that Allotey is seeking a way of embracing change. Sackey's response is also written in double-speak, where the opposite of what is said is what is meant:

'Now for your problem: there's only one way to beat the earth . . . control it, control it, and control it again!'

The two men went out, and left their laughter uneasily in a corner. 'You are giving me the same old "modern" medicine!' . . . 'But you need the modern, nothing scares away the ghosts and the dwarfs more than the deadness of gadgets and processes . . . you either live fragmented and half yourself, half your heart, or you keep slow, and whole, and die!' Sackey said. 'Well, Professor,' Allotey replied, surprisingly sadly, 'it's a choice I don't accept. There must be a middle way somewhere . . . no matter who or what is inhabiting me, I want to find this balance!'

(pp. 79–80)

Sackey is suggesting, although not believing, that the only way to overcome the menacing power of the land over his body is for Allotey to modernize entirely by way of technology. However, purging the land of the ghosts and the dwarfs, of the magic, of the spirits and ancestors, is to continue to live in a fragmented way – the ultimate defeat for a fiction that yearns for wholeness. You either continue to love the past or you keep up with the present by purging the past. These alternatives are rejected by Allotey – the author's voice – who demands a third way.

Thirds – the third eye, the third leg and now the middle way. Allotey continues the search for a balance that will enable him to experience transformation, while retaining the magic – the sense of wonderment at earth so blue. Here is the kernel of the novel, although we will once again be disappointed as Allotey's discoveries are ultimately reduced to romanticized micro-solutions that are not dissimilar from personal love and messianic salvation. At first, Allotey's rebellion against the stranglehold of the old rural ways is revolutionary; he seeks to remain on the land but on new terms. He asks Sackey whether he is

> angry that I come from a long line of fetish priests, and that I want to make alive my own type of farmer-priest? Sir, how many herbs have you analysed in your long sociological life?
>
> (p. 149)

What do they want from each other? Sackey undertakes a pilgrimage to Allotey's farm to warn him that their little trade agreement might bring him trouble because Sackey, and those close to him, are being victimized by corrupt politicians, particularly Dr Boadi. This is so because Sackey refuses to be drawn into bribery and political graft. Both he and Allotey are brave and honourable men and their refusal to buckle has authorial approval. Allotey's response to Sackey is simple – an unambiguous moral stepping stone in this novel of rapids; 'How can I run away from a friend when others are attacking him? We'll go on as we are!' (p. 148).

While Sackey's code of professional conduct is upright and clear, his quest is opaque. He is uncomfortable when he is outside the city and the university. Before even arriving, he is regretting 'setting out into "this wild nonsense of trees" '. He feels in 'an inappropriate place!', that he is 'swallowed by these valleys!' He feels 'absolutely crowded out, with all these leaves and branches marching up and down'. The hills take up too much space and he hates their 'motionlessness!', concluding resoundingly that:

> I don't want any of this nature worship on the soil of Ghana. I am amazed you've been able to stay up here so long!
>
> (p. 144)

However, quite contradictorily, he says a little further on: 'I have a secret desire to farm, I want the earth to yield to me before I finally yield to it in my death' (p. 148). It is perhaps the struggle to relieve this tension between rejecting and partaking of rural romanticism that makes it so difficult for Laing to enable Allotey to find what he seeks. Allotey wants from Sackey, the sociologist, help in understanding the riddles of the country: 'Professor, help me! I can't understand this country! And that's why I'm in the leaves here!' (p. 149). But in the end Allotey seems to work it out for himself, and his solution is peculiar and limp. Suddenly a voice seems to enter his mind and to tell him to leave the hills immediately and to go back to the village. He is in great crisis, deeply split and turned upside-down, like the inversion of the soil and the sky – 'the hills were revolving' and 'his back had become his front, and his front had almost vanished' and he strides into his beanfield 'frontless and headless, carrying his own head in his hands' (pp. 200, 201). His internal civil war has reached a crisis point. One side wishes simply to succumb to the past and tradition:

> 'Allotey!' he heard a voice shout, 'Allotey, come back to us at Kuse, come back to the earth in the way of your ancestors. Bury your questions!'
>
> (p. 201)

With great effort he literally pulls himself together. Again reminiscent of the man with the mask of glass in *The Satanic Verses*:

> his neck found his head, at last . . . as he touched his father's old talisman. But his body stiffened, for when he wanted to smile, he had to tear his lips apart. And he did smile on and off, for that was the best way to keep his head on.
>
> (p. 201)

However, his shadow still separates itself from his body and moves 'of its own accord' and in a new version of topsy turvy, the sun rises from the west and 'was met by the darkness from the east of his head' (p. 201).

Now there enters 'the black goat with the perfumed beard'. It is a menacing goat; in fact, as Allotey suddenly realizes, it is himself, objectified in an animal, an emanation of the negative, evil side of his spirit. It is the part of him that is moved to surrender. It is the alluring and simultaneously fatal pull of the past and temptation to abandon his quest and his mission. Destroying his own internalized doubts is the cathartic resolution of the agony:

> A sudden understanding rose in 1/2-Allotey's head; his head rolled back with the heat of the last answer: with a scream, he stuck the dagger lightly into his own left arm. He watched the goat intently. And from it came an enormous bleat: 'Leave me alone, leave me alone. We are Kuse. You can't destroy a whole village. Who told you the secret, the great secret?' Allotey raised the knife and plunged it into his arm again. The goat fell down, and was rolling downhill. He chased it, stabbing it several times in the beard . . . where the blood and the perfume met . . . and in the left side. He dragged it back up the hill, throwing it with a curse into the fire. The words burned: 'Allotey, you have killed us, you have won your peace. Come back to Kuse!'
>
> (pp. 202–3)

The point where the blood and the perfume meet is the most powerful and potent spot. It is redolent with meaning in a cultural moment focused on borders; in fiction structured around syncretisms the mingling of blood and perfume is highly suggestive. The goat's perfume carries vapours of decadent pungence and the spilling of blood carries the sweet odour of victory. Within this perplexing and poetic image comes the crossover for Allotey, as he appears to be liberated from his doubts. However, the solution of how to syncretize the old and new still remains abstract and oblique. It is given to us metaphorically:

> He saw how to burst through the propriety of ancient ways, then boldly
> sew the bits together again in different patterns.
>
> (p. 203)

An element of surrender pervades this solution, given that the rural romanticism Allotey earlier eschewed seems to be the cloth from which the bits are cut. The metaphor is even the old patriarchal one, linking earth to woman's body. The different patterns are contained 'within the womb of the earth, Assase Yaa':

> The earth was the basis, the earth was still the boss . . . even when you
> flew, you left your footmarks on it first, even if you would land on a
> different slope. He felt complete peace standing beside his herbs, and
> thinking: you would invent the impossible, you would make your life
> move fast; but you would always come back to the earth.
>
> (p. 203)

Added on to this anti-climax is another. Much like the betrayal of Osofo by his people, when he returns Allotey finds that all the villagers are there simply to see him 'driven away in disgrace'. His answer to them is both bizarre and mundane:

> So, I now understand why you are all here. You want to see me driven
> away in disgrace! Well, let me tell you: I will soon start a drug store here.
> No one is going to drive me away anywhere again!
>
> (p. 210)

The drug store, presumably, will stock the herbs he knows so well, the knowledge of which he has inherited from the ancestors, and will make money and take Allotey into the modern world and economy, which he already knows about through his trade in fish and beans. This all makes 'the lines of his life clearer' (p. 211) but does not, I think, bear the weight of the enormity of the problems and existential crises leading up to it.

Allotey, then, has found his solution in the womb of the earth and looks forward to passing this on to Professor Sackey 'in spite of any scorn that his friend would pour on it' (p. 203). Again this leaves open the nature of Sackey's resolution of his own philosophical difficulties. Adwoa may have found Kofi and Osofo bonded with Budu, but Sackey, and with him the purpose and usefulness of intellectual work, remains ambiguous in the narrative point of view. This is very apparent when we return to the interviews that Sackey grants Sally Soon. After all Allotey's revelations, we would expect Sackey to have had something more clear and wise to say. Instead he appears to become embroiled in contorted academic postures and needs to be calmed down by his son. He pontificates about the Ghanaian psyche such that it is unclear as to whether he is simply being parodied. At the same time, he does make the very important and cynical observation about his fellow country-people that links up with the march that we saw disintegrate at the sight of the food bribe:

> But seriously, how many would choose a soul rather than a Benz, if given the choice? The god of your shrine asks you: would you, Owura so-and-so, like a perfect soul or a brand new super-dupe Mercedes Benz 450 automatic? No doubt, all Ghanaians . . . almost all . . . would prefer to postpone their souls, and rush after the Benzes!
>
> (p. 238)

This does not take us much further than we were before. Sackey still lacks the concept of a boundary between 'the factual' and the supernatural. What continues to endure is the paradox, given that the source of endurance and survival is also the stumbling block for Ghanaians:

> the Ghanaian is indestructible because he has got formed in his head, deep ravines of opposites; if he feels too hot with one being or with one presence, he just hops onto another, thousands of miles away if necessary. And there's something I find very odd: there is no territory between the supernatural, and the purely factual . . . you get the factual explanations that do not fit the superfactual situations, and you get supernatural answers that fly off at a tangent to the merely factual; and all in the usual polemical stew, with no insight at all for any salt of any worth!
>
> (p. 240)

Again and again there is the chorus that there must be change but that tradition must be retained – 'our soil can grow completely new things here too' but 'the weight of our past seems to be crushing the present . . . and the future will not be born!' And again – 'You keep the drum, you keep the paraphernalia, but all relationships with them must change, must move' (p. 241). Given the plot insubstantialities and anti-climaxes, we have to assume that it is the writer himself who is stuck in the groove of a damaged tune.

One thing, however, that Laing is unambiguous about is political corruption, and the barometer of a character's narrative reliability is the extent to which that person actively and visibly defies that corruption. This is shown in the conflict between Sackey and Dr Boadi in relation to the modern Nigerian state; this is the familiar site to which all writers, almost without exception, return, and which bonds them in their search for solutions to national questions and crises.

Like Sackey, Dr Boadi is an academic – 'One of the fine sights of Accra' is that of 'Dr Boadi wearing his whaaaaat silver jacket, and lecturing with exaggerated gestures to students of Regional Planning' (p. 81). Like Okri, Laing avoids stereotypical polarities, and his critique of Dr Boadi is not a version of anti-intellectualism. Laing respects the genuine intellectual quester like Professor Sackey, contrasting him with the likes of Dr Boadi:

> As soon as Dr Boadi got his doctorate, he dropped his research and his reading, just like the pot that one threw away after finishing a hasty stew in it. Soon after, his body grew and his skin and eyes took on that carefully scrubbed, oiled look that certain chiefs and businessmen had acquired to bluff through life with . . . a flowering of ebony that was skin jazz and that outshone the even brighter colours they wore.
>
> (p. 83)

But Boadi is not to be dismissed simply. When he asks Sackey – 'Professor, who is more Ghanaian, you or me?' (p. 91), Sackey cannot answer, but merely storms out of the house. Kojo Laing's answer is clear. They are both Ghanaian. Boadi is not an aberration, and Beni Baidoo begs and receives from Boadi as much as from anyone.

If the marketplace is the crossroads traversed by the living and the dead, the spirit and the mortal, who exchange easy and profitable transactions, then the women who dominate trade are the sensitive point at which tradition and change approach each other. Throughout the fiction we have been assessing, gender has been the Achilles heel tripping up progressive writers. Who are the questing women in this novel and what is the role of women for the questing men?

The white woman, Sally Soon, had been a witch and loses her witchiness in rejecting colonialism and racism, thereby gaining her humanity. Adwoa Adde was a witch, who loses her powers in becoming fully womanly in through her relationship with Kofi Loww; the man of the land, Allotey, suspects that all his women are witches and have cursed him. Mothers abandon their children and bare their buttocks, cursing their men; there are women without husbands, strong and independent, who drive men mad with desire. Again we have an author who fears the power of women to emasculate and destroy men.

It is true that, in the case of Adwoa and Kofi, relations between man and woman provide the model for that unity between opposites that Laing seeks. This is reinforced by Laing's hope of the possibility for unity across the races, in the friendships that Sally Soon forges with Adwoa, Professor Sackey and his son. However this is not given unambiguously. Sally Soon and Adwoa Adde are reformed witches and therefore carry the potential to regain their unnatural and fearful powers. It is also true that Laing does not, in general, script his women as symbolic of the nation or of the race, in the manner of both Cheney-Coker and Okri. Laing, more than the others, holds passionately that the search for wholeness involves change, cultural and social interaction between Europe and Africa.

EsiMay and Sally Soon are women who travel across circumscribed national boundaries. But Sally Soon and Adwoa Adde carry the overtones of unnatural power. This stereotyped tendency to portray women as witches is evident again in the portrayal of the three generations of powerful women without men: Araba Fynn, her mother Ewurofua, and grandmother, Nana Esi.

In one sense it is clear that these women are Laing's ideal, not only of Ghanaian womanhood, but of the synchronisms that he seeks for the nation as a whole. Araba Fynn, for example, combines many contrasting influences and qualities as part of the depth of her allure:

> When she spoke English in the aeroplanes, her Mfantse touched it, and her Ga touched her Mfantse; so that in this world of languages touching, her mouth became complex yet beautiful, even when pressed shut in anger: at those who suggested that her money – not as much as they thought – was inherited. She made her money fresh, her mother made it fresh, and her grandmother made it with fresh fish. The three of them still lived together in the family house at Asylum Down, living like three flowers of different seasons.
>
> (p. 94)

She will become the heroic 'woman of the aeroplanes' of the next novel, a wonderful mosaic of modern woman and traditional market mamie. Women have always had economic independence and these women are no different – traders in cloth, fish, clothes, crafts and yam. But they are also sophisticated and part of the modern money economy, something Laing clearly admires. Araba knows many languages including English, and is in touch with the latest technology, including aeroplanes. But on the other hand these same women retain the overtones of witches – a threesome of powerful women without men resounding with Shakespearean foreboding, with the power to curse and humiliate men. Araba's suitor, John Quartey, provokes her with his claim to have 'a powerful hoof between his legs', but Araba pulverizes him with 'an expression of triumphant mirth', 'slight turn of the hips', and with 'we wish the hoof would gallop away to other pastures, fast!' (p. 98). Even on first meeting Pol, who will play a big part in her life, Araba 'almost laughed' at him because he is 'so thin and defenceless, so earnest'. The poor man is about 'to walk back out' but Araba

> grabbed his hand playfully and said, 'Little messengers do not leave without unloading their message. Come in . . . sir!' The last word burst with the force of sarcasm in it.
>
> (p. 99)

Laing tries to mitigate this with the emphasis on the mother's softness and the daughter's 'strange touch of mercy' (p. 97), but this is mercy shown to men who have been brought to their knees. Words repeatedly occurring in relation to these women are 'ridicule', 'laughter' usually at the antics of men, 'irony' and the like. Nana Esi refers to Pol as 'that mouse' (p. 103), and Araba herself warns him that she is 'too big for you, I am a woman of miles and miles that men can't reach' (p. 110). It is not surprising that Pol suddenly wonders 'what he was doing out of his depth' in the home of 'the Mfantse matriarches' (p. 171). They project the image of larger than life goddesses – some of the fisher-dealers who worked with Nana Esi think of her as a matriarchal Christ, believing 'that she could sometimes walk on the sea!' (p. 194).

All three women are attracted to weak men. Is it because there are no strong men in Ghana, or is it Laing's fear of what men lose when women like these emancipate themselves? Does the strengthening of the women result in the weakening of the men? This is what seems to be implied. They seem both to hamper and inspire questing, but are not, I think, questers themselves. They seem complete in their circle and do not have the restlessness which spurs the men. Only Sally and Adwoa are questers in their own right – and what they find are the conventional female stereotypes of home and family. They exhibit the quite traditional qualities of womanliness, as defined by Laing – the urge to mother and nurture, to bond and cook – and enable the connections to be made across the mortal and supernatural, and across the races.

Sally and Adwoa's traditional virtues are reinforced by the novel in its criticism of women who do not conform in this way. A recurrent theme in Laing's fiction is how the women let the family down by abandoning them, by having a destructively ambiguous attitude to mothering. The most powerful example is of Kofi Loww's mother, who leaves his father for another man and does not take the young Kofi with her, and who curses them both when she loosens the cloth around her waist and 'pulled her underwear down, and completely bared her buttocks' (p. 4). Again this is no grotesque body, bared in feminist protest against the patriarchy. Here is an evil witch, bent on the annihilation of the men:

> The hearts of father and son became one, turned and turned in their one desperate chest. In Erzuah's head Maame had become fire, had become a witch with her powers turned in evil towards his destruction. He rushed across the compound with his batakari flying, and covered the tear-stained face of his son. 'Kofi don't look, don't look. She's mad, she's mad in the buttocks!' Maame still followed Erzuah backwards, in her abomination.
>
> (p. 4)

The novel opens with this scene of the abandonment of the husband and son and colours Kofi's search and helps to account for his dispersal of focus, having been split apart in this manner at a tender age. Similarly, there is the bad and vicious wife of 1/2-Allotey who insults him sexually in public, in as humiliating and dramatic a way as Kofi's mother had done:

> And there to my amazement was Mayo standing at the head of the crowd of women mainly. She was talking fast, as usual, and had picked an okro

181

– o my god, I thought, it was *the* okro – which everyone was closely examining. They had not yet seen me. 'You are right, Mayo, he is big for nothing! As soon as you see this okro you can tell that its owner's copy is a useless thing . . . it may excite you as a woman, but there's nothing under it!' 'Yes yes yes,' laughed another, 'so all his boldness that some of us secretly admire is nothing but a power that cannot rise, Ooooooo! Poor Mayo, all these years without action.'

(p. 78)

The theme of betrayal, by the crowd or the women, of the ideals of the heroic characters, undercuts the men's and novel's own searches and values and accounts for much of the ambivalence that clouds the authorial point of view.

Less judgementally given, but also problematic, is Professor Sackey's wife, Sofi, who leaves her husband and who is pleased that he will take the children when he is on sabbatical. While Sofi is far more sympathetically portrayed, provoked by Sackey's obsessiveness and irascibility, we are nonetheless left with the poignant picture of the motherless Kwame, the child who stays with his father, and has to cook for him and run the household, and who in a lovely twist of the stereotype, is mothered by the white woman, Sally Soon, who becomes very fond of him. A further example of the domestic strife that provides a metaphor for splitting, isolation and polarity, is that of Dr Boadi's wife:

For Boadi, for practical purposes, politics and economics were the same ampesi. But his wife was lost somewhere in between, for the years of bending to his will had finally bent her angles away from the 180 degrees of his life. She now seemed to know only half of his cloth, half his head, and half his heart . . . the other half of which, on the slimmest of rents, belonged to other women.

(p. 83)

Here the portrayal is entirely sympathetic to the wife, but this marriage intersects with the critique of Boadi and the social and political corruption of the country. It is also notable that this wife does not leave her family, no matter how repulsive her husband is. The suspicion that Laing is critical of women who leave, no matter what the provocation, is confirmed by the change in the perception of Kofi's mother only once she returns to her family and in much more acceptable motherly terms helps to get Kofi out of jail and fights to get to know and to claim her grandson. Given that Laing is sympathetic to women who are oppressed and harangued by their husbands, this simultaneous judgement against those who act against their oppression by leaving, results once again in ambivalence in his position.

As with the other roads and their destinations, gender relations provide a very partial and contradictory way forward. Women are powerful and embody the potential for transformation of the society and their men. But that very power makes them threatening and also potentially destructive. Women threaten to become, or revert to being, witches with vicious tongues and cold hearts whose power to humiliate and emasculate men and hamper their questing is as great as their ability to enhance it. While women are present and important in the novel, Laing seems to be advocating quite traditional roles for them, rather than championing the transformation that the novel so desperately seeks in other areas. Women tend to have relationships with the major questers, rather than being searchers and discoverers in their own right.

This brings us to the relationship between Araba Fynn and Okay Pol. Pol takes over Beni Baidoo's role as the soul of modern Accra. Beni himself warns Pol 'that if he Pol were not careful, he would turn into an old man like Baidoo himself'. Pol, meanwhile

> would abuse Baidoo for bathing infrequently, and drag the old man in an absent-minded way to the nearest tap and soak him . . . and then he would regret it as the Beni shivered as hard as the abuse leaving his old mouth.
>
> (p. 165)

Cleanliness battles the verbal abuse of the old trickster, whose power of language weakens Pol and makes him regret his sanitizing efforts. However, Beni's time is up. When he gets sick and dies, it is Pol who 'used to go for medicine for Beni, and discovered the old man's body' (p. 246). It is suggested that Beni Baidoo 'never recovered from the betrayal of Osofo at the Freedom Arch' (p. 246); the old city dies with Beni, as betrayed as Osofo, and the new Ghana has to be searched for with a modern quester, one who can handle a camera and a motorbike, which he significantly buys with 'the sad arrears Boadi had paid him' (p. 243). The underbelly of degradation is never far from the surface.

Trickster, then, has turned photographer and binds the city's people, goats and buildings together, not with jokes, riddles and inexplicable comings and goings, but with photographs. He cuts a strange, only half believable figure – 'and as he went around Accra, he was said to look like a cross between a policeman and a scampering squirrel, all fezzed, FEZZED' (p. 243). Pol is an enigmatic figure of a man, physically and intrinsically. He is very tall, but very thin – both big and small. He appears to be very weak, innocent and indecisive, but this seems to be the source of his strength. As Araba Fynn perceives him, he looks 'ridiculous' but constantly frees himself from this ridicule (p. 100). Intriguingly, it appears that being split is here positive, enabling the problem parts to hive off from the strengths – 'paradoxically, it was this way he had of abandoning or forgetting parts of himself – even important parts, such as a basic uncertainty in his aims' – that enabled him to be bold. 'When you forgot the limits of your strength, nothing stopped you from trying to lift an elephant' (p. 101).

Pol can only begin to develop as someone of substance in the novel after he resigns his job as Dr Boadi's lackey and errand boy. The break from Boadi is inspired by Kofi Loww's steadfastness and necessitated by the relationship with Araba, which Boadi threatens. However, and this point is critical, Araba's primary function seems to be to deepen and strengthen Pol, as much with love as with sorrow, to enable him to fulfil a much broader function and destiny than a personal relationship. Pol, for example, is described as 'tall and open' but his thinness is the metaphorical fact that 'his heart was yet narrow, it needed space for some of his own suffering' (p. 246). That suffering will in part follow on giving Araba Fynn up because 'the secret for both of them now was to burst through someone else's life' (p. 249).

By the end of the novel, in other words, Laing appears to be insisting upon bigger quests and broader, more structural, solutions than salvation by way of personal relationships, such as that between Kofi Loww and Adwoa Adde, or between the latter and Sally Soon. Pol has a destiny to fulfil for Accra, for Ghana, in the new role of photographer, reminiscent of Okri's *The Famished Road*. 'Photographers could make money, but he had to move a woman out of his head first' (p. 247). In fact, quite early on, Araba prophetically says to Pol:

> Don't speak of love yet, innocent people like you shouldn't speak of it. You have to do something first, you have to find some of that new Ghana you speak of!
>
> (p. 112)

Quietly, almost surreptitiously, Pol metamorphoses into the central quester. Pol 'would sometimes forget the Kojo in his name because he was confused' and when he does so, it is Beni Baidoo, his forefather, his roots in the past, who 'would shout it back against his surname, with the Kojo shaking' (p. 165). Nor can it be by chance that Kojo also happens to be the name of the author. Pol may still be confused, but we await his emergence from the chrysalis of his love for Araba Fynn. This occurs in the final chapter of the novel.

Pol is a man of many disparate parts. He is a bit of Boadi on his motorbike, with overtones of the decadence of the corrupt police; a bit of the Muslim North embodied in his fez, a bit of the land in his aura of scampering squirrel. He too battles, as did Kofi Loww and Adwoa Adde before him, 'to offer drink to himself, to the gods, and to the ancestors', which is 'getting more and more difficult' to do (p. 243). Like Adwoa, 'he flew through Accra' (p. 243) and like her, he seeks to purge the badness out of himself:

> Pol was now looking for a contract with a dog, to bark the thieves and witches of his soul away. Or perhaps he could ride his bike into the sky, for he had earned a little goodness there.
>
> (p. 245)

The answer to what he, and his namesake Laing, are searching for, as the solution to the sweet country, still seems to lie in the ability to bring together the culture's disparate mosaic of parts. A whole lot of mixing has already happened and Laing warns that 'you would not want to divide this . . . city into tribal groups' because 'it had devoured all the different tribes long ago'. Even the mosques were absorbed and incorporated, built as they were 'on swallowed mouths' (p. 245), the mouths of the city that had gobbled up all the different tribes. All of this mosaic Pol tires himself out with filming, day and also night – 'the evening came in a flash, and that was what he had to use for more pictures from his camera' (p. 247). On his exhausted way home,

> all the lights showed the different angles at which the rain cut this city into bits; into jig-saw puzzles, in restrained African razzle-dazzle; and through the beams, there was yellow rain and white rain, but most of the vast stretches of wall where the concentrated light could not reach were shadows, were black rain.
>
> (p. 247)

The camera's flash, the city lights, gleaming through the rain, highlight the natural weather embracing technology of film and electricity. What is lit up is both difference and unity as Africa's mix of white, black and yellow people are both cut up bits of a puzzle, but also a puzzle that fits together into a pattern. That pattern is African razzle-dazzle, authorial ironic distancing *par excellence*. The seriousness of the combinations and interactions, the relationships and cultures is undercut by the fickleness, the love of partying, the betrayal by the temptation of a feast that sent the procession amok and killed Beni Baidoo's hope. The razzle dazzle turns the writer with a dream of change into an ironic elitist, steeling himself for the next betrayal by the dancing masses. Pol 'tried and tried, but he could not heal the whole of Kaneshie' (p. 248). The messianic is itself undercut by the refusal to entirely abandon the society as a structural whole and to retreat into the quiet internal spaces of individualized solutions – 'if Pol had a yet unfinished sunsum, a yet unfinished soul, it was because Accra was the same' (p. 249).

The tension between hope and disillusionment, between finding the sweet country and abandoning the search, is written into the narrative, as we have now come to expect, in the language of riddle. The very last paragraph of the novel is densely symbolic and profoundly difficult to understand, so that we as readers end the book with our own search for its meaning:

> A few months ago, it was the harmattan – with its strange and suspended dusts and lights – that he shivered and stared meanings through, with ancestors breathing their ancestry all over the islands of city grass; and that was when the black skin took on an astonishing number of colours. After all, there was some hope under this haha sky . . . where people usually laughed their troubles away though the fund of laughter was finishing.
>
> (p. 249)

Again, then, we have nature, but the opposite of rain, the dry and dusty harmattan, the breath of the ancestors, breathing colour into being black, into the richness of the black past, of tradition. This is not the image of many races and cultures, but of the black race, shining in the rainbow glory of its past and traditions, bringing hope, hope which our ambivalent writer immediately dispels with frustration at the frivolity of the Ghanaian psyche, as Professor Sackey would call it. The haha sky echoes the laughter of the reckless people, who do not confront their problems seriously, and ominously, face the crisis of when the supply of laughter runs out.

The arch of the beautiful rainbow is also the shape of the ironically named 'Freedom' Arch, the shameful site of the betrayal of the messiah on the part of the people. The rainbow becomes a fleeting moment, an illusion of hope. Pol realizes that:

> if he were not careful, the rainbow would continue to dress him up again and again, to give his skin beauty, only while the colours were there, only while they lasted so sad . . .. For after all, if you placed a thousand pairs of trousers empty and upright in ascending angels as blue as the sky, all through the city up to the Freedom Arch, random legs, with their kenkey perfume, would eventually force their flesh into the thousand pairs – hanging like angels or witches – and then swagger in their easy symbols, as if something had at last been achieved. And what was that something? After all, the purveyors of the Arch were typical and waakyiful, had betrayed all time before and after it, were worth just one tutu-ni . . . , tomorrow was Okay Pol snoring through his own ideas, chacha by national chacha . . . .
>
> (p. 249) [Here ends the novel.]

Empty clothes filled with swaggering flesh full of waakyi, of rice and beans, the food with which the policeman bribe the crowds at Freedom Arch. The rainbow, lending the skin such beauty, is only as lasting as the already evaporating drops of rain that make prisms from the light. The silliness, the lack of commitment, renders irrelevant whether the people are good or bad, angels or witches; they are all worth just one prostitute – 'tutu-ni' [sic!] Even Pol, with all his ideas, is sleeping through them, snoring to the rhythm of the national chacha, a pun on the European dance and the local word for gambling. The haha sky, the razzmatazz, razzle-dazzle of a dancing, gambling, laughing, sleeping nation that betrays its messiahs, its Osofos, Pols, writers, Kojo Laing himself.

However, the harmattan supplements the rain image earlier of the many colours, of blacks, whites and browns. All the different seasons make up the year, and the rainbow coming out with the dry wind, links quite directly to the rain. The association is that the culture is a rainbow of races, and within the black majority, there is a bright and colourful past, purveyed through the ancestors. The extended metaphor of colour and light, modifies the pessimism of the grey, gloom of the gutters and open sewers.

Metaphors, poetic images, perplexing puzzles, inversions and riddles, linguistic manoeuvres and paradoxical hula hoops are, in fact, themselves the colour and light of creativity. It is not surprising that it is with language itself that Laing comforts himself and projects a more unambiguous direction for the future.

> The problem that I wished to explore in the book was that we do have a long oral history in literature and in other areas of endeavour, but when it comes to the written word, and when it comes to encapsulating the modern world that Ghanaians live in at present, I think that what our intellectuals are doing is twofold: firstly, taking over information, usually second-hand, from other cultures; and, secondly, thinking that the effort used to master this information is an end in itself. But I think that the rub comes when you assess the fact that there's a gap between written history and oral history. That gap should be the source of an original thrust in ideas, in invention, in creation, but it's a gap that's not being made use of, it's not a source of originality.[10]

Throughout this chapter we have seen the enormous energy, and also the difficulty, posed by Laing's enigmatic language. He speaks in deeply symbolic poetry, in riddle and paradox, with a forked tongue that inverts reality and often says the opposite of what it means. What we have also seen is Laing's difficulty in identifying a solution to the problems of modern Ghana through the choices and relationships of his characters. A link between the highly stylized, symbolic language of the novel and this authorial distancing from the people who populate it has been made by Quayson. He describes the gulf between characters and the omniscient, third person narrator, whose descriptions are surrealistic and which have 'little impact on the ways in which the characters perceive setting or the events in which they are involved'. Thus the 'poetic quality of the writing' is specifically 'aimed at disrupting the reading process' thereby drawing attention to 'the narrative representation as problematic'. Laing is, in other words, deliberately disrupting a seamless, realistic style in order to enact the tower of babel cacophony of his culturally mixed and unevenly developed society. However, the characters themselves have only a 'limited perspective' on this. The gap between their perception, that of ordinary people inserted into their everyday reality, and the perception of the magical realist, with his awareness of the disparities and hybrid peculiarities, results in the ironic nature of the authorial point of view, which is by now familiar to us. In Laing, however, it takes a particular form, given the role played by his language and style:

> In relation to characterization, the characters are themselves presented to us as partaking in the surreal exchanges of the narrative's discourse, but this is not evident to them. Because of this dichotomy between how the narrator describes things and how the characters perceive their world,

the narrative institutes a subtle level of irony into the unfolding of events.[11]

If the characters cannot provide solutions to the problem of change with roots in the past, then it is language itself that becomes the major player and actively attempts to demonstrate, through the means of the novel itself, how this synthesis might be achieved. Throughout the analysis of the novel we have seen the crucial role of language in, for example, the depiction of Beni Baidoo, Kofi Loww and others.

Asked about his radical experimentation with the novel form, with language, images and technique, Laing replied: 'Read my long poems and you will see where my novel form(s) come(s) from. Also dragging two continents along creates its own "newness" '.[12] Syncretized newness that binds the splits together is, then, a hard, 'dragging' process. Loww's cumbersome feet are thus 'clumsy' and 'broad'. Laing's poetry in its very form enacts the splits, the gulfs, the spaces, that are the pages on which his fiction is written. For example, 'Funeral in Accra':

Over there where the cross   quarters the sun
The sick bishop rents   his knees to heaven
Praying in minor keys   for a simple death,
As drums detonate in incense,   clocks are anachronistic![13]

The middle space is inscribed on the poem as the Christian cross splits the African sun in four, tearing the bishop apart as his prayers for unity and joining are unanswered. He is blown apart by the African cultural power of the drums and history is not forged in a new time – the clocks have no place.

In other poems, such as 'More Hope   More Dust', the reader is split as two voices speak simultaneously, voices that are separate and also interwoven:

Three Ghanaians have taped goats' backs, they block the dung

I

By the dust-blown koobi stands a chief on one leg,

AM

taped goats grunt and move their dust onto the flat fish,

OBSESSED[14]

This poem enacts more dust than hope. The image of the taped up goats, painfully blocked up beasts of the African rural way of life, is a powerful one. The past is not harmoniously transformed and integrated into the present. The chief, traditional power holder, does not have Loww's three legs; he too, like the goats, is crippled with one leg only. The poet, whose first person has to be read between the lines, is obsessed with the touch of the rural animals, but also shamed by a 'forgotten future', a future that is built on an obliteration of the past. Many of Laing's poems, in their form and their content, enact this painful, most often hopeless, struggle to span the gulf. Is the fiction more successful?

In a paper entitled 'Search Sweet Country and the Language of Authentic Being', M.E. Kropp Dakubu demonstrates how language serves this healing purpose and cuts through the surrealistic, ironically distanced and cynical voice of its author:

> the solution is paradoxically seen to lie in the transformation of language. That is, the creation of an authentic language is advanced as a necessary condition of change. Beni Baidoo's failure is the failure of the country, and must be reversed. To accomplish this, the country must abandon empty and half-understood slogans.[15]

Kropp Dakubu explains that Laing attempts a synthesis between

> the techniques and traditions associated with the Concrete Poetry movement (especially as practiced in Scotland during the 1960s) and with the techniques of figurative language characteristic of formal language use in Akan.[16]

In his next novel, Laing will centre the theme precisely on the interaction between fictional towns in Ghana and in Scotland. Here he is attempting to effect this global exchange linguistically. Not only globally, but nationally, Laing incorporates, juggles and juxtaposes language from Ga, Akan, English and slang.[17]

> Although Laing's purpose is not to make a sociolinguistic statement, he in effect does just that: his Accra is polyglot and multi-ethnic almost to the point of being non-ethnic. Its language is the mixed language of a nation-in-the-making, not the language of any single group, traditional or otherwise.[18]

Kropp Dakubu does acknowledge Laing's own recognition that change needs to come about within the framework of the past:

> In *Search Sweet Country*, Accra is multifaceted and multivoiced, like the country that it represents. This quality of the city is reflected and displayed in names and local vocabulary; however, in a novel that is preoccupied with using the past to get beyond the past, 'traditional Ga' cannot be displaced or ignored.[19]

The point is that the new language that Laing speaks – a language which wishes to integrate old and new, modern and traditional, magic and science – attempts to do so in the style of the traditional rhetoric of the oral tradition. To this extent, he shares a cultural national project with other African writers in general, and fellow Ghanaians like Ama Ata Aidoo and Ayi Kwei Armah in particular. These writers are battling to undo the psychological damage wrought by a cultural takeover that declared that there was nothing of cultural value in Africa, prior to colonialism.

For example, there are deep reverberations with the observations made by Richard Priebe about the rhetorical style of a 'traditional' Northern Ghanaian myth, that of Bagre, a secret society of the Lo Dagaa, and the writing of Laing:

> Operating here is a meaningful play between sense and nonsense. Through a process of symbolic inversion the lie becomes truth and foolishness becomes wisdom that results in the restructuring of the neophyte's worldview.[20]

There are also overtones of Henry Louis Gates Jr's proposal of the existence of a black tradition of language play that cuts across Africa and the Americas, that 'the black tradition is double-voiced'.[21] Within this tradition, who else is Beni Baidoo if not a variant of Gates's trickster figure, the 'signifying monkey'? At one point in the novel, Beni attempts to mediate between Professor Sackey and 1/2-Allotey. He tricks Sackey into waiting for him by stealing his car keys. As Gates says, 'as tricksters they are mediators, and their mediations are tricks'.[22] The Signifying Monkey, American version of the West African trickster, is 'he who dwells at the margins of discourse, ever punning, ever troping, ever embodying the ambiguities of language'.[23]

There is, then, a black intellectual drive to re-claim oral tradition as a strategy to combat Western culture. I think that Laing has both aligned himself with the type of argument put forward by Gates, but also distanced himself from it. As Kropp Dakubu points out, Laing refuses boundaries and divisions, such as between poetry and prose, those within or between Ghanaian languages, between Ghanaian languages and English, and even between variants of English:

> Laing considers himself free to exploit words of any source, from Hausa to Scottish. This deliberate catholicity of language recalls his earlier quarrel with false and destructive divisions, as manifested in one of the long poems:
>
> > But I do not know how long I am condemned to speak in old distinctions and new distinctions. ('Resurrection')[24]

Laing walks a narrow line between an inward looking cultural nationalism and an attempt at transformation that nonetheless holds onto its roots. He is aware of the pitfalls and states categorically:

> I have a strong link with my tribe, but I treat that purely as something which is ontologically equal to any other experience.[25]

But if there is a gap between Laing and his characters there is also one between Laing and his readers. His aim was to make his medium his message and to construct a new poetic language in the spirit of the oral tradition, with influences from English and a number of other languages spoken in Ghana. He has, however, created a language that is somewhat impenetrable to all but a few intellectuals, who are themselves challenged to decipher the messages of his riddles.

Search Sweet Country is best summed up, perhaps, by the words of Kofi Loww's father, Erzuah, speaking of what he has learnt from his son. His words stand for change and inversion as the elder prepares to bow to the wisdom of the younger. Erzuah realizes the importance of the balance between opposites, about the old and the new, about change:

> We must keep that wide wide experience that finds almost nothing odd, now . . . we accept the old, we move with cripples, we rub shoulders with the mad. Even some taboos must stay, or at least their spirit must stay, not necessarily each real one. Then we must continue to modernise faster . . . look at an old man like me talking about something like modernizing. But there's been so much change already in my life that I want more and more! Change everything except the roots that do the changing! And in change we must look both backwards and forwards.

> (p. 189)

This is no clear and optimistic message; only the urge to connect, to syncretize, is unambiguous. The substance of what is connected, what is born, remains opaque and anti-climactic, notwithstanding images of light and rainbows. Kojo Laing struggles to express his insistence that a syncretism with the past, free from foreign contamination, must nonetheless take place; the ancestors must leave their traces in the roots that have to survive transformation.

It is very unclear how foreign elements are to be avoided in the huge changes that Laing foresees and welcomes. The hint is that modern magic, in the form of technology, must be harnessed to intrinsic realities within the society – technology as opposed to foreign ideology. Okay Pol replaces both Adowa and Baidoo and with his camera, and his humanity restored by love and by abandoning corruption, he will photograph, salvage and record, and thereby save the heterogeneous aspects of the African city.

It is appropriate, then, to conclude discussion of this novel by pausing a moment on this image of the photographer. I suggested in relation to Okri's *The Famished Road* that photography is defined by its ambivalences and that in some ways photography could be seen as the paradigm of the postmodern. However, we also saw that Okri lowered the ironic postmodern gaze of photography and that the postmodern gave way to the postcolonial as the photographs played an increasingly political role. This links to a point made by Fredric Jameson that can be applied to *Search Sweet Country*, and serves as a bridge to Laing's next novel. Jameson suggests that photography reveals 'an unsuspected Utopian vocation'[26] in its wish to redeem physical reality, to reveal a 'visible world which was also . . . the latter's unmasking'. Pol's role as photographer potentially captures the rainbow's moment and redeems it, even if in reality the beauty is fleeting. The utopian impulse becomes the fictional structure in Laing's next novel, *Woman of the Aeroplanes*.

Woman of the Aeroplanes is situated within the relationship of two towns – Tukwan in Ghana and Levensvale in Scotland. Both towns reject the corruption and racism of their respective countries at large, but only because their inhabitants are, in a sense, not human – they are immortal, much like the gods. The novel charts the process by which, through their fertile interaction, the inhabitants of both towns become mortal and enter historical, rather than eternal, time. This new-found mortality and humanity carries enormous consequences which the novel explores. Like Adwoa, who loses her supernatural powers as she becomes mortal, Tukwan cannot simply remain a utopia, outside of time, space and reality. Significantly, Tukwan seems able to enter time only by way of a global embrace with another town in a different country and culture, far from Africa. But as the novel progresses, its author appears to fear that traditional roots may be strangled in this embrace.

To explore the issues that preoccupy him, Laing takes his country back and forwards in historical time. As Rohrberger points out, 'It is perhaps 1965 but three other watches register different years. Thus, time is both free and absurdly controlled'.[27] One of the crucial time registers is, in fact, the point of independence from Britain, the same moment as Okri's *Famished Road*. On this brink of historical change, the question of the new nation pervades the book, expressed in Laing's notion of the relationship between utopia, magic, technology and politics. I will trace these themes by visiting Laing's fictional sites – the Tukwan with which the novel begins, Levensvale to which the inhabitants of Tukwan journey, the intermediate space between the two towns on the first return journey, the second trip to Levensvale and eventually the Tukwan to which the Ghanaians return and with which the novel ends.

I choose to focus on fictional sites because the relationship between space and utopia is organic. Like the sacred grove of the gods, utopias are holy, freed from the shackles of historical time and place. Jameson suggests that 'in all these varied Utopian visions as they have emerged from the sixties' we can see 'the transformation of social relations and political institutions' projected 'onto the vision of place and landscape'.[28] While utopianism may threaten history, as mythical spaces overwhelm concrete historical time, it can also provide the energy and vision for social change:

> Spatialization, then, whatever it may take away in the capacity to think time and History, also opens a door onto a whole new domain for libidinal investment of the Utopian and even the protopolitical type.[29]

The energy released in the imaginings of ideal places, freed from the stresses and cruelty of reality, is paradoxically a 'protopolitics'. If utopianism character-ized the sixties – the flower children's peace sign a weapon against Vietnam – then flower power has undergone a rehabilitation in the era of postmodernism and postcolonialism. Utopia has become an imagined alternative to racist imperialism and its corrupt legacies, a device for postcolonial writers who refuse simply to abandon the political. What Jameson says about surrealism surely applies to magical realism:

> The Utopian vocation of surrealism lies in its attempt to endow the object world of a damaged and broken industrial society with the mystery and the depth, the 'magical' qualities . . . of an Unconscious that seems to speak and vibrate through those things.[30]

The 'object world' of the magical realist is not so much a damaged industri-alism; it is rather the uneven transportation of this late twentieth century industrialization to the Third World. And so in Jameson's *Postmodernism, or the Cultural Logic of Late Capitalism*, the use of the term 'utopia' has been transformed from a cynical critique of idealism to the embrace of a moral and at least quasi-political stand:

> Utopian representations knew an extraordinary revival in the 1960s; if postmodernism is the substitute for the sixties and the compensation for their political failure, the question of Utopia would seem to be a crucial test of what is left of our capacity to imagine change at all.[31]

Thus '*Utopian*, in First World postmodernism, has become a powerful (left) political word rather than its opposite'.[32] 'The language of Utopia' has almost become a secret 'code word for the systematic transformation of contemporary society'.[33] However, Jameson appropriately retains questions regarding the concrete politics of the utopias under question, and so must we in examining Laing's novel. Jameson 'wants to insist very strongly on the necessity of the rein-vention of the Utopian vision in any contemporary politics' but 'it must be acknowledged that Utopian visions are not yet themselves a politics'.[34]

Raymond Williams, in his 'Utopia and Science Fiction', is very positive about the political possibilities of utopia, for reasons similar to Jameson's. For Williams, the most progressive, and therefore political, utopias emphasize human agency, '*the willed transformation*, in which a new kind of life has been achieved by human effort'.[35] In this context, technological progress, which is necessary and desirable, is not merely mechanical, not a 'new energy source, or some industrial resource of that kind', but heralds 'new *social machinery*'.[36] Technology must be driven by, and serve the ends of, social transformation. In short, the 'central sense' of the meaning of utopia is that 'of a transformed social life of the future'.[37] What is crucial for Williams, and what distinguishes revolutionary from reformist utopia, is that the new society must be 'fought for', must lie 'at the far end of generations of struggle and of fierce and destructive conflict':

> This is not the perspective of reformism, which in spirit, in its evasion of fundamental conflicts and sticking points, is much nearer the older utopian mode. It is the perspective of revolution – not only the armed struggle but the long and uneven development of new social relations and human feelings. That they have been developed, that the long and diffi-cult enterprise has succeeded, is crucial; it is the transition from dream to vision.[38]

There is, however, more to the politics than the struggle, and I am not sure whether Williams has not used the concept of revolutionary politics prematurely. What has to be examined quite closely is the nature of the society that emerges and which the struggle has achieved. In his critique of a late-nineteenth-century utopian fiction, Williams himself describes different kinds of utopian outcomes when he explains, regarding a novel that he is examining, that it is neither 'a socialist or an anarchist utopia'. It is 'a projection of the idealized social attitudes of an aristocracy'.[39] Another way of characterizing this aristocratic solution is that of the benevolent elite, the messianic mode, to which we have seen that some writers are vulnerable. We will see, furthermore, that Laing is ultimately not immune from recourse to this mode in his utopian Tukwan.

To sum up the characteristics of politically enlightened utopias, we can say that they link social transformation to technological change, that social agency domi-nates technological developments, and that they are born in struggle. But what are the historical and social conditions that tend to give rise to utopian impulses? For Jameson they include Vietnam and the rampant materialism and loss of hope of late capitalism. What are the parallels within the African context and how do these relate to magical realism?

Williams's description of the sixties helps us to answer that question. Williams writes of a generation of Western radicals who enjoyed a 'privileged affluence' that enabled them to know 'from inside' just how 'lying and corrupt' the rich and powerful of their society were. They were inspired to learn and imagine 'the condition of the excluded others'. This resulted in 'the move to drop out and join the excluded', to become materially poorer and thereby gain 'a clear moral advantage'.[40]

This has enormous resonance with the position of African writer-intellectuals. They see the abuse of power by some African leaders and privileged classes, also with an insider's eye, given their access to these classes through their own privileges and status. They too empathize with the impoverished masses, from whom, however, those privileges separate them. They therefore construct solutions in the form of utopias, which may be anchored in mythical pasts and secured from foreign Others by strong moats and walls; or perhaps they are utopias steeped in magic, where borders are entry points which embrace change. There is Soyinka's Aiyero in *Season of Anomy*, Achebe's Abazon in *Anthills of the Savannah*, or Kojo

Laing's Tukwan and Levensvale in *Woman of the Aeroplanes*. The nature of Laing's utopia will become clearer shortly. In the meanwhile, it is true to say that Williams' portrayal of the sixties utopianism echoes Laing's journeys from Ghana to Scotland and back, and is an inspirational beginning to my own investigation of the utopias of *Woman of the Aeroplanes*:

> Indeed it is probably only to such a utopia that those who have known affluence and known with it social injustice and moral corruption can be summoned. It is not the last journey. In particular it is not the journey which all those still subject to extreme exploitation, to avoidable poverty and disease, will imagine themselves making: a transformed this-world, of course with all the imagined and undertaken and fought-for modes of transformation. But it is where, within a capitalist dominance, and within the crisis of power and affluence which is also the crisis of war and waste, the utopian impulse now warily, self-questioningly, and setting its own limits, renews itself.[41]

Laing himself, in answer to my question as to whether Tukwan is a utopia, a dream, or an embodiment of an alternative politics, insists that

> Tukwan is realistically possible in terms of cross-cultural interchange. In terms of hope it is a realisable utopia.[42]

His novel opens with a puzzling inversion which confuses the reader with regard to the fiction's moral centre of authoritativeness. An omniscient third person narrator declares that 'Kwame Atta was the bad twin' (p. 1).[43] We discover, however, that this is radically untrue, or at least that 'bad' has to be re-defined to incorporate his scientific brilliance, adventurousness, courage and flair. The clue to the disjuncture between the word and its meaning lies in the fact that this character immediately becomes more authoritative than the omniscient narrator – Kwame Atta takes over the narration and helpfully and truthfully introduces us to Tukwan and its major inhabitants.

If the power of omniscience is called into question in this way, so is the genre boundary between novel, play and poem. The novel opens dramatically, as if presented on the stage, creating the sense of performance, or ritual. We become aware from the start that the events we are about to witness are cathartic, portentous moments in history. Kwame Atta is addressing a stranger to Tukwan, a man who is a spy on behalf of the authorities outside Tukwan. He is supposed to pull down a building, to damage Tukwan. This man, however, is also unpredictable, given that he is attracted to Tukwan and its ways and may well defy his bosses. Is he is a hero or a sneak? We are immediately in the realm of the labyrinthine point of view that has characterized all the magical novels we have discussed so far, and of the language games that are distinctive to Laing's fiction in particular.

We are also introduced to the subversiveness and originality of Tukwan, a town that has been banished by the centre of power, by Kumasi:

Have you no pity for this *strange*

strange

town that has been banished here by Kumasi? Have you ever heard of a whole town being banished, land, goats, elephants, ducks, lakes, latrines and lawyers?

(p. 1)

Many layers of strangeness are stacked upon each other. A play within a novel written in the language of poetry blurs genre distinctions along with narrative reliability. Toilets named along with elephants and lawyers are part of the fabric of the town's democracies and reinforce African traditions that refuse the border between animate and inanimate beings.

African traditions may be invoked in this way, but Laing emphasizes Tukwan's inclusive heterogeneity. It is not inhabited by one community – 'its ancestors had moved and stolen people from region to region' (p. 8). Surrounded in mist, invisible to the corrupt power centre of Kumasi, Tukwan is a unique space. The town is not only politically and ideologically distanced from Kumasi, it is also spiritually distanced from the world in that it is inhabited by immortals, by the ancestors themselves. Not, however, by stern and conservative ancestors, like those who plagued Allotey with their punitive, rigid customs; these are more like Allotey's father, who encouraged him to be different and to change the past while incorporating it. To qualify to live in Tukwan, a person must be different, non-conformist – 'everybody had to have one element of originality before he or she could continue to stay in the town' (p. 11).

At the outset of the novel, then, to be different is not to be human. But processes are already in action to change this, change that rests with four main actors. There is, first, the so-called bad twin, Kwame Atta, who is the scientist with inventive abilities. Without the technological advances that characterize utopia, the town cannot enter history. There are ninety-nine houses in Tukwan. With the hundredth house, the nature of the town will be transformed and it is Atta's inventiveness that will enable this to happen:

the houses grew into forties fifties sixties seventies eighties and nineties, but created a dam for history when they go stuck at ninety-nine. It was a shame that the pressure to break this history rested with the bad twin.

(p. 8)

Even more than the scientific inventions that will enable the hundredth house to materialize, the birth of mortality in the town seems to rely on Pokuaa, second pillar, town leader and creative entrepreneur. She has been trading with a town in Scotland called Levensvale, and has procured the two aeroplanes from this town that provide the central motif and title of the novel:

> The planes were owned in trust for the town by Pokuaa: she bought them, and had arranged for the town to buy them back by exporting palm-nuts and cassava to a sister town in the UK. She was a kind of buy-and-sell woman. (p. 6)

In order to appreciate the image of these aeroplanes, we must recall that the novel is set in part in the 1950s, when the style and substance of aeroplanes were like great birds, making their ponderous way through Africa. The proposed journey in these planes to Scotland, the choice of travellers from the town and the establishment of ties with Levensvale, are crucial to the town's gaining of its humanity. This journey must be blessed by religion, the responsibility of the third major player, Kofi Senya, 'the spiritual shrinemaster' of Tukwan (p. 2). Senya approves of religious syncretisms arranged by the pastor, Korner Mensah, who is highly reminiscent of Osofo of the previous novel:

> we have churchified the shrine and we have enshrined the church . . .
> Kofi Senya has agreed to this temporary union to help make the coming journey easier for the soul.
>
> (p. 15)

If Kofi Senya is the custodian of the shrine, the other, the 'good', twin, Kwaku de Babo, is the custodian of language, the town historian and our fourth major actor. The 'large Minutes Book of the town' rest on his strong knees – 'Babo was the chief secretary to the town, and he wrote everything with his pen and his chalk' (p. 3). He is an historian who recognizes the mediating power of language, the relative autonomy of text. If Kofi Senya is not afraid of newness entering his shrine, then Kwaku de Babo revels in his use of, and power over, English. When Korner Mensah asks de Babo 'What will happen to the English language when we arrive among the natives?' given that, as Mensah puts it, he has appointed himself 'as the custodian of the English language', de Babo replies that

> you are not going to get me to be defensive about a foreign language that I knew before I could walk.
>
> (p. 62)

Kwame Atta, de Babo, Kofi Senya and Pokuaa may be the main actors in terms of Laing's priorities, but they are not the only bosses of the town. Even in this utopia, unsavoury ambitions peep beneath the surface in the form of Lawyer Tay and the cola farmer, Moro. There is also hierarchy; issues such as who will travel and what rituals will be performed are not decided democratically, despite an insistence that 'every animal, human, thing, or presence was to be treated as equal in being, in principle, to everything else' (p. 58). Nevertheless, Tukwan is a true paradise, a beautiful place whose natural splendour is appreciated by its foremost scientist:

> Kwame Atta walked on assessing the avenues with their ice-plant hedges. Very few of the streets were tarred, but they were neat and could be touched. The pawpaw trees had shortened by the dwarf banana shoots, so that both trees held their fruit at the same height . . . but below the skin-ringed neck of Tukwan's chief inventor; the tiny pink-flowered stomach herbs, the milk-juice rabbit leaves, the blackberry thorns, the velvet-leaved cough bush all grew in lines of deliberately controlled weed; circular rows of wild crabgrass tightened the streets and met the yellow-flowering milk bushes, daring the planners of the streets to continue to use weeds creatively.
>
> (p. 42)

Creativity and destruction, the wild and the tamed, environmental planning and nature are all held in balance. This is Laing's ideal of the unity and beauty of opposites working in harmony. But it is achieved only out of time and space. Tukwan is a border space, about to make the crossing. Time is erratic, changing with the impending journey and the promise of the eternal becoming historical. In true magical realist fashion, this historical reality mediates the fantasies and narrative experimentation:

> the same year somewhere in the 1950s had shown itself for the last three weeks, during which the sun had been saved from the sweat of running in and out of different decades in the same week . . . and it sometimes became so bad that two different houses experienced two different parts of the same breathless calendar; and when Tuesday finally caught up with Wednesday, it was a different year altogether. Time was slowing down before the journey, was jumping about less.
>
> (p. 49)

Some year 'in the 1950s', as we have seen, is not random. Ghana just prior to independence was on the threshold of entering a new historical dimension, as is Tukwan on the brink of its pioneering travels. It can no longer stand aloof from time and mortality as Ghana enters self-rule.

Even its magic is 'intermediate', bonded with scientific skills and technological advancement. The aeroplanes are wonders of modern technology but, with their bizarre trailers, they are endowed with magical powers. Earlier, I suggested that the intermediate magic of this novel stands as an image for the third, the interstitial space in which Laing's fiction plays out its dramas. In this vein, Tukwan is the 'land of the recycled immortals . . . where to be immortal is not to cease to be

human; where magic is made in bits but you don't become superhuman making it'
(p. 154).

The first stage in the journey to mortality is to travel to Levensvale:

> when Levensvale found that it had a magical link with Tukwan in central
> Ghana, it had to increase the production and consumption of Scotch
> broth . . . in order to build the courage not only to live beyond its means,
> but to live beyond itself, ampa.
>
> (p. 63)

Both Tukwan and Levensvale are doubly oppressed and peripheralized.
Tukwan is persecuted from Kumasi, whose corruption is itself a product of its
colonial heritage. Levensvale too has been banished from the economic centre and
finds itself out of time in that it is peripheral to Clydebank, which within the
British economic context, is itself marginalized. Like Tukwan, Levensvale has to
transform itself. This it has to do in two ways. First, it has to become human, like
Sally Soon of the last novel, in the sense of purging itself of racism and colonizing
practices. Secondly, it has to become economically viable and independent. Both
of these aspects – the material and the spiritual – are complementary, like the two
towns, the twin brothers and the twin aeroplanes:

> So both towns wanted a prosperity of the pocket to go with the reincar-
> nating prosperity of the soul, as if to remain immortal took too long, and
> that money would shorten things a bit.
>
> (p. 92)

Like lovers, the towns have to entwine and embrace, syncretize and mix:

> Now since a snore in Levensvale could originate in Tukwan, and since an
> elbow in Tukwan could have its counterpart in Levensvale, everybody
> was free to be and do what he or she liked. There was a blast of freedom
> from freely-mixed bodies and worlds, ampa.
>
> (p. 86)

Food and cooking, which we have recognized as such an important signifier for
cultural nationalism, are also integrated and 'Nana Kasa would tell Nana Bontox
whenever he demanded home food . . . "But I love the food here!"' (p. 87). And
when the Scottish Shebelda later cooked, her cooking 'included abenkwan, gari
foto, dried snails, crabs from Aba Yaa, and fufu' (p. 110).

But 'there was yet no talk of the business deal' (p. 87). Before the crucial trade
deals and commercial transactions, the spiritual embrace has to be emotionally
deepened. Two concrete images represent this deepening. The first is religious.
This religious fusion is not easily achieved. Korner Mensah has symbolically to

struggle to climb the resisting magical hill, which is one of those inanimate objects endowed with life, as in African tradition, and of which Laing is so fond. This hill is capable of opposing and finally, through his persistence, allowing him 'to put round it a huge necklace of polished pine cones', recalling Christ's crown of thorns, as a kind of shrine. He then tops it with the Presby church tower – the recognizable syncretized Afro-Christianity so dear to Laing. The other image of spiritual union between the towns, is the 'cross cultural corset' (p. 121). Sala, Lawyer Tay's son, finds a discarded corset, which he passes on to his new found Scottish friend, Donald with the red hair and the freckles. He says 'gravely' to the corseted Donald:

> Never forget when you grow up that you played with a boy called Sala, with a different skin, and with as much life and play in this skin as you have in yours, never forget!

> (p. 89)

As a prelude to the trade about to happen between their towns, the boys seal their friendship and 'exchanged one guava one plum, and swore to meet later' (p. 89). Sala undergoes the same ritual with Mackie's son, Ian, who he urges never to forget 'that however different my food or my worship is, [note what is chosen] we are the same!' (p. 89).

All this is the context for, and the prelude to, 'the tug-of-war of business talk' (p. 90). The negotiations around equitable and fair trade agreements, covering many pages, is itself a utopian fantasy. It is imagined in contrast to the underdevelopment thesis, which exposes how Europe enriches itself at the expense of Third World countries. This is an exchange between equals, who nonetheless recognize historical inequalities, which demand reparations and redress to be built into their trade agreements, into how to arrive at 'a just exchange rate' (p. 93). In other words, both towns may well have been doubly oppressed, but the European Levensvale is nonetheless still perceived as having been part of the colonizing power of Britain.

While the Scots have to pay one percent of net profits for 'historical sins', Pokuaa insists that a quarter per cent should come off those reparations because of the guilt suffered by 'those of us here . . . for what some of our ancestors did to the slaves so-called of Africa' (p. 94). The two towns will enrich each other spiritually and materially and break old historical patterns, while remembering and acknowledging those realities. At this point, a telegram arrives from Moro back in Tukwan, requesting that de Babo invent a 'stupidity machine' because, in their absence, the town's inhabitants have become out of control and require this scientifically magical machine to keep them in line. This precipitates the journey back to Tukwan to deliver the machine and to find out what is happening.

Again there is the typical inversion, the paradox and riddle. Just as the 'bad' twin is not bad, so the 'stupidity' machine is not stupid. Its naming, however, distances it ironically from the author's moral and authoritative omniscience. De

Babo constructs a machine which develops a life and intelligence of its own. It exposes the truth about individuals, both the players in the plot and the political players in the country. It exposes some hard realities about Korner Mensah's vulnerabilities, as well as those of Mackie and Pokuaa herself. In the familiar mode of cynicism about party politics and political leaders, it insists that Nkrumah and Busia were identical in the violence they inflicted on the people:

> And then there were Kwame Nkrumah and Kofi Busia engaged in a furious waltz over Tukwan . . . but forgetting that it was the people's heads they were dancing on: squashed heads, bleeding heads, swollen heads, bruised heads, kwashiorkor heads and totally crushed brains. The basket was overheating in its binding metal, but the mad history coming out of its entrails refused to stop.
>
> (p. 128)

Disillusionment with the new nation threatens the fragile connections. Reminiscent of Okri's virtually indistinguishable Parties of the Rich or the Poor, Laing equates Busia and Nkrumah as equally murderous and culpable. In this context, and just prior to the publication of *Woman of the Aeroplanes*, Laing has himself described how:

> Living in Ghana I catch myself saying that I'm not 'interested' in politics. The true position is that I am only interested in politics for specific reasons: in relation to literature; in relation to specific issues that crop up in my own life and in the lives of others; and as a 'waiting game' over the modern political history of Ghana, manifested as deep psychological resentment of power and translating this resentment into the desire to witness the demise of that power as exercised by successive regimes. Let them all die; I have seen this need to 'outlast' regimes to be widespread. And who can blame us? The power holders, whether before, during or after colonialism, have displayed a massive blindness in their own ridiculous postures.[43]

This mad history, bringing the stupidity machine almost to burn-out, renders the efforts of Tukwan fragile and vulnerable. This vulnerability expresses the difficulties these writers experience in their hatred of their successive dictators and their inability to construct political solutions beyond utopian dreams and individualized human relationships. Ultimately, the utopian dream cannot withstand the demands of the nation state, as we shall see, increasingly as the novel plays itself out. The syncretisms with Levensvale fly in the face of the menace of Kumasi and the mad politicians, who threaten carelessly to dance over and trample the town. In this situation border spaces are dangerous points of entry for the enemy. In a profound reversal of Laing's drive to break down divisions and borders, the national boundary has to be safeguarded against the invasion of corrupt power.

201

The urge towards openness and cross-cultural celebration is countered by the terror of enemy invasion and from here onwards the novel fights a losing battle to placate both urges.

On their journey home the Tukwanians enter an African terrain unmistakably reminiscent of the bush invoked by Amos Tutuola, with all its labyrinthine, surrealistic terrors. Their aeroplane, willfully and of its own volition, lands where there is

> a forest bordered by the vast desert and in between was a tiny natural tarmac, the size of which tested its landing ingenuity.
>
> (p. 140)

The plane makes two such stops along the way. Both places are populated by strange and unsavoury characters, who threaten the travellers' safe arrival back in Tukwan. The first place turns out to be a time zone, the future. A 'wizened brown old man' with 'a high threatening voice', who himself stands 'with one foot in the forest and one foot in the desert' along with 'several similar old men, brown, black and white',

> rushed onto the travellers and tied them with steel nets. There was a strange and overpowering urge not to resist: Mackie had a gun, but could not use it.
>
> (p. 141)

Caught in a magical iron labyrinth, brought to this place by the insubordination of the anthropomorphic plane, the travellers find themselves in the future, a bleak place where technology has run rampant, and the corrupt political leaders of all races have united to inhibit progress. The Tukwanians are saved, significantly, by their historian, by the keeper of time, who is able to smash the net. He interrogates their captors as to the time of day, the day, month and year of the calendar and establishes that they are in the future. The future can only be safeguarded by way of historical understanding and conception of time. Babo questions the old man:

> And you know what happens to those that break the march of time by stealing events in advance, do you not, old man?

The old man does indeed know the answer and replies

> Yes the desert advances against the forest, and all our luck would be destroyed in advance.
>
> (p. 142)

They are freed and take off, only to have the unrepentant aeroplane decide to land again. Once more they are in what is for them the future, although the reader can recognize it as the current crisis of politics in Africa. They land in a totalitarian state, a composite of many African countries, ruled cruelly and despotically by a power-mad king. They first encounter a grasscutter-cum-bush animal, with one silver and one gold eye, who comes 'from several countries in golden Africa' (p. 144). This creature warns them about the king, who 'has ears to hear everything that is said in his countries' (p. 145). The grasscutter takes them to a football match, symbolic of life's struggles, where the opposing teams are contrasting political tendencies which – by now predictably, like the Party of the Rich or of the Poor, like Nkrumah or Busia – amount to exactly the same thing. Both are inept and are killed by the cruel king for his sport. This time they are saved by their resistance to despotism – they derive energy from publicly insulting the king, calling him a rat and a monster. Their parting advice to the people of that place is that they too should resist and kill the king 'and start anew!' (p. 146).

This Tutuolan interspace between the two towns, peopled by menacing and supernatural creatures, narrated in circles of endless, winding and repetitive threats and dangers, stands, I think, for the gulf between the two towns, character-izing the hazards of the embrace across cultures and continents. A sense of history and a commitment to resisting totalitarian politics may have rescued the travellers, but this zone has been full of 'terrors' and Babo, his pen ominously suspended in that limbo of the journey, asks when 'the peace of Tukwan will be reached' (p. 146). Their glimpse into a possible future has shaken the Tukwanians and when they do reach that haven of home, they will build their fortifications against invaders. But simultaneously, a powerful image critical of boundaries is built into this Tutuolan interspace. This is described in Laing's inimitable satirical style. The travellers are warned by the weird grasscutter that

> before you can come to the football match you must cross a gorge of goats that guard the king against strangers like yourselves. Now these goats that love imported jelly are dangerous: they have small ladders tied to their backs, and when they bleat, the bleats climb the ladders which amplify them to dangerous decibels against the enemy.
>
> (p. 145)

The language once again enacts the sentiment; there are no distinctions between the life force of goats, ladders and even bleats. The corruption in the gorge of watchgoats – the boundary – is equated with the excesses of the king.

Nevertheless, the lesson in Tutuola's world of myth, of the consequences of change and of the free flow of traffic, has been well taken. This is apparent on arrival in Tukwan where the town is under siege and its boundaries have to be fortified. Kumasi is threatening that 'this time when we find your land, we will not banish you; we will crush you' (p. 154). And the stupidity machine warns them 'to check the maze around the town' because the inhabitants had not sufficiently strengthened the borders and fortifications protecting it from attack. They had not had 'the creative stupidity' to 'make it impregnable' (p. 155). In securing the town

Babo checks the string he had threaded through the hills to lower them, but 'rats had eaten it', causing 'a small haemorrhage of small rocks through the holes made for the string' (p. 163). The hills must be secured with new string to prevent the loss of blood foretold by the haemorrhage of rock. In the process of fortifying their border maze the Tukwanians capture two Kumasi spies. One of them, in classic intertextual style, is called Koomson; the same name as Laing's fellow countryman Ayi Kwei Armah gave to his greedy political villain in *The Beautyful Ones Are Not Yet Born*.

The creation of a border safeguards the town, freeing the travellers to return to Levensvale. Along with its syncretisms and welded newness, the narrative structure from here on increasingly splits open and finds solutions to its conflicts by constructing spatial separations between what is permissible in Tukwan and in Levensvale. But at the same time, neither Tukwan nor Levensvale can achieve their humanity or their material well-being without the other. Tukwan alone is only half a utopia. As in *Search Sweet Country*, images of twinning dominate the novel and supplement images of enclosure and capture; humanity, it appears, can only be achieved by way of the creative and enriching embrace of other cultures, races and nations.

This is a position, however, that the novel finds it increasingly difficult to sustain. The paradox lies in the fact that the space that is being so jealously guarded is the ability to mix and cross races, countries and cultures. Eventually, paradox begins to crack and become contradiction. The border zones, once fertile spaces, become areas of vulnerability that must be securely guarded from invasion. But before this transition is completed, and in order to understand fully what needs to happen in Tukwan, a final journey to Levensvale has to be undertaken, where a conference is to be held.

Levensvale's 'Conference of the humanity' celebrates the depth of the cultural syncretisms already achieved. There is the religion of the 'new Necklace Church' (p. 190) and lunch includes 'Brussels sprouts, yam chips and keta-schoolboys in shitoh', as listed by Jock, who surprises everyone with his graduation 'beyond fish and chips' (p. 191). It is announced at the Conference, moreover, that 'profits from our joint businesses so far amount to more than one million pounds each town' (p. 194). In the midst of all this harmony, sweetness and light, however, what emerges at the Conference is Kofi Senya's urgency, 'an agitation that was not customary', to return to Tukwan. He wishes to return to 'the shrine at Tukwan', where the changes need to be sanctified. Interestingly, for the first time a kind of spiritual hierarchy between the two towns is expressed, which is that 'any other problem that arises here must be solved from Tukwan' (p. 197).

Laing is here focusing on two issues. There is, first, the old question and ultimate goal – how to have change and newness, without losing one's roots? The second issue is that of technology and the social relations giving rise to it and which are mediated by it, as the aeroplanes zoom back and forth and take unilateral decisions, and as the stupidity machine gives advice and knows more about history and the novel's characters than they do about each other. The technological inventions are crucial to the whole process of transformation. They come from both lands, ensuring that the false polarity – technology as Western and human relations as African – is sundered. The aeroplanes may well be part of the trade from Scotland, but they are in Tukwan from the very outset and Pokuaa, the central character, the 'woman of the aeroplanes', has power over them. The planes themselves, with their trailers, are steeped in the magical, along with lakes that can be rolled back, magical ducks and elephants and the marvellous stupidity machine itself. In other words, this novel questions the polarity between magic and science in a way reminiscent of Marquez's *One Hundred Years of Solitude*.

Laing's technology is magical and the magical inventions are scientific – and both are governed by the spirits. However, what is increasingly lost is that critical cutting edge between belief in the magic and ironic distance from it and from the characters that espouse it. I suggested in Chapter 2 that it is within this crucial and fertile tension that magical realism is born. In other words, reminiscent of Syl Cheney-Coker's myth of the bloodline of strong Malaguetans, Laing ultimately deals with his dilemmas and tensions by way of a group of heroic, positive leaders, like Pokuaa, the woman of the aeroplanes herself, and the priestly Kofi Senya. While Laing's tongue-in-cheek satirical surrealism tended to mask this lack of ironic distancing, there is an increasingly strong and central authoritative and morally unambiguous voice at the core of the novel's narrative structure. It is this voice that will harness the magic, the science and the global interactions and keep them on the tightrope of the novel's political and ideological aspirations, which are increasingly linked to the national project, which, by definition, is situated locally in Tukwan, and at the expense of the global embrace.

To see how this develops, we must go back to Levensvale and Kofi Senya, who is insisting on the urgent need to return to Tukwan. Kwame Atta attempts to calm Kofi Senya with assurances that Tukwan is fine because 'the stupidity machine is there shaping things' (p. 197). Senya, however, 'declared flatly' that 'some of the soul' that he had given this machine 'has to be renewed' (p. 197). Laing, like Raymond Williams, recognizes that the technology has to be subordinated to human struggles. However, what Senya is insisting on is that this grounding of science has to take place in the shrine at Tukwan. This is Laing's answer to the question of how to have change that is rooted in the past. Atta is stung by all of this:

> Now what is Papa Senya saying? Is he saying that anything I invent, he must give some soul to? Now why should he do this without telling me? Is he telling me that there is a dimension to my science that I do not know? So the soul is getting finished in the stupidity machine indeed! I would like to see the mechanics and the electronics finishing too! Memmaaaaeeeii! they now want to pollute my science!
>
> (pp. 197–8)

Senya, speaking 'with an authority that was definite and final' insists that he is 'not reducing' his science, but 'making it longer and stronger in time' (p. 198). There is no ambiguity in the narrative point of view here. Senya speaks with an authority that is emphasized and underlined. Any invention

> had to have parts that were highly perishable, so that the renewal of these parts led to the addition of some soul, some vulnerability before the intimidating neutrality of your own invention.
>
> (p. 198)

He rejects the 'vast and mindless energy' of science and

> it was in articulating these truths that Senya became passionate *and author-itative*, his wiry frame looking like hundreds of thousands of restrained diamonds.
>
> (p. 198; my emphasis)

We have established that it is enlightened to limit the autonomous power of scientific invention by way of human intervention. However, the human intervention that is proposed here is the traditional shrinemaster, priest and custodian of the people's well-being, who is carrying the whole weight of the social relations and the social struggle necessary to bring about change. This elite solution increasingly characterizes the nature of Tukwan and the novel's authoritative voice.

The concept invoked by Laing is that of a necessary new 'orthodoxy'. This orthodoxy could be called the moral centre that emerges in the novel's narrative point of view. The intimation that ultimately the novel's point of view is not as oblique as one at first might imagine was there in the bogus confusion of calling the wise machine and the clever twin stupid and bad respectively. Here words simply mean their opposite, rather than carrying opaque and ambiguous perspectives.

> The secret was this: once a town had created the new, it had to allow the new to create value and principle by enforcing its own orthodoxy. And this new orthodoxy became only a framework over which all the ordinary everyday living passed.
>
> (p. 173)

There is a hasty return to Tukwan, which is indeed now under dire threat of invasion from its enemies. There is an air of chaos and violation of the utopia – 'the weeds, expertly mixed with the tamed flowers, had now overgrown their borders, there was no order to their roots in the avenues' (p. 209). The town is in ugly, untidy disarray, contrasting with the beautiful harmony of opposites in balance which hitherto characterized it. Mortality has already made its appearance – 'there had begun a relentless morality: when the flies died, they didn't rise again' (p. 213). This is a critical transitional phase where change and metamorphosis are in progress, but as yet unborn. It is the gulf that Soyinka looks down in terror, breathlessly awaiting Ogun's saving leap. For Laing too these border moments have become dangerous and terrifying:

> you had to ask what exactly were the gods and the ancestors doing: What was the essence of giving *cruel images for the transitional phase* between the immortal and the mortal? Cruel: for a whole morning, any man who wanted to shave had to move his jaws up and down against a stationary blade; and women who were bathing had to rub themselves against the soap on the bath floor. And try as they could people could not use their hands to eat; they had to put their mouths to the food direct, and this was for a whole day.
>
> (p. 215: my emphasis)

There is still the ironic distancing from the terror, given how bizarre and anti-climactic the examples of the cruelty in fact are. This relates to Laing's real commitment to change and the growth that follows on attaining mortal status. However, the moment of change remains unstable and vulnerable. The terror lies, of course, as it did in the last novel, in the possibility that radical change, which is desirable, carries the risk of sweeping away the spiritual roots and cultural fortifi-cations of the whole society. And so Kofi Senya sets about constructing an orthodoxy to enable the new to operate within an older framework, 'to create value and principle' and to govern and organize 'all the ordinary everyday living' (p. 173). When Kofi Senya lit his pipe what comes out 'with the smoke' is 'the orthodoxy of the new'. And so he summonses Babo, the man who keeps the histor-ical record, to document the changes within the new Law:

> Senya called Babo from the hills to bring his chalk and write what was both a tragedy and a triumph: change, *change that should be living the new way with the old spirit.* . . . The town was being tidied up again, and yet he felt that the real war with the Kumasi people, and perhaps even with Accra, had not yet started.
>
> (p. 214: my emphasis)

What is highly significant is that, with these historical changes and the entry of modernity and mortality, once again the power of magic begins to wane and give way to the rational: 'magic was becoming small steps in rational processes, wrote Babo' (p. 214). Magic might give way to the rational, but in its place, science has to be pinned down to the shrine. So Zolozolo, Senya's assistant in the shrine

> had been so sobered by the stupidity machine's powers that he truly started to work hard under Kofi Senya the shrinemaster. . . . Everyone woke up to a surprise from Zolozolo one morning: he had made terrazzo on the shrine floor, and had transferred the invention room to a fine hut at the back, in which would live the stupidity machine.
>
> (p. 217)

Like the loss of witchy power that Adwoa and Sally Soon experienced in *Search Sweet Country*, the magical has to be replaced by a new spirituality into which science is inserted and subjugated.

The 'real war', the onslaught of the sick nation in the making that still threatens, requires further social and spiritual fortifications and these are achieved by reorganizing the town into a new elite leadership, with overtones of hereditary power and our old foe of essentialized female reproduction, as metaphor for social rejuvenation. In fact, superior beings like Senya himself and the priestess figure of Pokuaa have not entirely lost their immortality – Senya 'laughed at Pokuaa preparing her grave, for he knew she was still immortal, and could thus eat in peace with her jaw over the centuries'. This is so because she is 'in the vanguard of the spirit, as he was' (p. 217). What this means is that

> he was the culmination of the transient, with the eternity of truth in one eye, and the lie of mortality in the other eye . . . you Senya with the sparkling eyes with the vulture reflected in them, you Senya with the huge frown that made waves on the constant tides of skin on the forehead.
>
> (p. 217)

History will, after all, be only very partially embraced as the universality of the mythical dimension of gods and their messianic saving powers are retrieved. The all-seeing Senya, man-god, larger-than-life, does not see with the third eye that perceives history and magic, politics and pleasure. Laing, whose authority Senya carries, sees here with the eye of myth, of the universality of past wisdom, of the role of exceptional gods and healers, who being in the spirit of the vanguard, are above ordinary mortals. Ultimately, roots are not endangered because the changes become quite superficial. Without a doubt, the global embrace with Levensvale is highly significant and atypical in African fiction. But ultimately the borders are hazardous and the future lies in the nation – at the shrine in Tukwan.

How does this relate to the politics of utopia – of a 'socialist or an anarchist utopia', as opposed to 'the idealized social attitudes of an aristocracy'?[44] In my view the novel degenerates into a patriarchal and aristocratic ideal at an alarming rate. It turns out that Senya is the biological father of Pokuaa, implying that their extraordinary powers are hereditary. Senya wants another child to carry on this superior bloodline, selecting a strong and purposeful woman, Maimuna, as a suitable vessel for his superior procreation:

> I want you to have my second child, because Pokuaa's mother disappeared in another region long ago . . . Maimuna looked at him with a terrible surprise bordering on horror. 'But I have sworn never to marry . . . ' She began. 'The gods have already broken that vow!' he interrupted, 'and I, yes I, am the one to take you. Believe me!'
>
> (p. 221)

Pokuaa herself, in a startling plot manipulation, turns out herself to be pregnant, but without the father of the future child's knowledge that he had slept with her. Carrying all the overtones of the immaculate conception – of Pokuaa as virgin Mary, selected by the ancestors to bear the prophet whose coming will save Tukwan – it appears that she manipulated the calendar and mated with Babo in another time dimension. Maimuna's and Pokuaa's babies are obviously destined to be mortal-gods, whose good governance and leadership is ordained – Pokuaa declares that 'I will bear my child into my authority' (p. 232). Magical realism is becoming the science fiction of Laing's next novel.

If Pokuaa is a syncretized virgin Mary, then her counterpart Maimuna is a reincarnation of the blind woman Maimuna in Sembene Ousmane's *Gods Bits of Wood*, archetypal mother, brave and sacrificing for her child. In Sembene Ousmane's novel of resistance and worker pride and rebellion, the baby is called 'Strike':

> Maimuna, the blind woman, remained behind, in the compound at N'Diayene. She still had milk and had begun to nurse the baby who had been called Strike. 'I am nourishing one of the great trees of tomorrow,' she told herself. At night she liked to sit in the courtyard, surrounded by the children, singing one of her old songs to them or telling them the story of the girl and the curious little man who had lost their lives on the road at the entrance to the city.[45]

In a novel of vast historical understanding, Sembene's blind woman, mythical receptacle of the future in her womb, custodian of ancient songs and maker of new myths, is a tension. *God's Bits of Wood* ends with the ancient song of Maimuna:

> As the crowd scattered into the shadows of the rapidly descending night, Lahbib heard someone singing. It was the *Legend of Goumba*, the old song of Maimuna, the blind woman.[46]

Laing's novel, which in many ways strove for progressive ideals, invokes this problematic aspect of Sembene Ousmane's work to buttress the search for roots of the past.

Thus the gods have dictated that Senya will be the one 'to take' Maimuna and impregnate her. It is no surprise that, notwithstanding all the new food and religion, Maimuna and Senya have a 'traditional' wedding (p. 229). This leads to a detailed description of how Tukwan, transformed utopia, will be organized as an elite oligarchy following a new orthodoxy. Senya explains that

> we are not just trying to go back to an old time, so right. We are trying not to return to the heart of the old ancestors only and the old spirits, but to the new joy that we created less than one handful of years ago.
>
> (p. 235)

To effect this Senya makes five unilateral pronouncements. He states that 'the first thing we must do is to make Pokuaa the formal leader of this town'. She will 'lead from the front' while, and second, Senya 'will continue to be in the background behind the pregnant president'. Third, 'the next thing is to make Kwame Atta our ambassador to the cities and countries outside us' while

> The next solution is to create a new maze by spreading the truth of your book, which is a fitting chronicle of all that we have been trying to do, and whose spirit would be behind the most tortuous maze ever created.
>
> (p. 235)

This fourth edict is to strengthen the moat, the protective border ring around Tukwan, preventing attack and entry. This maze is constructed by the fortifying threads of history, woven by Babo in the truth contained in his book. This truth, which reflects the new and unambiguous authority and Law and orthodoxy governing the town, will keep the enemy out. Finally, and very belatedly:

> after that we must have an election to choose what to do, where to go with our spirit and morals and inventions, and to decide finally what we can tolerate and what we cannot!
>
> (p. 235)

Thus democracy is to be mediated by the tenets of the ruling, hereditary group. And with this version of the familiar benevolent elite, Laing comes much more in line with his more culturally nationalistic fellow writers, who search for cleansing rituals in order to regenerate their ailing nations. In taking this path, Laing moves somewhat away from the embrace of open borders, which welcome travellers to cross over, away from migrants, mongrels and hybrids. He moves, in other words, away from the magical realism of the earlier parts of the novel, as the ironic voice is muted and Kofi Senya's monolithic pronouncements reverberate with the godly certainty of purifying myth. Deandrea appears to concur quite precisely with this interpretation when he states that:

> notwithstanding his revolutionary style, Laing still belongs to that descent of African artists who have brought to the fore their preoccupation with the state. The main theme of his writing could be summarized in one question: how could a new Ghana – and consequently a new world – be built? Although Laing's anti-realism and problematization of history might easily be assimilated by some postmodern or post-colonial critics, the pervasive national project supporting his style cannot be traced back to the constant dismantling of such projects theorised by postmodernist academics like Homi Bhabha.[47]

It is, of course, not so simple, given that Laing is a highly complex writer, with many conflicting tensions and agendas. Deandrea therefore qualifies his earlier comment with:

> On the other hand, both Laing's socio-political quest and stylistic influ-
> ences succeed in going far beyond any Ghanaian or African boundary,
> therefore rejecting any potential label of 'nativism'.[48]

In other words, as the borders close in Tukwan, as the maze is strengthened, Laing does not so much abandon his global cosmopolitanism as deflect it to a safer space, out of Africa and back to Levensvale. Here the border territory is one that Bhabha would embrace and recognize – a cross-cultural space that admits traffic:

> There existed this tunnel, the last creation of the Levensvale stupidity
> machine, which allowed natives out, and allowed strangers in, if both
> swore to be faithful to the open values of the town whether within it or
> without it. And the first thing the two strangers from Glasgow said when
> they entered was, 'How can you keep up with the computers when there
> is such conscience here, such a balance between the old and the new, such
> a whimsical reverence for a vital Necklace religion and a culture so wide
> that almost anything can fit into it?'
>
> (p. 231)

This contrasts with Tukwan where, while the curious do come from Kumasi, they enter the town as a fortified and self-contained space where the new is firmly harnessed to the ancestors, the shrine and tradition. With Tukwan firmly established, the dangerous Tutuolan borders encountered on the journey between it and Levensvale have been secured. Mackie's son, Angus, on his journey to Tukwan from Levensvale 'had travelled the same route as his father had done with the Tukwan group' and he finds 'the old mercenaries were all doubly dead' and

> When he reached the land of the Football King and the golden-eyed
> grasscutter, he saw that it was now the grasscutter that was ruling in a true
> burrowing akrantie fashion with a degree of wisdom that fitted nicely
> into its silver eye; the awam football matches had ceased, and cassava and
> even yam had multiplied to such an extent that they threatened the sky
> with their leaves. And the King was dead: slaughtered on his own
> slaughter; and the gorge of goats was free!
>
> (p. 247)

Once Tukwan, the African centre, has secured itself and its roots in the past, then in the safer zone, far from home, Levensvale, originally Siamese twin with Tukwan, becomes the space where crossover, cultural hybridity and border traffic is enabled. In the process, a division of labour between the two towns, as opposed to their syncretization, is effected. Highly symbolic of the fact that Levensvale inherits the mantle of the original utopian vision, is the gift that Angus makes to Tukwan of fifty more years of immortality. Levensvale, in other words, buys Tukwan time:

> And he [Angus] had given his immortality freely . . .. After all, the ances-
> tors had decreed in their diminishing power that any residue immortality
> ought to be given in transfer not to another human being, but to an idea:
> the idea that Tukwan should exist at least for the next fifty years with the
> power to regulate its own rate of change, and its own way of change.
>
> (p. 247)

This device of splitting the vision into what is feasible at home and what can be dreamt about in Levensvale damages the very core of Laing's own mission of twinning and entwining, on a global scale. In other words, Laing's abhorrence of being torn by the cacophony of cultural unevenness, rips his narrative apart into separated spaces. There has been a genuine urge towards change and transforma-tion, an enlightened celebration of cultural difference, but at the crucial moment of transition, Laing loses his nerve and clings to the old gods and ancestors in the guise of Kofi Senya.

Laing attempts to resolve the chasm that has opened up in his narrative by constructing individual romantic alliances. Cross-cultural marriages attempt to heal the rift of the novel's sad conclusion regarding the impossibility of cross national syncretism. This echoes Kofi Loww's searches for big solutions to his sweet country's problems as finally resting within his love for Adwoa Adde, in the previous novel; it confirms Laing's comment that he is only interested in the poli-tics that affect his own life and the lives of others. And so, Mackie's son, Angus, marries Aba and is 'quite at home, resplendent in his kente joromi, and with a new wise look' (p. 247), and Kwame Atta marries a white woman from Levensvale. These couples, however, like the machines that have to be installed in the shrine, are based in Tukwan and ultimately cannot conceal the novel's jagged edges. This is what Rohrberger fails to understand when he suggests that these marriages can act as the symbolic solution for the people as a whole:

> The symbolic joining of Angus and Aba is, at the end, the salvation of the
> people; for the major thrust of the novel is toward an inevitable return of
> Tukwan and Levensvale to their own geographies.[49]

Why was this geographical split inevitable? Moreover, while these happy unions do contest the Tutuolan fear of, and warning against, strangers, they do so on a reduced and individualized site, on the edge of a chasm, in which a vast sea sepa-rates Tukwan from Levensvale, by the novel's end.

Woman of the Aeroplanes ends on a high utopian note, full of hope and joy: 'the joy of forests and the joy of machines' (p. 249). *Major Gentl and the Achimoto Wars*, Laing's next novel, moves from utopia to science fiction. The political and ideological difference between the two genres is suggested by Raymond Williams:

> So that while the utopian transformation is social and moral, the science-fiction transformation, in its dominant Western modes, is at once beyond and beneath: not social and moral but natural; in effect, as so widely in Western thought since the late nineteenth century, a mutation at the point of otherwise intolerable exposure and crisis: not so much a new life as a new species, a new nature.[50]

Major Gentl and the Achimoto Wars was published in 1992. Set as science fiction in the year 2020 in a place called Achimota City, its chapters are called 'Zones'. In this novel, Laing has, I think, succumbed to the pleasures of the linguistic devices and philosophical riddles and paradoxes to the extent of creating a fiction that is almost unreadable. This leads one reviewer to call it an 'awful novel', which 'goes nowhere, which makes it, kindly speaking, pure surrealism'.[51] Here, I will not go beyond the iceberg's tip of this novel's puzzles and mazes. All I wish to emphasize, as a conclusion to this chapter, is that its politics take to their logical conclusion the path chosen by Laing in *Woman of the Aeroplanes*.

For Williams, where social transformation is central in utopia, science fiction tends towards the position that the technological makes the new life; people are more powerless and human struggle is superseded by scientific advance. However, the aspect of the difference between the two that I wish to focus on here is the question of the Other that intersects intriguingly with the issue of cultural nationalism. In science fiction we have 'mutation' – 'not so much a new life as a new species, a new nature'.[52] In utopia, the actors are people like ourselves; in science fiction there is the divide between ourselves and the aliens, the mutated species, which is a caste system of Manichean opposition – 'the paradisal and hellish planets and cultures of science fiction are at times . . . deliberate, often sensational presentations of *alien* forms'.[53] I am suggesting that *Major Gentl and the Achimoto Wars* retreats from the possibilities inherent in the utopia of *Woman of the Aeroplanes*, to the genre of science fiction, where the divide between ourselves and the aliens is unambiguous.

As in the other novels, the country or the town is the quest, be it Tukwan, Ghana or Achimota, that is being battled over. The 'wars' are always about values, the struggle for modernity which is African and incorporates the rituals and culture of the past. However, this novel is far more reminiscent of the bitterness of an Ayi Kwei Armah against a generalized and stereotypical European culture than are Laing's other novels. Major Gentl sees through his 'magic binoculars'

> a Europe that had finally given up language and humanity to what it thought were the poor areas of the world . . .
> 'It's as if they are saying that only the poor can afford humanity, Major, no?' asked the golden cee, still expecting no answer from the major. (p. 2)[54]

Europe as a whole appears to be populated by 'the rich' – an alien, ahuman species that has relinquished language. The poor – African people – are 'us', the humans. The villainous West and greedy East have conspired to rob Ghana – 'western fun with eastern backing or indifference'. This had resulted in a 'tragic history that had stolen the people and lands of this country' (p. 137). The 'cities abroad', always as wholes, suffer from a rapacious greed that is pathological, a component of their essential lack of humanity, rather than economically or rationally motivated:

> And this power wasn't even wanted intrinsically by the bosses; all this power was for processes that led beyond the earth. Can you put such a massively sick spirit back on course?
>
> (p. 155)

Like the invocation of 'The Way' in Ben Okri's sequel to *The Famished Road*, the 'massively sick spirit' could have been taken directly from Ayi Kwei Armah's classic of exclusivist cultural nationalism, *Two Thousand Seasons*. These unnatural, alien Europeans are simply bored and want 'our happiness' (pp. 155–6).

Cold climates are symbolic of cold humanoids. Gentl looks through his magic binoculars from the paradise of Achimota to the hell of 'the frosty lands' where 'humanity was declared as something truly belonging to another century altogether, something completely out of date'; where 'truncated human beings – half puzzles – wishing they were more whole than they were' believed that 'brains were everything and the truest and broadest intelligence was nothing'.

> Don't mind them! thought aMofa Gentl, for residues of the true African drum, of the subtleties of true African movements, width and intelligence, would follow them like obsessive ghosts that would haunt the universe forever.
>
> (p. 164)

But Gentl cannot console himself, given his spirit and soul, and so finds himself 'crying on the moon; he was wetting the craters with humanity' (p. 166). In the same vein, near the end when the war is very much in earnest, the enemy are Roman soldiers, despicable mercenaries, who are fighting on behalf of 'the frosty nations' of 'France, Germany, Japan, America, Britain and South Africa'. By contrast:

> Amassed on the home army's side were the thousands of fighting men and women, the sparrows, the crows, the camel's six cousins that had suddenly appeared, goats, hundreds of rabbits, termites, the train engines, the snakes, two rivers diverted into the army with their intelligent water power, belligerent bananas, pineapples.
>
> (p. 167)

The African army is strengthened by its animism – its belief in the sacred life force of all humans, animals and objects, as opposed to the cold inhumanity of Europe and America. The novel ends with an unashamedly superior Achimoto City, which 'was the standard that they all had to follow' (p. 180). Why the world has to follow it is because here

> power was the last resort, and humanity and invention allowed even the smallest human being to open out into the trees and into the universe, to see the whole, to touch the inner.
>
> (p. 180)

And here summed up is the contradiction scarring the ultimate nature of Tukwan and its new orthodoxies. It, too, becomes the standard, its shrine the new global headquarters. However idealistic Laing's hopes for cultural entwine and global embrace, as long as he resorts to the roots of a superior culture, his writing is vulnerable to being swept away by the maelstrom of conflicting ideologies, strategies and dreams.

Laing seems at times to have forgotten the knowledge, with which he himself endowed Major Gentl, that

> fighting the enemy, even in a war of existence, was fighting yourself, provided you started from the footage, Ewurade, that humanity was one; and that those who dealt in outdated distinctions were merely thieves of conclusion and betrayers of premise.
>
> (p. 159)

Major Gentl's knowledge is Kojo Laing's own wisdom. Laing's conflicts and tensions lead to the betrayal of some of his finest aspirations. These are expressed by Mackie, in his advice to Jock, with which I will end this chapter:

> And the little secret, Jock, is that listen to all the ideas, yes, but just take what you want and leave the rest. After all we have to take some. They take some of ours and we take some of theirs, that's the way to the new toughness of the world . . . and don't forget that we all have our little obligations to be new, new for this town to prosper, new to be mortal and free again.[55]

7

'OLD GODS, NEW WORLDS'

Some conclusions

Science provides mankind with its magic, light, guidance, and miracles. It's the religion of the future.

Naguib Mahfouz[1]

African discourses have been silenced radically or, in most cases, converted by conquering Western discourses. The popular local knowledges have been subsumed critically by 'scientific' disciplines.

V.Y. Mudimbe[2]

Magical realism arises out of particular societies – postcolonial, unevenly developed places where old and new, modern and ancient, the scientific and the magical views of the world co-exist. It grapples with cultural syncretism and accepts it to a greater or lesser extent. Where syncretism is rejected, it is usually the result of pressure arising out of national disaster, which insists on the writer's obligation to engage in national liberation.

In other words, as elsewhere in the Third World, the unevenness of Western capitalist development, the co-existence of disparate ways of living and of seeing life, have fundamentally determined African fictional politics and aesthetic choices. Among these choices is that of the magical realist mode with its strange relationships, weird linkages and multi-dimensional spaces. This mode contests boundaries, seamless unities and ethnic purities and can therefore co-exist only very uneasily with cultural nationalism.

And co-exist, however contradictorily, ambiguously and uneasily, it does. We have seen how, in fascinating ways, Okri, Laing and Cheney-Coker all occupy ambiguous fictional spaces, suspended between Bhabha's cosmopolitan celebration of border traffic, on the one hand, and Soyinka's or Achebe's decolonizing boundaries, as national fortifications, on the other. What has become clear, as the many varied, multi-shaped and coloured pieces fleetingly settle, only to take off again into space and time, is that magic turns to myth and back again, in a kinetic kaleidoscope of fictions of dizzying, daring and brave narrative experimentation. All these novels, but especially Okri's and Laing's, teem with images, symbols, mysteries and interpretative puzzles. The density of the writing, and at times the

216

frustrating difficulty of the reading, can be accounted for in terms of these frenetic journeys.

The unevenness of the development of their societies is reflected in the positioning of the writers themselves. Insiders and outsiders, traitors and champions of resistance, these writers are cultural hybrids, who grapple with the demands created by national atrocity and with the attractions inherent in contributing to national pride; these writers inscribe in the narrative guts of their fictions their moral and political uncertainties. Many voices clamour; when one rises above the din, it usually speaks for greater certainties and unities, taking fright at the maelstrom of borders, change and cultural weldings. We saw the narrative chain reserved for the Malaguetan founders in Cheney-Coker's novel, that increasingly became an epic, a myth of national regeneration; we saw Tukwan's blood elite speak of a new orthodoxy; we saw Okri dare to travel along the dangerous, famished road, only to arrive at The Way, the mythical path of African purity and superior spirituality.

All three writers shy away from organized politics; all are sickened by corruption. There is a startling similarity in Laing's and Cheney-Coker's recourse to utopias governed by benevolent but autocratic ruling elites, with blood claims to sovereignty. These lead inevitably to healing myths that compromise the challenges of magical, open borders, along which newness is free to enter the world. The messianic solution, including that of Okri's photographer, is compelling to writers, who are torn between their hatred of the theft, despotism and corruption of many of Africa's current rulers, and their simultaneous distance from the multitude, who suffer the brunt of the crimes of those rulers and their mandarins. In other words, and paradoxically, this rejection of the debaucheries of their respective governments binds these writers into the nationalist project, which struggles for solutions to the national malaise, even as their fictions strain to forge new alliances.

In Chapter 2 I set up a distinction within postcolonial writers, between cosmopolitan and decolonizing tendencies. I suggested that the trend among African writers was commitment to decolonizing their cultures, as part of a national project of reconstruction. I suggested that this project encouraged the excavation of myths of return to an idealized past and the orthodoxy of the ancestors, and which discouraged admixture with other cultures and continents. I also insisted that this distinction was not a fixed polarity, but that there was traffic back and forth across these positions. The bulk of this book has explored the fiction of three writers, who magnificently demonstrate the nature of this traffic.

The dominant cultural mood in Africa, however, certainly once the hard reality of the betrayal of the hopes and dreams of independence has sunk in, has been a revived negritude and a heightened cultural nationalism. This I illustrated in Chapter 3, by way of the example of Chinua Achebe's latest novel, and I have substantiated elsewhere in relation to Wole Soyinka, Ayi Kwei Armah and Ngugi wa Thiong'o.[3] As V.Y. Mudimbe puts it:

no one will disagree that a nationalistic trend is present. More and more African scholars seem to rely on the hypothesis of African unity.[4]

Mudimbe, too, links this trend to 'the ideological significance of the failure of contemporary African society' and suggests that it results in priority being given 'to questions that have been asked again and again about tradition'. This fosters the urge 'to create myths which would give a meaning to [Africa's] hopes for improvement'.[5] This urge towards the creation of these healing myths is present in all three writers. Carnival in Laing and Okri becomes the Tutuolan warning against change, and in Cheney-Coker, the fair admits the Arab invaders and dwarf-like cultural purifiers.

At the same time, magical realism in West Africa, as elsewhere in the world, is crucially inspired and poetically enriched by local stories, beliefs, tales and wisdom. As well as being potential sources for healing myths, oral traditions, the language of rhetoric, riddle and doublespeak, enable the fictional medium to enact its message of opposition. Western scientific and technological developments are contested by these writers and characterized as in cahoots with colonizing advances, which seek to obliterate indigenous ways of seeing, with the blinding light of so-called progress. The ritual journey and the masquerade, allowing for the masked secret space in which spiritual discovery may take place, have been springs of healing inspiration for these writers. This comes with a price. The folkloric tradition, for all its transformations in the modern world, carries a conservatism and a cultural exclusiveness that also shuts down the vision of the third eye, even as it champions its magical possibilities of vision.

Nothing sums up the ambiguity of the politics better than the ambivalent attitude to women shared by all three writers. Here, the fear of what the inevitable changes might bring finds its object as the women emasculate men, abandon their families and terrify with the power of their bodies. The daunting matriarchs always carry a mixed message – priestess hints of witch. Lurking beneath the gender ambivalence of these fictions is the *abiku* – strange unnatural child, image of labyrinth, repetition and woman's fertile and unreliable body. Okri's *abiku* breaks out into history essentially as an existential act of self-liberation. Cheney-Coker's *abiku* survives the terrible round of dying and being re-born only by assuming the mantle of purified and cleansed African being, the opposite of Garbage, of the name he carries as reminder of the dangers of cultural contamination.

Two philosophers – travellers like Cheney-Coker, Laing and Okri – are Kwame Anthony Appiah and V.Y. Mudimbe. Their philosophical prose writing can help us, I think, to capture the essence of what the fiction has been struggling with.

Kwame Anthony Appiah is a hybrid product of wonderfully mixed parts. As mentioned in Chapter 2, his father was a Ghanaian statesman and brother-in-law of the King, his mother, Peggy Cripps, daughter of a British aristocrat.[6] Brought up in Ghana, educated in Britain and now living in America, he shares the cosmopolitan migrancy and revels in the panoramic smorgasbord of his family and his culture. I must quote this inspirational and poetic celebration of hybridity in full:

> If my sisters and I were 'children of two worlds' no one bothered to tell us this; we lived in one world, in two 'extended' families divided by several thousand miles and an allegedly insuperable cultural distance that never, so far as I can recall, puzzled or perplexed us much. As I grew older, and went to an English boarding-school, I learned that not everybody had family in Africa and in Europe; not everyone had a Lebanese uncle, American and French and Kenyan and Thai cousins. And by now, now that my sisters have married a Norwegian and a Nigerian and a Ghanaian, now that I live in America, I am used to seeing the world as a network of points of affinity.
>
> This book is dedicated to nine children – a boy born in Botswana, of Norwegian and Anglo-Ghanaian parents; his brothers, born in Norway and in Ghana; their four cousins, three boys in Lagos, born of Nigerian and Anglo-Ghanaian parents, and a girl in Ghana; and two girls, born in New Haven, Connecticut, of an African-American father and a 'white' American mother. These children, my nephews and my god-children, range in appearance from the colour and hair of my father's Asante kinsmen, to the Viking ancestors of my Norwegian brother-in-law; they have names from Yorubaland, from Asante, from America, from Norway, from England. And watching them playing together and speaking to each other in their various accents, I, at least, feel a certain hope for the human future.[7]

Like all three of the writers under discussion, however, Appiah both celebrates his cultural syncretism, as a human ideal, and also asserts the existence of an identifiable, homogeneous and superior African cultural identity. He writes that 'the African writer's concern is not with the discovery of a self that is the object of an inner voyage of discovery'. The problem, as he sees it, for all African writers 'is finding a public role, not a private self'. This he contrasts with 'European intellectuals'. Appiah goes on to describe the African writer's refusal to ignore the past or to avoid the 'difficulty of this decolonization of the mind':

> That past and their people's myths of the past are not things they can ignore. When Ngugi wa Thiong'o says that 'the novelist, at his best, must feel himself heir to a continuous tradition', he does not mean, as the Westerner might suppose, a literary tradition: he means, as any African would know, 'the mainstream of his people's historical drama'. It is this fundamentally social-historical perspective that makes the European problem of authenticity something distant and unengaging for most African writers.[8]

219

Appiah's book contests boundaries at every turn, and yet here falls into the rigid polarities between public and private, into the denigration of personal quests as European isolation from a sense of community, into the assumption that all African and European intellectuals think the same as their own kind ('any African would know'). If Appiah has demonstrated that his own cultural experience is fundamentally European *and* African, how can he polarize it in this way?

The ambiguity of his positioning, the masks that he dons to conceal his contradictions, are most acute in two of his also most poetic and powerful chapters – 'Old Gods, New Worlds', which provided the title for this conclusion, and 'The Postcolonial and the Postmodern', which I discussed in Chapter 2.

The stated purpose of 'Old Gods, New Worlds' is to examine 'some aspects of traditional culture', which is defined simply as 'culture before the European empires' and then 'to look at some of the ways in which the experience of colonization and extended interaction with the West has produced a culture in transition from tradition to modernity'.[9] In other words, Appiah is scrutinizing the so-called indigenous culture and the effects on it of the unevenness of capitalist modernization.

In this vein, Appiah describes a traditional ceremony of installation of a spirit in a shrine 'somewhere in rural Asante'. What becomes clear is his unwillingness to clarify what exactly he thinks about those traditional believers in the spirits, for which they build shrines. He states that while 'most intellectuals outside Asante think they know . . . that there are no such spirits',

> that for all the requests in the priest's prayer, no unseen agent will come to inhabit the shrine; no one will answer the questions 'What made this person ill?' 'Would we win if we went to war?' or 'How should we cure the king's elder?' Yet here is a culture where, for at least several hundred years, people have been setting up just such shrines and asking them just such questions and asking the spirits they believe are in them to perform just such tasks.[10]

Appiah goes on to question 'Surely, by now, they should know, if they are rational, that it won't work?'[11] Appiah builds up the argument that it is not good enough to explain such rituals as simply symbolic. While they use symbolic devices, like the sprinkling of valuable gold dust as a sign of respect to the spirit, the ritual is based on the firm belief 'in traditional Asante culture [in] the existence of disembodied departed spirits'. He repeats and emphasizes this argument, that 'practices arise from the belief, literal and not symbolic, in the powers of invisible agents'.[12]

Can we assume that Appiah is speaking as a 'scientific' thinker when he explains that the fundamental difference between scientific and non-scientific thinkers is that the latter will not accept that unfortunate events have no explanation – nothing is meaningless – 'the cosmos works to a plan?'[13] Can we assume that 'the point of view of the Western intellectual' is not his own when Appiah advances the opinion that it is reasonable to accept and hold onto beliefs from one's culture when there is an absence of 'countervailing evidence', even though, from the point of view of Western intellectuals, such views are 'wildly false'?[14] He explains, somewhat defensively perhaps, that traditional society lacks an 'alien alternative [Western] point of view' and there is plenty of evidence from within the culture that spirits do, in fact, exist. It remains quite hard to gauge Appiah's stance on whether spirits do exist, given his own abundant access to such an alternative point of view.

The relationship between the magical and the scientific is, in fact, at the cutting edge of the themes and viewpoints of our writers. It is the narrative space where the educated writer's simultaneous ironic distance from, and acceptance of, pre-scientific worldviews negotiate the magical realist stance. We saw Laing contest the polarity, invent magical machines, but also insist that the embrace of global modernity entailed a loss of magical power. We saw Okri refuse the linear view of progress as his road, car, electricity, spirits and bush dizzyingly engage in a dance of changed partners and positions. Ultimately, however, his photographer acts for the oppressed by way of his camera, a camera shared by Laing's Okay Pol, the ultimate seeker after the 'sweet country' of Ghana.

Postcolonial writers are at pains to illustrate that their pre-colonial societies were not backward because they did not develop Western forms of technology. They show that magical beliefs had spiritual roots that acted rationally in keeping the society together. Hence Gustavius Martins had to undergo cleansing rituals and Kofi Senya had to rush back to his shrine where the scientific inventions are ultimately contained. These are difficult areas, often prising the writers away from the hazards of dangerous journeys with unknown destinations, into the lager of safe and secured national certainties.

Linked to this, Western science and technology have been implicated in the conquest of colonies. Appiah resists the superiority of science over magic, as does Laing, as a strategy of resistance to cultural imperialism and its racist assumptions about the superstitiousness and inferiority of indigenous beliefs and customs. As Brian Conniff points out in relation to One Hundred Years of Solitude, 'once the people believe that science, like all uplifting things, must come from elsewhere, that the outside world is better because it is more "advanced" then imperialism becomes much easier to justify'.[15]

Appiah goes on to compare the 'traditional' ceremony with another, the wedding of his sister. He explains that unlike the other, this was a 'non-traditional' ceremony because it co-existed with 'a degree of belief in the Christianity that came with the colonials' and also 'some familiarity with the vision of the natural sciences'.[16] It was a Methodist ceremony at which the Catholic Archbishop of Kumasi said prayers after which 'one of the king's senior linguists' poured 'libations to my family ancestors'. This notwithstanding, 'these ... are modern Africans'. The bride and groom met at Sussex University, England, 'and were, respectively, a medical sociologist and a Nigerian merchant banker'.[17] Appiah then poses a question about all of this in the most telling way:

What are we to make of all of this? Or rather, what are Europeans and Americans to make of it, since it is all so familiar to me – to most contemporary Africans – that I find it hard to recover the sense of contradiction between the elements of this no-doubt remarkable synthesis.[18]

Appiah is being less than candid with us. Firstly, there is the 'we', all of us readers, which becomes the ethnic, cultural nationalism of 'we Africans' who are spiritually in advance of 'them' who are all Europeans and Americans. Simultaneously, and contradictorily, he emphasizes, in the best tradition of an avowed cosmopolitan, that the co-existence of all these elements taken from many cultures, including the European and American, gives rise to a rich and remarkable synthesis. The mixture is a 'resource for a tremendous range of cultural activity'.[19]

Seeing with a third eye entails putting a limit on the endlessness of possibilities, given that certain ways of conceptualizing reality cannot co-exist because they are mutually exclusive. The magical can be a device for exposing reality, but only if there is a degree of critical, ironic distance from it which prevents supernatural explanations being proffered to elucidate historical processes. The fervour of cultural nationalism ultimately mutes the irony of Laing, Cheney-Coker and Okri, and results in Appiah finally constructing his own ethnic melting pot. Appiah reveals his hand only to throw in the cards. He insists that 'most Africans cannot fully accept those scientific theories in the West that are inconsistent with [beliefs in invisible agents]'. He goes on to say that 'If modernisation is conceived of in part as the acceptance of science, we have to decide whether we think the evidence obliges us to give up the invisible ontology'. He answers the question of 'how much of the world of the spirits we intellectuals must give up' with the evasion that he does not think that 'the answer is obvious'.[20]

Laing also passionately espouses the syncretism between African religion and Christianity, but finally retreats into the sacred shrine of old. 'Ambiguity' remains the keyword for the moral or authoritative narrative voice, 'ambivalence' for the past and its role in the present, for the magical and its transcendence by science, for the future and its global networks.

V.Y. Mudimbe, Professor of Romance Languages and Comparative Literature at Duke University, lives a cosmopolitan life not dissimilar from Appiah's. His erudite writing is steeped in the knowledge and traditions of intellectuals throughout the world and history. He demonstrates, however, in his *The Invention of Africa*, that this intellectual history itself gave rise to the discourses, be they of anthropology or history, that have, in fact, invented Africa itself.

Mudimbe's book is to Africa, what Edward Said's *Orientalism* was to the East. Mudimbe sees 'a dichotomizing system' as having arisen out of 'the colonializing structure' consisting of oppositions such as traditional versus modern; oral versus written and printed; agrarian and customary communities versus urban and industrialized civilization; subsistence economies versus highly productive economies.[21]

He suggests that 'between the two extremes there is an intermediate, a diffused space in which social and economic events define the extent of marginality'.[22]

> Marginality designates the intermediate space between the so-called African tradition and the projected modernity of colonialism. It is apparently an urbanized space in which, as S. Amin noted, 'vestiges of the past, especially the survival of structures that are still living realities (tribal ties, for example), often continue to hide the new structures (ties based on class, or on groups defined by their position in the capitalist system)'.[23]

While I have been suggesting that this space is a highly creative one, the very arena in which magical realist dramas are played out, Mudimbe, by contrast, does not characterize it as a fertile border interstice; it is the maelstrom, the chasm. It is the arena of developmental failures and of confusion:

> This space reveals not so much that new imperatives could achieve a jump into modernity, as the fact that despair gives this intermediate space its precarious pertinence, and, simultaneously, its dangerous importance.[24]

Mudimbe, at this moment, does not wish to venture into intermediate spaces, which are the vulnerable entry points of Western aggression, reminiscent of the boundaries that Laing ultimately erects to protect his utopia from invasion. That 'marginal space' which

> has been a great problem since the beginning of the colonializing experience; rather than being a step in the imagined 'evolutionary process,' it has been the locus of paradoxes that called into question the modalities and implications of modernization in Africa.[25]

Our writers have attempted, with great difficulty, to confront the paradoxes and to operate upon that intermediate and diffused space. Mudimbe's pessimism is driven by the ever-present sovereignty of European thought, of Western culture, of whites who simultaneously represent blacks in their own image and distance them through the construction of their exotic difference from themselves.

In other words, Africans are doubly represented, just as they were in European art in the sixteenth and seventeenth centuries. Mudimbe illustrates this by way of Hans Burgkmair's painting of 1508, entitled *Exotic Tribe*, a family portrait of three black figures – mother, father and child. 'All are naked and have either bracelets around their arms or a string around their necks, clear signs that they belong to a "savage" universe'. However, 'the structure of the figures, as well as the meaning of the nude bodies, proclaim the virtues of resemblances' – the painter has represented 'blackened whites'. Thus 'all differences' are reduced and neutralized into 'the sameness signified by the *white* norm'.[26] On the other hand, and simultaneously, 'the excellence of an exotic picture' rests on its ability to create 'a cultural distance, thanks to an accumulation of accidental differences, namely, nakedness, blackness, curly hair, bracelets, and strings of pearls'.[27]

Mudimbe's portrait of Burgkmair's picture is a huge canvas that stretches across his entire book. It is the backdrop for the sophisticated theories of a Lévi-Strauss or Foucault. It comes to life with the depiction of modern black intellectuals who perpetuate what Mudimbe calls 'epistemological ethnocentrism'.[28]

Mudimbe is a global intellectual, a postmodernist, who believes that 'history is a legend, an invention of the present'.[29] He is, however, simultaneously himself captured by the 'grid of Western thought and imagination' in those moments when he is unable to see in anything other than black and white.

And always there is some truth in this picture. In our discussion, for example, of the grotesque as transgression, the work of Bakhtin and its applicability to magical realism, it became clear that the physically grotesque was implicated in the degradation of the woman's body. If grotesque realism became potentially reactionary as regards gender, then Mudimbe illustrates the same point in relation to race:

> the black color of a horned woman, a monstrous animal with a human face surrounded by serpents and bizarre birds. The African has become not only the Other who is everyone else except me, but rather the key which, in its abnormal differences, specifies the identity of the Same.[30]

This may be an eighteenth-century representation, but for Mudimbe it remains pertinent.

In his conclusion to *The Invention of Africa,* however, Mudimbe utterly rejects 'the static binary opposition between tradition and modernity, for tradition . . . means discontinuities through a dynamic continuation and possible conversion of *tradita* (legacies)'.[31]

It is this insight that Mudimbe carries with him into a later book – *The Idea of Africa* – in which some of the most profound and inspiring hopes of the magical realist project are expressed. In a fascinating chapter entitled 'Reprendre', Mudimbe comments on the exhibitors in a show of contemporary African artists:

> most of them belong to a second generation in the field, and if they consciously relate to earlier African art they know how to distort it, how to submit it to their own creative process. In fact, they discover in the African past simply art that has preceded them, art both beautiful and ugly. If the past inspires them, it does not bind them.[34]

He questions 'why should one *a priori* decide that the ancient art was best?' The answer is that only a nationalistic agenda dictates such a preference as part of a political drive to construct a legitimizing genealogy of the ancient tales, customs or art. In fact, as Mudimbe continues, 'discontinuity . . . doesn't necessarily mean the end of African art; it seems, rather, that the ancient models are being richly adapted'.[35] The nature of this adaptation is what we have been exploring within a particular kind of fictional experiment. Again with reference to contemporary African artists, Mudimbe magnificently captures the goals and frameworks of our writers:

> The artists of the present generation are the children of two traditions, two worlds, both of which they challenge, merging mechanics and masks, machines and the memories of gods.[36]

Mudimbe appears to have overcome his earlier terrors of the interspace and concludes with an emphasis on the 'historical and intellectual discontinuities, social ruptures, and political negotiations of African traditions'. What 'discursive formations in Africa' offer is 'tables of intellectual and epistemological dissensions witnessing to fabulous acculturations'.[37]

While they draw heavily on the past for inspiration, the magical realists can either aspire to these 'fabulous acculturations', or they can generate new myths as part of the plan of national reconstruction. This distinguishes them from the more nationalistic decolonizers, who more unambiguously rely on their interpretations, modifications and reconstructions of indigenous beliefs and myths, in order to contribute towards the creation of national cultures. Okri, Laing and Cheney-Coker battle creatively and courageously to open the borders and allow for change. Laing declares passionately in his poetry that

> And down where the blind myth heals,
> it heals only its own intensity,
> for the great silence cannot accept its answers.[38]

Out of that silence softly come the beautiful strains of his new piano concerto. This is not the piano of Gabriel Okara's classic poem, 'Piano and Drums', published nearly three decades earlier:

> And I lost in the morning mist
> of an age at a riverside keep
> wandering in the mystic rhythm
> of jungle drums and the concerto.[39]

This 'piano and drums' theme was an enduring shorthand for the clashing of cultures – the foreign, colonial invasion of indigenous African lifestyles and values. The poem stereotyped images of Africa and Europe, but in doing so, it expressed powerfully and poignantly the reality of how many African intellectuals saw their personal fates and their continent's history. The poem also accurately expressed the shock of the colonial encounter before its incorporation into the fabric of post-colonial life.

Today the imagery is radically outdated. 'Culture clash' no longer has resonance with the reality of life in the African city or of African intellectuals teaching in New York, winning Nobel Prizes or fulfilling writer-in-residencies in London or Paris. The more appropriate and inspirational symbolic shorthand is of Okri's photographer with his piano of black and white keys combining to play a global tune; it is of Laing's own 'new song' sung through the 'wild piano' drowning out the discordant note of racial disharmony.

However, Laing, Okri and Cheney-Coker, are ultimately themselves contradictory hybrids of cosmopolitan magical realism and nationalistic decolonization. For all the enormous intellectual challenge of their works, Okri and Laing all too often fall into the labyrinthine web of their own linguistic threads and leave the reader stranded. Cheney-Coker's novel struggles with similar life and death questions, but enthrals and enchants. It is he, then, who must have the last word:

> Because life in my part of the world is so utterly complex and exasperating, even while I was writing, I was having to learn things anew. And you must also remember my exposure to various cultures, which are quite different from mine. . . .
>
> There is so much spiritual vitality in what one sees around oneself. *The Last Harmattan of Alusine Dunbar* would not have been possible if I had narrowed myself to a kind of ethnic or cultural preoccupation that some people say you find in other African writers' work.[40]

NOTES

1 Seeing with a third eye

1 Ben Okri, 1992, p. 229.
2 Colin Bundy, 1996, p. 33.
3 Fredric Jameson, 1991, p. 400.
4 Ibid., p. xii.
5 Homi Bhabha, 1994, p. 222.
6 Ibid., p. 222.
7 Ibid., p. 4.
8 Ibid., pp. 4–5.
9 Fredric Jameson, 1991, p. 318.
10 Michele Barrett, 1991, p. 93.
11 Ibid., p. 151. Barrett is here quoting Nancy Fraser on Foucault.
12 There are notable exceptions, such as Monica in Wole Soyinka's *The Interpreters*, 1970.
13 Alice Walker, 1983.
14 Kwame Anthony Appiah, 1992.
15 Jamaica Kincaid, 1991, pp. 29–30.
16 Ngugi wa Thiong'o, 1981, p. 36.
17 Jamaica Kincaid, 1991, p. 29.
18 Chandra Mohanty, 1988, p. 64.
19 Ibid., pp. 62–3.
20 Michele Barrett and Anne Phillips, 1992, p. 2.
21 Chandra Mohanty, 1992, p. 74.
22 Michele Barrett and Anne Phillips, 1992, Preface.
23 Julia Watson, 1992, p. 147.
24 Manicheism is defined in the Collins Concise dictionary as 'the system of religious doctrines taught by the Persian prophet Mani about the third century AD. It was based on a supposed primordial conflict between light and darkness or goodness and evil.'
25 Abdul R. JanMohamed, 1983, p. 283.
26 See, for example, Ngugi's chapter entitled 'Her Cook, Her Dog: Karen Blixen's Africa' in Ngugi wa Thiong'o, 1993, pp. 132–5.
27 Sidonie Smith, 1992, p. 413.
28 Ibid., p. 413.
29 Ibid., p. 431.
30 Suzanne Chester, 1992, p. 443.
31 Ibid., p. 443.
32 Ibid., p. 446.
33 Ibid., p. 446.

34 Ibid., p. 452.
35 Ibid., p. 437.
36 Sylvia Walby, 1992, p. 48.
37 Robert Young, 1990, p. 127.
38 Ibid., pp. 19, 20.
39 Gayatri Chakravorty Spivak, 1990, p. 60.
40 Gayatri Chakravorty Spivak, 1992a, p. 774.
41 Gayatri Chakravorty Spivak, 1990, p. 62.
42 Ibid., pp. 42, 43.
43 Ibid., p. 42.
44 Ibid., p. 43.
45 Ibid., p. 62–3.
46 Robert Young, 1990, p. 171.
47 Ibid., p. 155.
48 Ibid., p. 158.
49 Gayatri Chakravorty Spivak, 1990, p. 61.
50 Robert Young, 1990, p. 160. Young quotes here from Spivak's *In Other Worlds*, 1987, p. 198.
51 Ibid., p. 156.
52 Tzvetan Todorov, 1985, p. 374.
53 Jamaica Kincaid, 1991, pp. 162–3.

2 'Sacred names into profane spaces': magical realism

1 Homi Bhabha, 1994, p. 225.
2 On the matter of terminology, I accept, along with Elleke Boehmer, that the term 'postcolonial', for all its difficulties, is useful 'as an umbrella term, a way of bracketing together the literatures written in those countries which were once colonies of Britain' (Elleke Boehmer, 1995, p. 4) and similarly 'the collective term *Third World* is used, as it is by the Non-Aligned movement, to signify its difference from the West' (ibid., p. 9). All of this is not to ignore difference and specificity. The purpose of these early chapters is precisely to set up some generalizations, some broad trends, from which the specific and more detailed case studies, later in the book, can take off.
3 Fredric Jameson, 1986a, p. 311.
4 Salman Rushdie, 1992, pp. 301–2.
5 See, for example: Suzanne Baker, 1991, pp. 56, 58; and Amaryll Beatrice Chanady, 1985, p. 19; and Geoff Hancock, 1986, pp. 33–4.
6 Fredric Jameson, 1986a, p. 302.
7 Amaryll Chanady, 1986, p. 50.
8 P. Mendosa, 1983, p. 59.
9 Amaryll Beatrice Chanady, 1985, p. 50.
10 Quoted in Amaryll Chanady, 1986, p. 55. The reference is to Jean Franco, *Historia de la literatura hispanoamericana*, 1975, Ariel publishers, p. 255.
11 Gerald Martin, 1989, p. 28 (his emphasis).
12 Elleke Boehmer, 1995, p. 4.
13 Timothy Brennan, 1989, p. 62.
14 Ahmad Aijaz, 1986, p. 10. See also Anne McClintock, 1993, p. 292, for a rejection of the concept of 'postcolonialism'.
15 Ahmad Aijaz, pp. 10–11 (my emphasis).
16 Ibid., p. 13.
17 Arif Dirlik, 1994, pp. 338–9.

18 Ibid., p. 339.
19 Ibid., p. 339.
20 Ibid., p. 342.
21 Ibid., p. 353 (his emphasis).
22 Timothy Brennan, 1989, p. viii.
23 Ibid., p. 40.
24 Ibid., p. 49.
25 Ibid., p. 50.
26 Ibid., p. 50.
27 Ibid., p. 95.
28 Ibid., p. 35.
29 Salman Rushdie, 1990, p. 4.
30 Salman Rushdie, 1988, p. 33–4.
31 Salman Rushdie, 1992, p. 15.
32 Ibid., p. 20.
33 Homi Bhabha, 1994, p. 225.
34 Ibid., p. 225.
35 Ibid., p. 226.
36 Ibid., pp. 226–7.
37 Ibid., p. 5.
38 Ibid., p. 218.
39 Ibid., pp. 218–9.
40 Ibid., p. 292.
41 Ibid., p. 4 (his emphasis).
42 Timothy Brennan, 1989, p. 52.
43 Ibid., p. 50.
44 Mikhail Bakhbin 1984a, p. 19–20.
45 Krystyna Pomorska, 1984, p. xi.
46 Michael Holquist, 1984, p. xvii.
47 Ibid., p. xix.
48 Krystyna Pomorska, 1984, p. x.
49 Mikhail Bakhtin, 1984b, p. 5–6.
50 Ibid., p. 7.
51 Ibid., p. 11.
52 Ibid., p. 5.
53 Peter Stallybrass and Allon White, 1986, p. 8.
54 Mikhail Bakhtin, 1984b, p. 25–6.
55 Ibid., p. 53.
56 Ibid., p. 52–3.
57 Peter Stallybrass and Allon White, 1986, p. 9 (their emphasis).
58 Gabriel Garcia Marquez, 1978, p. 9.
59 Ibid., p. 21.
60 Ibid., p. 21.
61 Robert Wilson, 1993, p. 110–11.
62 Mikhail Bakhtin, 1984a, p. 31 (his emphasis).
63 Ibid., p. 43 (his emphasis).
64 Peter Stallybrass and Allon White, 1986, p. 38.
65 Ibid., p. 38.
66 Ibid., p. 40.
67 Ibid., p. 29–30.
68 Ibid., p. 43.
69 Terry Eagleton,1981, p. 145.

70 Peter Stallybrass and Allon White, 1986, p. 43.
71 Ibid., p. 11.
72 Terry Eagleton,1981, p. 148.
73 Peter Stallybrass and Allon White, 1986, p. 201 (their emphasis).
74 Robert Young, 1990, p. 18, 19.
75 Biodun Jeyifo, 1991, p. 56 (his emphasis).
76 Ibid., p. 66 (his emphasis).
77 See Fredric Jameson, 1984, p. 60; Terry Eagleton, 1985, p. 61 and Perry Anderson,
    1988, p. 332. For a fuller discussion of this point see Brenda Cooper, 1991, pp. 127–8.
78 Homi Bhabha, 1990, p. 315.
79 Aijaz Ahmad, 1992, p. 85.
80 Ibid., p. 13.
81 Ibid., pp. 93–4.
82 Ibid., pp. 68–9.
83 Ibid., p. 135.
84 Ibid., p. 141.
85 Ibid., p. 139.
86 Jean Franco, 1988, pp. 505–6.
87 Ibid., p. 506.
88 Ibid., pp. 508–9.
89 Ibid., p. 509.
90 Ibid., p. 505.
91 Edwin Williamson, 1987, p. 86.
92 in John King, 1987, p. 142.
93 Geoff Hancock, 1986, p. 44.
94 Kumkum Sangari, 1987, p. 172.
95 Ibid., p. 176.
96 Robert R. Wilson, 1986, p. 70.
97 Ibid., p. 71.
98 Ibid., p. 72.
99 James Higgens, 1990, p. 144.
100 Amaryll Chanady, 1985, pp. 29–30.
101 Ibid., p. 149.
102 Ibid., p. 160.
103 Ibid., p. 41. The 'focalizer' in her vocabulary is the point of view from which the char-
    acters and their actions are presented to the reader.
104 Ibid., p. 162.
105 Hayden White, 1987, p. ix.
106 Ibid., p. xi.
107 Hayden White, 1980, p. 17 (his emphasis).
108 Ibid., p. 18.
109 Hayden White, 1987, p. 53.
110 Ibid., p. 157.
111 See Terry Lovell, 1987, chapter 4 for an analysis of the gothic subtext in realist fiction.

3 An endless forest of terrible creatures: magical realism in West Africa

1 Stephen Minta,1987, pp. 4 – 5.
2 Eileen Julien, 1992, p. 35.
3 Ibid., p. 45.

4 Ibid., pp. 41, 42.
5 Ibid., p. 26.
6 Brenda Cooper, 1994, p. 10.
7 Kojo Laing, 1992, p. 167.
8 Ibid.
9 Adeola James, 1990, p. 19.
10 Chinua Achebe, 1988, p. 22.
11 Afolabi A. Epega and Philip John Neimark, 1995, p. vii.
12 Ibid., p. viii.
13 Ibid., p. ix.
14 Margaret Thompson Drewal, 1992, p. 26.
15 Andrew Apter, 1992a, p. 98.
16 Ibid., p. 175.
17 E.N. Obiechina, 1980, p. 105.
18 A. Afolayan, 1975, p. 149.
19 Bernth Lindfors, 1973, p. 65.
20 D.O. Fagunwa, 1982, p. 14.
21 Ibid., p. 38.
22 Ibid., pp. 41–2.
23 Amos Tutuola, 1981, p. 151.
24 Ibid., p. 159.
25 Ibid., p. 163.
26 Bernth Lindfors, 1973, p. 67.
27 Ibid., p. 69.
28 Ibid., p. 70.
29 Ibid., p. 59.
30 Ibid., p. 59.
31 Margaret Thompson Drewal, 1992, p. 9.
32 Ibid., p. 20.
33 Ibid., p. 197.
34 Ibid., p. 198.
35 Andrew Apter, 1992a, p. 1.
36 Ibid., p. 166.
37 Ibid., p. 177.
38 Ibid., p. 193.
39 Ben Okri, 1996, p. 201 (my emphasis).
40 Chinua Achebe, 1980, pp. 261–2.
41 E.N. Obiechina, 1980, p. 89.
42 Ibid., p. 90.
43 Ibid., p. 99.
44 Viktor Beilis, 1987, p. 452.
45 Ibid., p. 455.
46 Ibid., p. 455.
47 Bernth Lindfors, 1973, p. 33.
48 Amos Tutuola, 1952, p. 18.
49 Ibid., p. 19.
50 Ibid., p. 19.
51 Ibid.,p. 25.
52 Ibid., p. 20.
53 Ibid., p. 21.
54 Bernth Lindfors, 1973, p. 55.
55 See Eldred D. Jones, 1992, p. 3.

56 V.Y. Mudimbe, 1991, p. 146.
57 Ibid., p. 148.
58 Ibid., p. 150.
59 Ibid., p. 150.
60 Andrew Apter, 1992a, p. 112.
61 Ibid., p. 113.
62 Ibid., p. 11.
63 Ibid., p. xvi.
64 Eileen Julien, 1992, p. 47.
65 I found Julien's discussion here very useful, albeit that I disagreed with her example of Ngugi's *Devil on the Cross*.
66 Ibid., p. 157 (my emphasis).
67 Ibid., p. 157.
68 Reed Way Dasenbrock, 1986, p. 313.
69 Kwame Anthony Appiah, 1992, p. 122.
70 See Brenda Cooper, 1995.
71 For a discussion of this, see Brenda Cooper, 1992, Chapter 2.
72 Anthony Arnove, 1993, p. 287.
73 Neil Lazarus, 1990, p. 204.
74 Ibid., p. 213.
75 Bill Ashcroft, Gareth Griffiths and Helen Tiffin, 1989, pp. 29–30.
76 Elleke Boehmer, 1995, pp. 237–9.
77 Biodun Jeyifo, 1991, p. 54.
78 Aijaz Ahmad, 1992, p. 3 (his emphasis).
79 Ibid., pp. 34–5.
80 Ibid., pp. 36–7.
81 Ibid., pp. 37–8.
82 Ibid., p. 35.
83 Ibid., p. 8.
84 Ibid., p. 38 (his emphasis).
85 Timothy Brennan, 1989, p. 52.
86 Ibid., p. 52.
87 Ibid., p. 166.
88 Ibid., p. 54.
89 Stuart Hall, 1992, p. 291.
90 Ibid., p. 309.
91 Ibid., p. 310 (his emphasis).
92 Ibid., p. 311.
93 Ibid., p. 313.
94 Ibid., p. 313.
95 See Brenda Cooper, 1995.
96 Aijaz Ahmad , 1992, p. 11.
97 Ibid., p. 37.
98 Ibid., p. 7.
99 Stuart Hall, 1992, pp. 293–5.
100 Ibid., p. 296
101 Ibid., p. 295.
102 Isidore Okpewho, 1983, p. ix.
103 Ibid., p. 155.
104 Ibid., p. 161.
105 Arjun Appadurai, 1996, p. 41.
106 C.L. Innes, 1990, pp. 171, 172.

107 Gareth Griffiths, 1987, p. 21.
108 Ibid., p. 22.
109 Ibid., p. 22 (my emphasis).
110 Ibid., p. 26.
111 Interview with Bruce Steele published in 1988 and quoted in Chimalum Nwankwo, 1991, p. 55.
112 C.L. Innes, 1990, p. 159.
113 Chinua Achebe, 1987, p. 127 (his emphasis).
114 Ibid., p. 195.
115 Ibid., p. 30.
116 Ibid., p. 32.
117 Ibid., p. 31.
118 Ibid., p. 33.
119 Ibid., p. 134.
120 Ibid., p. 153.
121 Ibid., p. 204.
122 Ibid, p. 102.
123 Ibid., p. 105.
124 Ibid., p. 110.
125 Ibid.,p. 114.
126 Ibid., p. 197. See also p. 199.
127 Kwame Anthony Appiah, 1992, p. 224.
128 Ibid., pp. 238, 239.
129 Ibid., pp. 238–9.
130 Ibid., p. 254.

4 'Out of the centre of my forehead, an eye opened': Ben Okri's *The Famished Road*

1 All references to the novel are taken from Ben Okri, 1992.
2 Biodun Jeyifo, 1988, pp. 277–8.
3 Ibid., pp. 280–1.
4 Ato Quayson, 1995, p. 155.
5 Camara Laye, 1956.
6 Chinua Achebe, 1975, p. 95.
7 Ibid., pp. 95–6.
8 Ato Quayson, 1995, p. 153.
9 (My emphasis).
10 Jane Wilkinson interview of Okri, 1992, p. 86.
11 (My emphasis).
12 Jane Wilkinson interview of Okri, 1992, p. 83.
13 (My emphasis).
14 Robert Browning, quoted from *The Oxford Book of Story Poems*, selected and arranged by Michael Harrison and Christopher Stuart-Clark, Oxford University Press, 1990.
15 Jane Wilkinson interview of Okri, 1992, p. 84.
16 Ibid., p. 85.
17 (My emphasis)
18 M.T. Drewal, 1992, p. 33.
19 Salman Rushdie, 1988, pp. 33–4.
20 (My emphasis).
21 Ayi Kwei Armah, 1969, p. 73.

22 Linda Hutcheon, 1989, pp. 44–5.
23 Ibid., pp. 121–2.
24 Ibid., p. 47.
25 (My emphasis).
26 Biodun Jeyifo, 1988, p. 281 (his emphasis).
27 Michael Gorra, 1993, p. 24.
28 Ibid., p. 24.
29 Ato Quayson, 1995, p. 154.
30 Ibid., p. 154.
31 All references to *Songs of Enchantment* are taken from Ben Okri, 1994 edition.
32 Ayi Kwei Armah, 1973, p. 1.
33 Kojo Laing, 1989, p. 10.

5 'The plantation blood in his veins': Syl Cheney-Coker and *The Last Harmattan of Alusine Dunbar*

1 All page references to the novel are taken from Syl Cheney-Coker, 1990.
2 Syl Cheney-Coker, 1980, p. 7 (*Hydropathy*).
3 Brenda Cooper, 1994, p. 9.
4 Ibid., p. 13.
5 Leo Spitzer, 1974, p. 3.
6 Ibid., p. 138.
7 Brenda Cooper, 1994, pp. 11–12.
8 Syl Cheney-Coker, 1980, p. 8 (*Hydropathy*).
9 Ibid., p. 16 (*Freetown*).
10 Leo Spitzer, 1974, p. 120.
11 Ibid., p. 122.
12 Brenda Cooper, 1994, pp. 10–11.
13 Syl Cheney-Coker, 1980, p. 16 (*Freetown*).
14 Brenda Cooper,1994, p. 12.
15 Eldred D. Jones, 1992, p. 3.
16 Brenda Cooper, 1994, p. 14.
17 Ibid, p. 14.
18 Ibid, p. 16.
19 Ibid, p. 11.
20 Ibid, pp. 15–16.
21 D.T. Niane, 1965, p. 41.
22 Ibid., p. 51.
23 Eldred D. Jones, 1992, p. 6.
24 Henry Louis Gates Jr, 1988.

6 Intermediate magic and the fiction of B. Kojo Laing

1 Kojo Laing, 1992, p. 1.
2 Personal correspondence, May 1995.
3 Note all page references from Kojo Laing, 1986.
4 Adewale Maja-Pearce, 1987, p. 28.
5 Pietro Deandrea, 1996, p. 164.
6 Ato Quayson, 1995, p. 148.
7 Personal correspondence, May 1995.

8 Ato Quayson, 1995, p. 148.

9 Ibid., p. 148.

10 Interview with Adewale Maja-Pearce, 1987, pp. 27–8.

11 Ato Quayson, 1995, p. 147.

12 Personal correspondence, May 1995.

13 Kojo Laing, 1989, p. 45.

14 Ibid., p. 38.

15 M.E. Kropp Dakubu, 1993, p. 34.

16 Ibid., p. 19.

17 Ibid., pp. 20–1.

18 Ibid., p. 21.

19 Ibid., p. 22.

20 Richard Priebe, 1980, p. 220.

21 Henry Louis Gates Jr, 1988, p. xxv.

22 Ibid., p. 6.

23 Ibid.,p. 52.

24 M.E. Kropp Dakubu, 1993, pp. 26–7.

25 Interview with Adewale Maja-Pearce, 1987, p. 28.

26 Fredric Jameson, 1991, p. 173.

27 M. Rohrberger, 1991, p. 915

28 Fredric Jameson, 1991, p. 160.

29 Ibid., p. 160.

30 Ibid., p. 173.

31 Ibid., p. xvi.

32 Ibid., p. xvi (his emphasis).

33 Ibid., p. 334.

34 Ibid., p. 159.

35 Raymond Williams, 1980, p. 196 (his emphasis).

36 Ibid., p. 203 (his emphasis).

37 Ibid., p. 202.

38 Ibid., pp. 204–5.

39 Ibid., p. 201.

40 Ibid., p. 211 (his emphasis).

41 Ibid., p. 212.

42 Personal correspondence, May 1995.

43   Kojo Laing, 1988b, p. 85.

44 Raymond Williams, 1980, p. 201.

45 Sembene Ousmane, 1970, p. 219.

46 Ibid., p. 245.

47 Pietro Deandrea 1996, p. 159.

48 Ibid., p. 159.

49 M. Rohrberger, 1991, p. 915.

50 Raymond Williams, 1980, p. 209.

51 Harold Waters, 1993, p. 427.

52 Raymond Williams, 1980, p. 209.

53 Ibid., p. 198 (his emphasis).

54 All references to this novel are taken from Kojo Laing, 1992.

55 Kojo Laing, 1988a, p. 130.

7 'Old Gods, New Worlds': some conclusions

1 Naguib Mahfouz, 1992, p. 96.
2 V.Y. Mudimbe, 1994, p. xiv.
3 See Brenda Cooper, 1992 and 1995.
4 V.Y. Mudimbe, 1988, p. 79.
5 Ibid., p. 96.
6 Godfrey Lienhardt, 1993, p. 12.
7 Kwame Anthony Appiah, 1992, pp. ix–x.
8 Ibid., pp. 8–9.
9 Ibid., p. 173.
10 Ibid., p. 175.
11 Ibid., p. 176.
12 Ibid., p. 194.
13 Ibid., p. 200.
14 Ibid., pp. 189, 190.
15 Brian Conniff, 1990, p. 174.
16 Kwame Anthony Appiah, 1992, p. 193.
17 Ibid., p. 193.
18 Ibid., p. 193.
19 Ibid., p. 194.
20 Ibid., p. 219.
21 V.Y. Mudimbe, 1988, p. 4.
22 Ibid., p. 4.
23 Ibid., p. 5.
24 Ibid., p. 5.
25 Ibid., p. 5.
26 Ibid., p. 8 (his emphasis).
27 Ibid., p. 9.
28 Ibid., p. 15.
29 Ibid., p. 195.
30 Ibid., p. 12.
31 Ibid., p. 189.
32 V.Y. Mudimbe, 1994, p. 163.
33 Ibid., pp. 163–4.
34 Ibid., p. 164.
35 Ibid., p. 207.
36 Kojo Laing, 1989, p. 56.
37 Gabriel Okara, 1963, p. 121
38 Brenda Cooper, 1994, p. 13.

BIBLIOGRAPHY

Achebe, Chinua (1959) *Things Fall Apart*, Heinemann.

—— (1960) *No Longer at Ease*, Heinemann.

—— (1964) *Arrow of God*, Heinemann.

—— (1966) *A Man of the People*, Heinemann.

—— (1975) *Morning Yet on Creation Day*, Heinemann.

—— (1980) 'Work and Play in Tutuola's *The Palm-Wine Drinkard*', in Bernth Lindfors (ed.) *Critical Perspectives on Amos Tutuola*, Heinemann, pp. 256–64.

—— (1987) *Anthills of the Savannah*, Heinemann.

—— (1988) *Hopes and Impediments, Selected Essays 1965–1987*, Heinemann.

—— (1990) 'African Literature as Restoration of Celebration', in Kirsten Holst Petersen and Anna Rutherford (eds) *Chinua Achebe. A Celebration*, Dangeroo Press, pp. 1–10.

Achebe, Chinua and Innes, C.L. (eds) (1992) *The Heinemann Book of Contemporary African Short Stories*, Heinemann.

Adam, Ian and Tiffin, Helen, (eds) (1993) *Past the Last Post: Theorising, Post-Colonialism and Post-Modernism*, Harvester Wheatsheaf.

Afolayan, A. (1975) 'Language and Sources of Amos Tutuola', in Bernth Lindfors (ed.) *Critical Perspectives on Amos Tutuola*, Heinemann, pp. 148–162.

Agovi, K.E. (1990) 'The African Writer and the Phenomenon of the Nation State in Africa', *Ufahamu* 18(1) 41–62.

Ahmad, Aijaz (1986) 'Jameson's Rhetoric of Otherness and the National Allegory', *Social Text* 1 (Fall) 3–25.

—— (1992) *In Theory*, Verso.

Alden, Patricia (1991) 'New Women and Old Myths: Chinua Achebe's Anthills of the Savannah and Nuruddin Farah's Sardines', in Holger G. Ehling (ed.) *Critical Approaches to Anthills of the Savannah*, Rodopi, pp. 67–80.

Amado, Georg (1989) 'Interlude of the Christening of Felicio, Son of Massu and Benedita or Ogun's Compadre', *Shepherds of the Night*, Collins Harvill.

Anderson, Benedict (1983) *Imagined Communities: Reflections on the Origin and Spread of Nationalism*, Verso.

Anderson, Perry (1984) 'Modernity and Revolution', *New Left Review* 144 (March/April) 96–113.

—— (1988) 'Modernity and Revolution', in Cary Nelson and Lawrence Grossberg (eds) *Marxism and the Interpretation of Culture*, Macmillan, pp. 317–33.

Anyidoho, Akosua (1991) 'Linguistic Parallels in Traditional Akan Appellation Poetry', *Research in African Literatures*, vol. 22, no. 1, 67–81.

Appadurai, Arjun (1996) *Modernity at Large: Cultural Dimensions of Globalization*, University of Minnesota Press.

Appiah, Kwame Anthony (1992) *In My Father's House: Africa in the Philosophy of Culture*, Methuen.

—— (1994) 'The Hybrid Age? Homi K. Bhabha, The Location of Culture', *Times Literary Supplement* 27 May, p. 5.

Apter, Andrew (1992a) *Black Critics and Kings*, University of Chicago Press.

—— (1992b) 'Que Faire? Reconsidering Inventions of Africa', *Critical Enquiry* (Autumn) 87–104.

Armah, Ayi Kwei (1969) *The Beautiful Ones Are Not Yet Born*, Heinemann.

—— (1973) *Two Thousand Seasons*, East African Publishing House.

Arnove, Anthony (1993) 'Pierre Bourdieu, the Sociology of Intellectuals, and the Language of African Literature', *Novel: A Forum on Fiction* 26(3) 278–96.

Ashcroft, B., Griffiths, G. and Tiffin, H. (1989) *The Empire Writes Back*, Routledge.

Baker, Suzanne (1991) 'Magic Realism as a Postcolonial Strategy: The Kadaitcha Sung', *Span* 32 (April) 55–63.

Bakhtin, Mikhail (1981) *The Dialogic Imagination: Four Essays*, University of Texas Press.

—— (1984a) *Problems of Dostoevsky's Poetics*, University of Minnesota Press.

—— (1984b) *Rabelais and His World*, Indiana University Press.

Barrett, Michele (1991) *The Politics of Truth: From Marx to Foucault*, Polity Press.

Barrett, Michele and Phillips, Anne (eds) (1992) *Destabilizing Theory. Contemporary Feminist Debates*, Polity Press.

Baucom, Ian (1991) 'Dreams of Home: Colonialism and Postmodernism', *Research in African Literatures* 22(4) 5–27.

Beilis, Viktor (1987) 'Ghosts, People, and Books of Yorubaland', *Research in African Literatures* 18(4) 447–57.

Bhabha, Homi (1985) 'Signs Taken for Wonders: Questions of Ambivalence and Authority Under a Tree Outside Delhi May 1817', in Francis Barker *et al.* (eds) *Europe and its Others*, University of Essex, pp. 89–106.

—— (1990) *Nation and Narration*, Routledge.

—— (1994) *The Location of Culture*, Routledge.

Boehmer, Elleke (1991) 'The Master's Dance to the Master's Voice: Revolutionary Nationalism and the Representation of Women in the Novels of Ngugi wa Thiongo', *Journal of Commonwealth Literature* 26(1) 188–97.

—— (1995) *Colonial and Postcolonial Literature*, Oxford University Press.

Brennan, Timothy (1989) *Salman Rushdie and the Third World*, Macmillan.

Brooke-Rose, Christine (1981) *A Rhetoric of the Unreal: Studies in Narrative and Structure, especially of the Fantastic*, Cambridge University Press.

Brown, Stewart (1981) 'A Poet in Exile', *West Africa* 21–28 (Dec.) 3055–9.

Bruchac, Joseph (1991) in Tracy Chevalier (ed.) *Contemporary Poets*, 5th edn, St James Press.

Bundy, Colin (1996) 'Sharing the Burden? A Response to Terry Lovell', in Brenda Cooper and Andrew Steyn (eds) *Transgressing Boundaries: New Directions in the Study of Culture in Africa*, University of Cape Town Press, pp. 39–56.

Carpentier, Alejo (1985) 'The Latin American Novel', *New Left Review* 154 (Nov.–Dec.) 99–111.

Chamberlain, Lori (1986) 'Magicking the Real: Paradoxes in Postmodern Writing', Larry McCaffery (ed.) *Postmodern Fiction: A Bio-Bibliographical Guide*, Greenwood, pp. 5–21.

Chanady, Amaryll Beatrice (1985) *Magical Realism and the Fantastic: Resolved versus Unresolved Antinomy*, Garland Publishing.

—— (1986) 'The Origins and Development of Magic Realism in Latin American Fiction', Peter Hinchcliffe and Ed Jewinski (eds) *Magic Realism and Canadian Literature: Essays and Stories*, University of Waterloo Press, pp. 49–60.

Cheney-Coker, Syl (1973 and 1980) *The Graveyard Also has Teeth,* with *Concerto for an Exile,* Heinemann Educational Books.

—— (1990) *The Last Harmattan of Alusine Dunbar*, Heinemann Educational books.

Chester, Suzanne (1992) 'Writing the Subject. Exoticism/Eroticism in Marguerite Duras's *The Lover* and *The Sea Wall*', Sidonie Smith and Julia Watson (eds) *De/Colonizing the Subject. The Politics of Gender in Women's Autobiography*, University of Minnesota Press, pp. 436–57.

Chinweizu, Jemie, O. and Madubuike, I. (1983) *Toward the Decolonization of African Literature*, Howard University Press.

Comaroff, Jean (1996) 'Late 20th Century Social Science: A Conversation', in Brenda Cooper and Andrew Steyn (eds) *Transgressing Boundaries: New Directions in the Study of Culture in Africa*, University of Cape Town Press, pp. 39–56.

Conniff, Brian (1990) 'The Dark Side of Magical Realism: Science, Oppression, and Apocalypse in *One Hundred Years of Solitude*', *Modern Fiction Studies* 36(2) 167–79.

Cooper, Brenda (1991) 'Does Marxism Allow for the Magical Side of Things? Magical Realism and a Comparison between *One Hundred Years of Solitude* and *The House of the Spirits*', *Social Dynamics* 17(2) 126–54.

—— (1992) *To Lay These Secrets Open*, David Philip Publishers.

—— (1994) 'Syl Cheney-Coker: *The Last Harmattan of Alusine Dunbar*, and an Interview', *ALA Bulletin* 20(3) 3–17.

—— (1995) 'The Two-faced Ogun: Postcolonial Intellectuals and the Positioning of Wole Soyinka', *English in Africa* 22(2) 44–69.

—— (1996) 'Postcolonialism Against the "Empire of the Discipline" ', Gail Fincham and Myrtle Hooper (eds) *Under Postcolonial Eyes: Joseph Conrad After Empire*, University of Cape Town Press.

Dakubu, M.E. Kropp (1993) '*Search Sweet Country* and the Language of Authentic Being', *Research in African Literature*, 24(1) 19–35.

Dasenbrock, Reed Way (1986) 'Creating a Past: Achebe, Naipaul, Soyinka, Farah', *Salmagundi* 68–9 (Fall–Winter) 312–32.

Deandrea, Pietro (1996) ' "New Worlds, New Wholes": Kojo Laing's Narrative Quest for a Social Renewal', *African Literature Today* 20, 158–78.

Diamond, Larry (1989) 'Fiction as Political Thought', *African Affairs* 88(352) 435–45.

Dirlik, Arif (1994) 'The Postcolonial Aura: Third World Criticism in the Age of Global Capitalism', *Critical Inquiry* 20 (Winter) 328–56.

Drewal, Margaret Thompson (1992) *Yoruba Ritual: Performers, Play, Agency*, Indiana University Press.

Drewal, Henry John and Margaret Thompson (1990) *Gelede: Art and Female Power among the Yoruba*, Indiana University Press.

Dunkerley, James (1987) 'Mario Vargas Llosa: Parables and Deceits', *New Left Review* 162 (March/April) 112–22.

Durix, J-P. (1987) *The Writer Written. The Artist and Creation in the New Literatures in English*, Greenwood Press.

Eagleton, Terry (1981) *Walter Benjamin or Towards a Revolutionary Criticism*, Verso.

—— (1985) 'Capitalism, Modernism and Post-Modernism', *New Left Review* 152 (July–August) 60–73.

Ehling, Holger G. (1991) (ed.) *Critical Approaches to* Anthills of the Savannah, Rodopi.

Epega, Alfolabi A., and Neimark, Philip John (1995) *The Sacred Ifa Oracle*, (translated and with commentary), San Francisco: Harper.

Fagunwa, D.O. (1982) *The Forest of a Thousand Daemons*, Surrey: Nelson.

Foucault, Michel (1980) *Power/Knowledge: Selected Interviews and Other Writings 1972–1977*, Harvester Press.

Franco, Jean (1988) 'Beyond Ethnocentrism: Gender, Power, and the Third-World Intelligentsia', Cary Nelson and Lawrence Grossberg (eds) *Marxism and the Interpretation of Culture*, Macmillan.

Gates, Henry Louis Jr (1988) *The Signifying Monkey*, Oxford University Press.

—— (1991) 'Critical Fanonism', *Critical Inquiry* 17(3) 457–70.

Gellner, Ernst, (1993) 'The Mightier Pen? Edward Said and the Double Standards of Inside-out Colonialism', *Times Literary Supplement* 19 February, pp. 3–4.

Gikandi, Simon (1991) *Reading Chinua Achebe*, James Currey.

Gorra, Michael (1993) 'The Spirit Who Came to Stay', *The New York Times Book Review*, 10 Oct, p. 24.

Griffiths, Gareth (1987) 'Chinua Achebe: When Did You Last See Your Father?' *World Literature Written in English* 27(1) 18–27.

Griffiths, Gareth and Moody, David (1989) 'Of Marx and Missionaries: Soyinka and the Survival of Universalism in Post-colonial Literary Theory', *Kunapipi* 2(1) 74–85.

Gunn, Janet Varner (1992) 'A Politics of Experience. Leila Khaled's *My People Shall Live: The Autobiography of a Revolutionary*', in Sidonie Smith and Julia Watson (eds) *De/Colonizing the Subject. The Politics of Gender in Women's Autobiography*, University of Minnesota Press, pp. 65–80.

Hall, Stuart, (1992) 'The Question of Cultural Identity', in Stuart Hall, David Held and Tony McGrew (eds) *Modernity and its Futures*, Polity/Blackwell/Open University Press, pp. 273–325.

—— (1993) 'Cultural Identity and Diaspora', in Patrick Williams and Laura Chrisman (eds) *Colonial Discourse and Post-Colonial Theory. A Reader*, Harvester Wheatsheaf, pp. 392–403.

Hancock, Geoff (1986) 'Magic or Realism: The Marvellous in Canadian Fiction', Peter Hinchcliffe and Jewinski, Ed (eds) *Magic Realism and Canadian Literature: Essays and Stories*, University of Waterloo Press, pp. 30–48.

Harlow, Barbara (1987) *Resistance Literature*, Methuen.

Harris, Nigel (1986) *The End of the Third World: Newly Industrializing Countries and the Decline of an Ideology*, Pelican Books.

Hassan, Ihab (1986) 'Pluralism in Postmodern Perspective', *Critical Inquiry* 12(3) 503–20.

Higgens, James (1990) 'Gabriel Garcia Marquez: Cien Anos De Soledad', in P. Swanson (ed.) *Landmarks in Modern Latin American Fiction*, Routledge and Kegan Paul.

Hinchcliffe, Peter and Jewinski, Ed (eds) *Magic Realism and Canadian Literature: Essays and Stories*, University of Waterloo Press.

Holquist, Michael (1984) 'Prologue', in Mikhail Bakhtin, *Rabelais and His World*, Indiana University Press, pp. xiii–xxiii.

hooks, bell (1993) 'Postmodern Blackness', in Patrick Williams and Laura Chrisman (eds) *Colonial Discourse and Post-Colonial Theory. A Reader*, Harvester Wheatsheaf, pp. 421–7.

Hurston, Zora Neale (1990) *Their Eyes were Watching God*, Perennial Library.

Hutcheon, Linda (1988) *A Poetics of Postmodernism: History, Theory, Fiction*, Routledge.
—— (1989) *The Politics of Postmodernism*, Routledge.
—— (1993) 'Circling the Downspout of Empire', in Ian Adam and Helen Tiffin (eds) *Past the Last Post: Theorising Post-Colonialism and Post-Modernism*, Harvester Wheatsheaf, pp. 167–89.
Ikegami, Robin (1991) 'Knowledge and Power: The Story and the Storyteller: Achebe's *Anthills of the Savannah*', *Modern Fiction Studies* 37(3) 493–507.
Innes, C.L. (1990) *Chinua Achebe*, Cambridge University Press.
Jackson, Rosemary (1981) *Fantasy: The Literature of Subversion*, Methuen.
James, Adeola (1990) *In Their Own Voices: African Women Writers Talk*, James Currey and Heinemann.
Jameson, Fredric (1981) *The Political Unconscious*, Methuen.
—— (1984) 'Postmodernism, or the Cultural Logic of Late Capitalism', *New Left Review* 146 (July–August) 53–92.
—— (1986a) 'On Magic Realism in Film', *Critical Enquiry* 12 (Winter) 301–25.
—— (1986b) 'Third World Literature in the Era of Multinational Capitalism', *Social Text* 15, 65–88.
—— (1991) *Postmodernism, or The Cultural Logic of Late Capitalism*, Verso.
JanMohamed, Abdul R. (1983) *Manichean Aesthetics. The Politics of Literature in Colonial Africa*, The University of Massachusetts Press.
Jeyifo, Biodun (1985) *The Truthful Lie*, New Beacon Books.
—— (1988) 'Ben Okri', in Yemi Ogunbiyi (ed.) *Perspectives on Nigerian Literature: 1700 to the Present*, vol. 2, Lagos: Guardian Books, pp. 227–8.
—— (1991) 'For Chinua Achebe: The Resilience and the Predicament of Obierika', in Kirsten Holst Petersen and Anna Rutherford (eds) *Chinua Achebe. A Celebration*, Heinemann, pp. 51–70.
Johnson, Barbara (1985) 'Thresholds of Difference: Structures of Address in Zora Neale Hurston', in Henry Louis Gates Jr (ed.) *'Race', Writing and Difference*, University of Chicago Press, 317–28.
Jones, Eldred Durosimi (ed.) (1980a) *African Literature Today*, vol. 11, Heinemann.
—— (1980b) 'The Palm-Wine Drinkard: Fourteen Years On', in Bernth Lindfors (ed.) *Critical Perspectives on Amos Tutuola*, Heineman, pp. 72–6.
—— (ed.) (1992) 'Myth and Modernity: African Writers and Their Roots', *African Literature Today*, 18, 1–8.
Julien, Eileen (1992) *African Novels and the Question of Orality*, Indiana University Press.
Kincaid, Jamaica (1991) *Lucy*, Plume Publishers.
King, Bruce (1988) 'Postcolonial Complexities', *The Sewanee Review* 96(4) xxxiv –xxxv.
King, John (ed.) (1987) *Modern Latin American Fiction: A Survey*, Faber and Faber.
Laing, B. Kojo (1986) *Search Sweet Country*, Heinemann.
—— (1988a) *Woman of the Aeroplanes*, Picador.
—— (1988b) 'History allow us to speak our minds', *Index on Censorship* 5(17) 85–6, 91.
—— (1989) *Godhorse*, Heinemann.
—— (1992) *Major Gentl and the Achimoto Wars*, Heinemann.
Laye, Camara (1956) *The Radiance of the King*, Fontana.
Lazarus, Neil (1990) *Resistance in Postcolonial African Literature*, Yale University Press.
Lienhardt, Godfrey (1993) 'From Ghana to Harvard', *Times Literary Supplement* 12 February, p. 25.

Lindfors, Bernth (1973) *Folklore in Nigerian Literature*, New York: Africana Publishing Company.

—— (ed.) (1980) *Critical Perspectives on Amos Tutuola*, Heinemann.

Liyong, Lo Taban (1980) 'Tutuola, Son of Zinjanthropus', in Bernth Lindfors (ed.) *Critical Perspectives on Amos Tutuola*, Heinemen, pp. 77–83.

Longley, Kateryna Olijnyk (1992) 'Autobiographical Storytelling by Australian Aboriginal Women', in Sidonie Smith and Julia Watson (eds) *De/Colonizing the Subject. The Politics of Gender in Women's Autobiography*, University of Minnesota Press, pp. 370–84.

Loomba, Ania (1993) 'Overworlding the "Third World" ', in Patrick Williams and Laura Chrisman (eds) *Colonial Discourse and Post-Colonial Theory. A Reader*, Harvester Wheatsheaf, pp. 305–23.

Lovell, Terry (1987) *Consuming Fiction*, Verso.

—— (1996) 'The Burden of the Disciplines', in Brenda Cooper and Andrew Steyn (eds) *Transgressing Boundaries*, University of Cape Town Press, pp. 14–30.

Mahfouz, Naguib (1992) *Sugar Street*, Doubleday.

Maja-Pearce, Adewale (1987) 'Interview with Kojo Laing', *Wasafiri* Spring/Autumn, 27–9.

Marquez, Gabriel Garcia (1978) *One Hundred Years of Solitude*, Picador.

Martin, Gerald (1989) *Journeys Through the Labyrinth*, Verso.

Maughan-Brown, David (1991) '*Anthills of the Savannah*: Achebe's solutions to the "Trouble with Nigeria" ', in Holger G. Ehling (ed.) *Critical Approaches to* Anthills of the Savannah, Rodopi, pp. 3–22.

McClintock, Anne (1993) 'The Angel of Progress: Pitfalls of the Term "Post-Colonialism" ' in Patrick Williams and Laura Chrisman (eds) *Colonial Discourse and Post-Colonial Theory. A Reader*, Harvester Wheatsheaf, pp. 291–303.

Mendoza, P. (1983) *The Fragrance of Guava*, Verso.

Minta, Stephen (1987) *Gabriel Garcia Marquez: Writer of Colombia*, Jonathan Cape.

Mishra, Vijay and Hodge, Bob (1993) 'What is Post(-)colonialism?', in Patrick Williams and Laura Chrisman (eds) *Colonial Discourse and Post-Colonial Theory. A Reader*, Harvester Wheatsheaf, pp. 276–90.

Mohanty, Chandra (1988) 'Under Western Eyes: Feminist Scholarship and Colonial Discourses', *Feminist Review* 30 (Autumn) 61–88.

—— (1992) 'Locating the Politics of Experience', in Michele Barrett and Anne Phillips (eds) *Destabilizing Theory. Contemporary Feminist Debates*, Polity Press, pp. 74–92.

Mudimbe, V.Y. (1988) *The Invention of Africa*, Indiana University Press.

—— (1991) *Parables and Fables: Exegesis, Textuality and Politics in Central Africa*, The University of Wisconsin Press.

—— (1994) *The Idea of Africa*, Bloomington and Indianapolis, Indiana University Press.

Nasta, Susheila (ed.) (1991) *Motherlands, Black Women's Writing*, The Women's Press.

Ngara, Emmanuel (1991) 'Achebe as Artist: The Place and Significance of *Anthills of the Savannah*', Kirsten Holst Peterson and Anna Rutherford (eds) *Chinua Achebe. A Celebration*, Heinemann and Dangeroo Press, pp. 113–29.

Ngugi wa Thiong'o (1981) *Writers in Politics*, Heinemann.

—— (1986) *Decolonising the Mind*, Heinemann.

—— (1993) *Moving the Centre. The Struggle for Cultural Freedoms*, James Currey and Heinemann.

Niane, D.T. (1965) *Sundiata: an Epic of Old Mali*, London: Longman.

Niven, Alastair, (1989) 'Achebe and Okri: Contrasts in the Response to Civil War', in Jacqueline Bardolph (ed.) *Short Fiction in the New Literatures in English*, Nice Faculty, Des Lettres et Sciences Humaines, pp. 277–83.

Nixon, Rob (1992) *London Calling: V.S. Naipaul, Postcolonial Mandarin*, Oxford University Press.

Nwanko, Chimalum (1991) 'Soothing Ancient Bruises: Power and the New African Woman in Chinua Achebe's Anthills of the Savannah', in Holger G. Ehling (ed.) *Critical Approaches to Anthills of the Savannah*, Rodopi, pp. 55–65.

Obiechina, E.N. (1980) 'Amos Tutuola and the Oral Tradition', in Bernth Lindfors (ed.) *Critical Perspectives on Amos Tutuola*. Heinemann, pp. 84–105.

Ogunba. O. (1975) *The Movement of Transition. A Study of the Plays of Wole Soyinka*, Ibadan University Press.

Okara, G. (1963) 'Piano and Drums' in G. Moore and U. Beier (eds) *Modern Poetry from Africa*, Penguin, p. 121.

Okpewho, Isidore (1983) *Myth in Africa*, Cambridge University Press.

—— (1988) 'African Poetry: The Modern Writer and the Oral Tradition', *African Literature Today* 16, 3–25.

Okri, Ben (1986) 'Soyinka: A Personal View', *West Africa* (27 October) 3608, 2249–52.

—— (1992) *The Famished Road*, David Philip Publishers.

—— (1994) *Songs of Enchantment*, David Philip Publishers.

—— (1996) *Dangerous Love*, Ad Donker.

Ondaatje. M. (1993) *The English Patient*, Picador.

Ojaide, Tanure (1992) 'The Half Brother of the Black Jew: The Poet's Persona in the Poetry of Syl Cheney-Coker', *CLA Journal* XXXV (1 September) 1–14.

Ousmane, Sembene (1970) *God's Bits of Wood*, Heinemann.

Patai, Daphne (1983) *Myth and Ideology in Contemporary Brazilian Fiction*, Cranbury, NJ: Associated University Presses.

Pomorska, Krystyna (1984) 'Foreword', in Mikhail Bakhtin, *Rabelais and His World*, trans. Helene Iswolsky, Indiana University Press, 1984b, pp. vii–xii.

Povey, John (1988) 'Review of Anthills of the Savannah', *African Arts* 21(4) 21–3.

Priebe, Richard K. (1980) 'Tutuola, the Riddler' in Bernth Lindfors (ed.) *Critical Perspectives on Amos Tutuola*, Heinemann Publishers, pp. 215–23.

—— (1988) *Myth, Realism and the West African Writer*, Africa World Press.

Quayson, Ato (1995) 'Esoteric Webwork as Nervous System: Reading the Fantastic in Ben Okri's Writing' in Gurnah Abdulrazak (ed.) *Essays on African Writing*, Heinemann Educational Books, pp. 144–58.

Rhys, Jean (1981) *Smile Please. An Unfinished Autobiography*, Penguin Books.

Richards, David (1991) 'Repossessing Time: Chinua Achebe's Anthills of the Savannah', in Kirsten Holst Peterson and Anna Rutherford (eds) *Chinua Achebe. A Celebration*, Heinemann and Dangeroo Press, pp. 130–8.

Rohrberger, M. (1991) 'Kojo Laing's Woman of the Aeroplanes', *Magill's Literary Annual*, Salem Press, pp. 914–8.

Rosenthal, Jane (1994) 'Where the Spirit World Meets Reality', *Weekly Mail and Guardian*, Supplement, April, p. 5.

Rushdie. Salman (1988) *The Satanic Verses*, Viking.

—— (1990) *In Good Faith*, Granta.

—— (1992) *Imaginary Homelands: Essays and Criticism 1981–1991*, Granta.

Sachs, Albie (1990) 'Preparing Ourselves for Freedom', in Ingrid de Kok and Karen Press (eds) *Spring is Rebellious*, Buchu Books, pp. 19–29.

Said, Edward W. (1978) *Orientalism*, Routledge and Kegan Paul.

—— (1986) 'Intellectuals in the Post-colonial World', *Salmagundi* 70–1 (Spring–Summer) 44–64.

—— (1989) 'Representing the Colonized: Anthropology's Interlocutors', *Critical Inquiry* 15 (Winter) 205–25.

—— (1991) 'Identity, Authority and Freedom: The Potentate and the Traveller', *31st T.B. Davie Memorial Lecture*, University of Cape Town.

—— (1992) 'The Politics of Knowledge', in Paul Berman (ed.) *Debating P.C. The Controversy Over Political Correctness on College Campuses*, Laurel, pp. 172–89.

—— (1993) *Culture and Imperialism*, Chatto and Windus.

Said, Edward, Buttigieg, Joseph A. and Bove, Paul A. (1993) 'An Interview with Edward W. Said', *Boundary 2* 20(1) 1–25.

Sangari, Kumkum (1987) 'The Politics of the Possible', *Cultural Critique* 7, 157–86.

Scholes, Robert (1979) *Fabulation and Metafiction*, University of Illinois Press.

Sharma, Govind Narain (1993) 'The Christian Dynamic in the Fictional World of Chinua Achebe', *ARIEL* 24(2) 85–99.

Simpkins, Scott (1988) 'Magical Strategies: The Supplement of Realism', *Twentieth Century Literature* 34(2) 140–54.

Slemon, Stephen (1993) 'Modernism's Last Post', in Ian Adam and Helen Tiffin (eds) *Past the Last Post: Theorising Post-Colonialism and Post-Modernism*, Harvester Wheatsheaf, pp. 1–11.

Smith, Sidonie (1992) 'The Other Woman and the Racial Politics of Gender. Isak Dinesen and Beryl Markham in Kenya', in Sidonie Smith and Julia Watson (eds) *De/Colonizing the Subject. The Politics of Gender in Women's Autobiography*, University of Minnesota Press, pp. 410–35.

Soyinka, Wole (1965) *The Road*, Oxford University Press.

—— (1970) *The Interpreters*, African Writers Series, Heinemann.

—— (1973) *Season of Anomy*, Rex Collings.

—— (1975) 'Neo Tarzanism: The Poetics of Pseudo-Tradition', *Transition* 48 (April/June) 38–44.

—— (1976a) 'Aesthetic Illusions', in H.A. Baker (ed.) *Reading Black: Essays in the Criticism of African, Caribbean, and Black American Literature*, Monograph Series 4, Cornell University, Africana Studies and Research Centre, pp. 1–12.

—— (1976b) *Myth, Literature and the African World*, Cambridge University Press.

—— (1988) *Art, Dialogue and Outrage*, Three Horn Press.

—— (1989) *Isara: A Voyage Around Essay*, Methuen.

Sparrow, F. (1988) 'Chinua Achebe, *Anthills of the Savannah*', *World Literature Written in English* 28(1) 58–63.

Spitzer, Leo (1974) *The Creoles of Sierra Leone*, University of Wisconsin Press.

Spivak, Gayatri Chakravorty (1985a) 'Three Woman's Texts and a Critique of Imperialism', *Critical Enquiry*, 12, 243–61.

—— (1985b), 'The Rani of Sirmur', in Francis Barker *et al.* (eds) *Europe and its Others*, University of Essex, 128–51.

—— (1987) *In Other Worlds*, Methuen.

—— (1990) *The Post-colonial Critic. Interviews, Strategies, Dialogues*, ed. Sarah Harasym, Routledge.

—— (1992a) 'Acting Bits/Identity Talk', *Critical Inquiry* 18 (Summer).

—— (1992b) 'Thinking Academic Freedom in Gendered Post-coloniality', *32nd T.B. Davie Memorial Lecture*, University of Cape Town.

Sprent, M. (1985) BBC Film of the series *Films Around the World*.

Stallybrass, Peter and White, Allon (1986) *The Politics of Transgression*, Methuen.

Swansen, Philip (1990) *Landmarks in Modern Latin American Fiction*, Routledge.

Tiffin, Helen (1978) 'Mirror and Mask: Colonial Motifs in the Novels of Jean Rhys', *World Literature Written in English*, 17.

—— (1993) 'Introduction', in Ian Adam and Helen Tiffin (eds) *Past the Last Post: Theorising Post-Colonialism and Post-Modernism*, Harvester Wheatsheaf, pp. vii–xvi.

Todorov, T. (1975) *The Fantastic: A Structural Approach to a Literary Genre*, Ithaca, NY: Cornell University Press.

—— (1984) *The Conquest of America. The Question of the Other*, Harper and Row.

—— (1985) ' "Race", Writing, and Culture', in Henry Louis Gates Jr (ed.) *'Race', Writing, and Difference*, University of Chicago Press.

Tutuola, Amos (1952) *The Palm-Wine Drinkard*, Faber.

—— (1981) *The Witch-Herbalist of the Remote Town*, London: Faber and Faber.

Udumukwu, Onyemaechi (1991) 'Achebe and the Negation of Independence', *Modern Fiction Studies* 37(3) 471–91.

Uwajeh, P.N. (1992) 'Orature in Literature: Myths as Structural Elements in Achebe's Anthills of the Savannah', *Neohelicon* 19(1) 297–306.

Walby, Sylvia (1992) 'Post-Post-Modernism? Theorizing Social Complexity', in Michele Barrett and Anne Phillips (eds) *Destabilizing Theory. Contemporary Feminist Debates*, Polity Press, pp. 31–52.

Walker, Alice (1983) *In Search of our Mothers' Gardens*, Harvest/HBJ.

Waters, Harold A. (1993) 'Review of Kojo Laing's *Major Gentl and the Achimota Wars*', *World Literature Today* 67(2) 427.

Watson, Julia (1992) 'Unspeakable Differences. The Politics of Gender in Lesbian and Heterosexual Women's Autobiographies', in Sidonie Smith and Julia Watson (eds) *De/Colonizing the Subject. The Politics of Gender in Women's Autobiography*, University of Minnesota Press, pp. 139–68.

White, Hayden (1978) *The Tropics of Discourse: Essays in Cultural Criticism*, Johns Hopkins University Press.

—— (1980) 'The Value of Narrativity in the Representation of Reality', *Critical Enquiry* (Autumn) 5–27.

—— (1981) 'Critical Response III "The Narrativization of Real Events" ', *Critical Inquiry* (Summer) 793–8.

—— (1986) 'Historical Pluralism', *Critical Inquiry* 12 (Spring) 480–93.

—— (1987) *The Content of the Form: Narrative Discourse and Historical Representation*, Johns Hopkins University Press.

Wilkinson, Jane (1992) *Talking with African Writers*, James Currey.

Williams, Patrick and Chrisman, Laura (1993) (eds) *Colonial Discourse and Post-Colonial Theory. A Reader*, Harvester Wheatsheaf

Williams, Raymond (1980) *Problems in Materialism and Culture*, Verso.

Williamson, Edwin (1987) 'Coming to Terms with Modernity: Magical Realism and the Historical Process in the Novels of Alejo Carpentier', in King, John, (ed.) *Modern Latin American Fiction*, Faber and Faber, pp. 78–100.

Wilson, Robert R. (1986) 'The Metamorphoses of Space: Magic Realism', in Peter Hinchcliffe and Ed Jewinski (eds) *Magic Realism and Canadian Literature*, University of Waterloo Press, pp. 61–74.

—— (1993) 'SLIPP PAGE: Angela Carter, In/Out/In the Post-Modern Nexus', in Ian *Modernism*, Harvester Wheatsheaf, pp. 109–23.

Young, Robert (1990) *White Mythologies. Writing, History and the West*, Routledge.

INDEX

Page numbers in bold type give the main reference to a subject.